Sai Baba
Faqir of Shirdi

Sai Baba
Faqir of Shirdi

Kevin R. D. Shepherd

STERLING

STERLING PAPERBACKS
An imprint of
Sterling Publishers (P) Ltd.
Regd. Office: A1/256 Safdarjung Enclave,
New Delhi-110029. CIN: U22110DL1964PTC211907
Tel: 26387070, 26386209; Fax: 91-11-26383788
E-mail: mail@sterlingpublishers.com
www.sterlingpublishers.com

Sai Baba: Faqir of Shirdi
© 2017, Kevin R. D. Shepherd
ISBN 978 93 86245 06 9
First Published 2017

All rights are reserved.
No part of this publication may be reproduced, stored in a retrieval system or transmitted, in any form or by any means, mechanical, photocopying, recording or otherwise, without prior written permission of the author.

Printed in India

Printed and Published by Sterling Publishers Pvt. Ltd.,
Plot No. 13, Ecotech-III, Greater Noida - 201306,
Uttar Pradesh, India

Preface

This book is a sequel to my *Sai Baba of Shirdi: A Biographical Investigation* (2015). The longer work is not actually a biography, but an analysis of fairly numerous components relating to the life of Sai Baba. There are many gaps and uncertainties in the record of his earlier years. Even some features of the last years are open to different, or more intensive, interpretations.

The title of this more compact book includes the phrase *Faqir of Shirdi*. That is a well known description for Sai Baba, but not always seen in perspective. He was a complex entity, difficult to classify under generalising criteria of spirituality. His moods were diverse, and his speech often very allusive. Sai Baba did not preach religious doctrines, but was nevertheless a teacher of a more discreet kind. His interactions with numerous devotees are on record to some extent, and require due attention.

In this book I have attempted to supply additional information and perspectives in relation to the Shirdi *faqir*. Some chapters revisit themes in *Biographical Investigation*.

I would like to thank Shri S. K. Ghai, the Managing Director of Sterling Publishers (New Delhi), for his benevolent interest in the publication of this book.

Kevin R. D. Shepherd
January 2017

Introduction

The basic context for Sai Baba is that of a *faqir*, an ascetic. One of his accoutrements was a *dhuni*, or sacred fire, which he kept burning at his rural mosque in Shirdi. This practice was shared in his time by both Muslim and Hindu ascetics, although better known in respect of the latter.

In the case of Sai Baba, there were no Vaishnava or Shaiva characteristics in his cultivation of the *dhuni*. Elsewhere, diverse *sadhus* and Yogis maintained a *dhuni* fire in a manner that made their religious or sectarian affiliation quite evident. Those renunciates included *naga sadhus*, who were distinctive for nudity, and whose background was Shaiva. The Nath Yogis were another Shaiva category of *dhuni wala* (fire man), and closely associated with various Tantric attitudes and customs.

A procedure which Sai Baba shared in common with the *sadhus* was that of gifting visitors with ash (*udi*) from the *dhuni*, a generally recognised form of benediction. He would sometimes apply ashes to the visitor's forehead. Yet he never daubed his own body with ashes, contrary to the habit of many *sadhus* and Yogis. In his case, there was no *trishul* (trident) or *damaru* (drum), trappings well known amongst Shaiva holy men.

An eyewitness reported that Sai Baba was daily "near the Dhuni, early morning facing south, leaning on a post.... People were not allowed to go near, i.e., even 50 feet.... He used to utter words like *Yade Haq*. They were seldom clear or audible to us at some distance. *Allah Malik, Allah Vali Hai*, i.e.,

God is the Master and Protector, he used to say often and at all times" (Narasimhaswami 2006:83).

A famous ritual of Shaiva *sadhus* is smoking of the pipe (*chilum*), a procedure in which a mixture of cannabis and tobacco is used. There are special *chilum mantras* to facilitate the desired communion with Shiva. Some *sadhus* will eat the *chilum* ashes, regarding these as *prasad* (holy gift) from Shiva. Shiva was, and is, quite commonly regarded as the patron of *charas* (cannabis resin), so often used in the *chilum*.

Sai Baba also smoked a pipe, but not in a Shaiva (nor a Vaishnava) context (Shepherd 2015:114–115). He did not employ *chilum mantras* (for example, *Alakh*). He is described in the sources as smoking tobacco; there is no reference to *charas* (or to *ganja*, meaning cannabis leaf). He wore the typical garb of Muslim *faqirs*, whose customs often differed from those of *sadhus* and Yogis. There was a degree of convergence between *sadhus* and *faqirs* in relation to smoking cannabis, but this tendency was not uniform. Variations amongst *sadhus* also require to be taken into account. A contemporary investigator has reported: "Many [Hindu] Babas do not smoke at all and may even condemn the habit as low caste and counterproductive" (Hartsuiker 1993:99).

Sadhus were generally known as Babas. The word *Baba* can mean a wise senior or father. "The majority of Sadhus belong to a sect or organisation. Besides these organised Sadhus there is also a small but important group of independent Babas, who actually follow the ancient tradition of solitary asceticism. They have usually been initiated by a Guru, but refuse sectarian membership" (ibid:66). Many of these independents are Nath (Gorakhnathi) Yogis.

There were also independents in the ranks of Sufi ascetics, persons who did not profess allegiance to any Sufi Order. The characteristics of such *faqirs* could easily assume a quasi-Hindu complexion, to varying degrees. This subject is not well known, but nevertheless relevant.

Introduction

A necessary exercise in presentation is to review, or probe, both the Muslim and Hindu dimensions of Sai Baba. This is not always done, and has led to an imbalance in a number of versions available. Some accounts prefer to dwell upon miraculous occurrences, a tendency which can be obscurantist.

Sai Baba was an exceptional instance of religious liberalism, crossing the divide between doctrinal formats, and eschewing all forms of intolerance (Chapter 5). He communicated with Hindu and Muslim devotees (Chapters 12 and 22), and also members of other religions. He is now noted for speaking in Urdu to his Muslim disciple Abdul Baba, who left a *Notebook* proving a strong Muslim Sufi dimension in the outlook of Sai Baba. The *Notebook* was very obscure until comparatively recently, when it was translated into English, revealing much that had been forgotten in earlier decades (Chapter 2).

It is not possible, in any presentation striving for accuracy, to ignore the Sufi aspect of Sai Baba. Nevertheless, he was not part of the milieu attaching to Sufi Orders, but instead a very independent mystic (Chapters 3, 7). This dimension will not easily be dismissed by hostile accusations that he was a Muslim, nor by the accumulating distortion of events found on some popular media.

Like many other subjects in Indian religion, a close study of detail is necessary in the case of Sai Baba. Unfortunately, we do not find this diligence in many of the popular errors gaining circulation (some of which are patently hostile). For instance, a misconception recently percolated Europe, leading some Westerners to believe that the *Shri Sai Satcharita* was written long after the death of Sai Baba by a person who never met him. In reality, the author of this work was Govind R. Dabholkar (d.1929), a direct devotee during the last years of the saint, and a poet who composed the *Satcharita* during the 1920s (Chapter 15).

A misleading story can be found that Shirdi Sai put his arm into boiling oil to bring out food for devotees. Undiscerning critics have described this action as a Tantric trick. The story is clearly a garbled version of a quite different occurrence. Shirdi Sai did put his arm into the hot water of a cooking pot when preparing food, but this was not a Tantric trick, only the trait of a resolute chef.

Shirdi Sai Baba was definitely not a Tantric Yogi. His reported encounter with a person in this category is frequently understated. Kusha Bhav (apparently a Nath Yogi) had dabbled in Tantric sorcery, and met with a stern response from the *faqir* of Shirdi (Chapter 27).

Various events in the life of Shirdi Sai Baba are not easy to define. A drawback is simplification, visible in some explanations. His early "expiry" at the mosque has been the subject of interpretations that are not always convincing, and invariably difficult to confirm (Chapter 9). His notable daily begging rounds certainly do set him well apart from affluent gurus with a relaxed lifestyle (Chapter 13). During his last years, he commenced a habit of asking for *dakshina*, resulting in gifts of money that he redistributed to others, not keeping anything for himself (Chapter 16). Too many gurus have, since, retained incoming funds, sometimes for purposes that are not beyond suspicion.

Sai Baba was not an enthusiast of *mantra*, and avoided giving initiation (Chapter 10). Such traits have perplexed some readers, but are attested in the literature on Sai Baba. For these and other reasons, he becomes additionally interesting.

Differing sources are revealing. The poet Das Ganu contributed a legendary depiction of Sai Baba's elusive guru, and this portrayal has caused many confusions (Chapter 8). The early memoranda of devotee Hari S. Dixit are more sober and factually informative (Chapter 14). The *Shirdi Diary* of Ganesh Khaparde is much better known, but still relevant to investigate in view of complexities (Chapter 31). The visit to

Introduction

Shirdi by Bal Ganghadar Tilak did not involve any political agitation on the part of Sai Baba (Chapter 30).

The controversial, but nonetheless relevant, work of Dr. Marianne Warren is capable of arousing both agreement and disagreement from the same party. Her presentation, profiling the Sufi background of Shirdi Sai, necessitates discussion of factors missing from more well known portrayals (Chapter 20).

A case has been made for the close relation of Shirdi Sai Baba to the eclectic trend evident in Maharashtra over centuries, and involving Bhakti *sants* and Sufis (Chapter 6). Consideration of *sants* like Eknath and Tukaram is surely relevant.

The temperament of Shirdi Sai Baba has often aroused comment, but too frequently in lop-sided terms. His explosive moods were accompanied by contrasting manifestations, sufficient to satisfy a prudent and exacting devotee like Ramachandra Tarkhad (Chapter 33). Less dramatically, the unusual attitude of Shirdi Sai to sacred books requires some attention (Chapter 18).

Swami Somdev (Somadeva) was one of the Vedantic contacts of Shirdi Sai. His first visit to Shirdi involved a misconception as to the nature of events. Superficial appearances can be misleading (Chapter 17). Recent criticism, from a Swami of the Shankara (or Dashanami) Order, attempted to label the Shirdi *faqir* as a Muslim, unfit for Hindu worship in temples (Appendix II). This opinion does not match the liberalism of Sai Baba, who incorporated Hindu worship at his mosque (Chapter 24).

One of the most frequently discussed events in the life of Sai Baba is a conversation with the *brahman* follower Nanasaheb Chandorkar, concerning a verse in the *Bhagavad Gita*. A prominent devotee commentator on this disputed episode was Govind Dabholkar, who supported the unorthodox dimensions of Sai Baba's *ajnana* argument. This matter has some philosophical interest, not the least because of different interpretations from Hindu and Muslim Sufi perspectives (Chapter 12).

An early contact of Sai Baba was Mohiuddin Tambuli, a Muslim inhabitant of Shirdi who proved resistant to Hindu activities at the mosque (Chapter 11). This drama was part of a recurring tension between Sai and Tambuli. The local opponent was at first victorious, but subsequently defeated. Sai Baba's own objective was a fraternal unity between Hindus and Muslims, a concord which he encouraged continuously amongst his followers (Chapter 23).

Individual reactions of new devotees were often revealing. Mulay Shastri was a fastidious *brahman*, at first too preoccupied with his private agenda of ritual and *asana*, which he considered more important than events at the Shirdi mosque (Chapter 19). Krishnashastri Bhishma was another caste-conscious *brahman*, influenced by conventional beliefs about contamination. He was initially averse to the pipe (*chilum*) featuring in the saint's routine at the Shirdi mosque (Chapter 32). Contrasting with such instances was the role of Bhagoji Shinde, a leper who became a personal attendant of Sai Baba. The Shirdi *faqir* is remarkable for the attention he gave to this man, thus defying social discrimination of an insidious type (Chapter 29).

The varied contacts of Sai Baba included entities who were not devotees, but saints existing outside his own activity. Some examples are Meher Baba, Bane Miyan, Gadge Maharaj, and Upasani Maharaj.

Meher Baba (d.1969) was an Irani Zoroastrian who encountered the *faqir* at Shirdi in 1915, thereafter demonstrating an unusual and varied vocation. He subsequently testified to the outstanding qualities of Sai Baba, who he regarded as the leading spiritual master of that era (Chapter 37).

Bane Miyan (d.1921) was an eccentric Muslim *faqir* of Aurangabad, whose early contact with Sai Baba remains

Introduction

obscure. Events in 1918 are an indication that some deep link existed between these two *faqirs*. The general biographical context for Bane Miyan exhibits complexities that are capable of different interpretations (Chapter 35).

Gadge Maharaj (d.1956) was a tireless worker in the cause of socially depressed people. Born a *shudra*, this saint of Maharashtra championed untouchables (*harijans*). His ideals were hard work and selfless service. The contact of Gadge with Sai Baba became, in part, legendary (Chapter 36).

Upasani Maharaj (d.1941) was a *brahman* disciple of Sai Baba who later gained autonomy at the Sakori ashram he inspired. Detailed information about him does exist, but is generally obscured. Whatever the debated religious origins of Sai Baba, Upasani Maharaj was one hundred per cent Hindu. A learned *shastri*, and a daunting ascetic, many features of his career are sufficiently unusual to merit a stronger interest than has so far been the norm (Chapter 38).

CONTENTS

	Preface	v
	Introduction	vii
1.	Early Years	1
2.	Abdul's Urdu *Notebook*	5
3.	*Qalandar* and *Majzub* Trends	13
4.	Arrival at Shirdi	18
5.	Intolerance and Liberality	21
6.	Bhakti *Sants* and Eclectic Sufis in Maharashtra	26
7.	An Independent *Faqir*	39
8.	Aurangabad, Gopalrao Deshmukh, and Jindewali	43
9.	*Nirvikalpa Samadhi*	46
10.	No Initiation or Mantra	48
11.	Mohiuddin Tambuli	52
12.	Hindu Devotees	55
13.	Daily Begging Rounds	60
14.	Memoranda of Hari S. Dixit	63
15.	*Shri Sai Satcharita*	72
16.	*Dakshina*	76
17.	Swami Somdev and the Flag	78
18.	Devotees Reading Books	80
19.	Mulay Shastri	84

20.	Marianne Warren and Sufism	87
21.	*Chilla-i-Makus*	100
22.	Muslim Devotees and Visitors	102
23.	Unity between Hindus and Muslims	104
24.	The Shirdi Mosque and *Chavadi*	107
25.	Affinity with *Bhakti*	110
26.	Professor Narke on What Sai Baba Taught	112
27.	Kusha Bhav, the Yogi	114
28.	Reincarnation and Hari S. Dixit	117
29.	Bhagoji Shinde	121
30.	Khaparde and Tilak	123
31.	Shirdi Diary	129
32.	Bhishma and the *Trikalajnani*	147
33.	The Amiable and Angry Saint	150
34.	Death and Burial	153
35.	Bane Miyan of Aurangabad	157
36.	Gadge Maharaj	168
37.	Zoroastrian Visitors	170
38.	Upasani Maharaj	175
	Appendix I Sufis and *Majazib* of Bijapur	178
	Appendix II Swarupananda Saraswati and Sai Baba Worship	187
	Notes	190
	Bibliography	227
	Index	235

1. Early Years

The early life of Sai Baba (d.1918) is very difficult to chart. The date of his birth is uncertain, and different theories exist about his birthplace. Furthermore, his early years at Shirdi are very sparsely recorded, and attended by reports which contain discrepancies.

A well known dating for his birth is 1838. This is uncertain, not definite, and based upon a devotee belief that Sai Baba lived to the age of eighty. This version is found as an approximate calculation in the *Shri Sai Satcharita*. (1) Various other dates of birth have also been proposed, including some in the 1850s.

The *Shri Sai Satcharita* (1929) is a relevant source. However, some (or many) hagiographical elements are discernible in this composition. The author was Govind R. Dabholkar (1856–1929), a devotee of Sai Baba, who wrote his book during the 1920s. (2) The *Satcharita* comprises over nine thousand verses in Marathi. This poetic work has been described as a religious text or *pothi*. "One does not look in it for historical truth or a chronological order of events." (3) This being so, the investigator has to correlate with other sources and attempt to place varied events in context.

In the second chapter of his book, Dabholkar refers to other compositions about Sai Baba that were known to him, (4) all of these being of a devotional and hagiological nature. In particular, Dabholkar refers to the works of Das Ganu, a poet and *kirtankar* who eulogised traditional saints, and who included Sai Baba in his elaborations. (5) Today, Das Ganu is not considered reliable as a historical source, whatever his talents as a poet and Vaishnava enthusiast. (6)

Dabholkar supplies very little information about the early years of Sai Baba. The celebrated "first and second arrivals" of Sai Baba at Shirdi are obscure, and attended by details which have been differently interpreted. The timeline for these events is contradictory, in that another major commentator gave a different date. The Dabholkar version is associated with the 1850s, whereas V. B. Kher refers to the period between 1868 and 1872. (7) The source for Kher on this point is Narasimhaswami, author of the lengthy *Life of Sai Baba*. (8) The difference is substantial enough to merit a cautious attitude.

A well known theory has named the birthplace of Sai Baba as Pathri, a village in the former dominion of the Nizam of Hyderabad. This version of origin argues for the identity of Sai Baba as a Hindu of the *brahman* caste. (9) The Pathri theory has been influential, but is not regarded as conclusive by all analysts. The status of plausible theory is not equivalent to confirmed fact. The same theory is attended by the consideration that, at a very early age, the young Sai left home to follow a Muslim *faqir*, thereafter leading a wandering existence for many years. In other words, Sai Baba is indicated to have changed religion.

Another theory attributed the birthplace to Jerusalem. At first sight, the geographical location specified here seems rather unlikely, but is certainly striking enough to merit comment. This rival theory is associated with the name of Shri Mittha Lakshmi Narasaiyya, a lawyer of Hyderabad. Sai Baba is here depicted as being born at Jerusalem in 1836, his parents being named as Vaishnava *brahmans* of Gujarat named Nandlal and Jamunabai. They are described in terms of associating with a Muslim *faqir* who took them to Mecca, where they visited the holy places of Islam. Afterwards they returned to India, and lived for a time at Pathri village in the district of Aurangabad. (10)

The Jerusalem theory has appeared in a variant. (11) The basic details are:

Early Years

The names of the parents are the same; this couple are said to have gone on a pilgrimage to all the sacred places in India, at one of which they met a Muslim saint who offered to take them to Mecca. Their pilgrimage to Mecca occurred in 1852, after which they proceeded to Jerusalem, where their son was born in 1858. The child was named Sai by the Muslim saint. They returned to India in 1862, after which the Muslim saint parted from them. (12)

A very late date of birth is supplied here. The Jerusalem theory has been viewed in terms of an attempt to explain the strong Muslim associations of Sai Baba, depicting his origin in relation to the Mecca pilgrimage (*hajj*), but maintaining a Hindu parentage. This little known report claims that the boy was named Sai by a Muslim saint, whereas the more celebrated version affirms that Sai Baba received his name from the Hindu priest Mhalsapati when he arrived in Shirdi.

Dabholkar has no reference to a military detail that is now of interest. A Professor of Sanskrit was interviewed in 1936, (13) and divulged:

> Sai Baba mentioned some autobiographical reminiscences of his own. He said he had been at the battle in which the Rani of Jhansi took part. He was then in the army. (Narasimhaswami 2006:230)

This detail was regarded as historical by Narasimhaswami, a major commentator. A problem exists in defining the context for this military phase. There is no indication, in the brief report available, as to what side Sai Baba joined during the Sepoy Rebellion of 1857–58. Different commentators have construed that this *faqir* fought in (a) the British army, and (b) the rebel Indian army. If the military episode has historical validity, then Sai Baba must have been born *circa* 1840 or earlier.

Sai Baba was early recognised as a Muslim *faqir*, this Arabic word denoting an ascetic. Throughout his life, many high caste Hindus were disconcerted by his Muslim characteristics, for example, his white *kafni* and headgear, his presence in a mosque, and his Islamic phraseology. He did not wear the ochre robe of Hindu ascetics, and spoke the Muslim language of Deccani Urdu. "A number of orthodox Brahmins adamantly refused to go too close to the saint in case they were ritually polluted." (14) A Sufi identity has been urged for the Shirdi *faqir*, but in different versions.

Sai Baba is often said to have expressed Muslim teachings to his Muslim devotees, and Hindu teachings to his Hindu devotees. Yet his predominant mode of communication was allusive, involving short stories or parables known as *goshtis*. In his last years, which are by far the most well documented, he gives no indication of being a systematic expositor to the many visitors who arrived at the Shirdi mosque.

Sai Baba was not a preacher of any kind. Instead, he demonstrated an attitude of religious tolerance that encompassed Hindus, Muslims, Zoroastrians, Christians, and Sikhs.

2. Abdul's Urdu *Notebook*

An early Muslim disciple of Sai Baba was Abdul Baba (1869/71–1954). He arrived in Shirdi as a young man in 1889, and served the saint for thirty years. During that period, Abdul wrote in Deccani Urdu a "notebook" recording the utterances of Sai Baba. The jottings have a fragmentary complexion, but abundantly reveal the Sufi affinities of Sai Baba. No dates are given for the many different entries; the earliest entries may have been composed during the 1890s.

This *Notebook* remained unpublished for over eighty years after the death of Sai Baba. There was a general ignorance of the contents. Many Hindus could not read Urdu, including the literate commentator B. V. Narasimhaswami, who briefly referred to this document. The manuscript was made known decades later in a book by the late Dr. Marianne Warren, who remarked: "The fact that the manuscript's Islamic nature does not fit in with the accepted Hindu interpretation and presentation of Sai Baba may explain why it has remained unpublished." (15)

Dr. Warren had the *Notebook* translated into English by several Urdu specialists. The contents are rather mixed. "Lack of organisation is only to be expected in a notebook never intended for publication." (16) Over 130 pages are presented, the most difficult being 28 pages in Modi script, "a very old short-hand version of Marathi in a script not read today." (17) The 109 pages in Urdu (and Arabic) afford many brief references to Islamic religion and law, *hadith* (traditions or sayings of the Prophet Muhammad), Sufi teachings, and Sufi Orders. Sai Baba was evidently familiar with the poetry of

Jalaluddin Rumi (d.1273) and the legends concerning Abu Yazid al-Bistami and Hallaj. (18) There are also references to Hindu religion, providing a significant indicator of Sai Baba's liberalism.

"The major portion of the text comprises Muslim and Sufi ideas, with lists of significant Sufi divines and their orders." (19) Some embellishments of Abdul are discernible, including a *qawwali* song which extols the power of Sai Baba to confer progeny. (20) This addition reflects a belief existing amongst devotees of the Shirdi saint.

A relevant observation is made by Warren: "It is often said that Sai Baba never gave discourses, but the *Sai Baba MS* [the *Notebook*] reveals that he gave quite extensive spiritual talks to Abdul" (Warren 1999:311).

In general, the strong impression conveyed by the sources is that the saint of Shirdi veered away from discourses. Abdul was evidently an exception to the rule, probably because he lived under the personal instructions of Sai, being a committed pupil who had renounced the world as a *faqir*. Most devotees were householders. We do not know if any other Muslims were present on the occasions when the saint made his disclosures to Abdul. These may have been purely private sessions.

Analysis of the *Notebook* is still at an early stage. There are several complexities not generally comprehended. The subject matter in this document varies from the *Quran* to the Sufi hierarchy of saints. The angle of Sufi discipline is firm. Sai Baba employs a few Hindu words such as *tapas* (an equivalent of the Arabic *riyaz*, meaning austerity).

> When a person practices *tapas*, divine insight (*marifa*) will automatically come.... He who performs *tapas*, I regard him to be on the path. It would not be proper to give him full knowledge about it [the path]. But before you proceed on the path of *Allah*, you must discipline the mind.... The heart is created for the realization of God. To find the way to attaining

a vision of God is a man's true task. For the vision of God, divine sight is necessary. (21)

This statement was evidently an instruction to Abdul, who himself lived as a *faqir*. The ideal was austerity, psychological discipline, and self-abnegation. Sai Baba appears to have prudently adapted some of his phraseology to the Hindu milieu without losing the Sufi thread. He also uses the Sanskrit word *prana* (life breath, subtle energy). "The [physical] body is under the control of *prana*." (22) He disputes materialism. "The people who equate the spirit with the [physical] body are wrong." (23)

Sai Baba uses the Sanskrit word *buddhi* for intellect or intelligence. This organ he compares in Islamic terminology to a *wazir* (prime minister), in the sense that bodily functions are servants of the intellect. Indeed, before "efforts" on the spiritual path are attempted, "one should understand one's thought processes." (24) Sai Baba refers to the brain in terms of analytical and memory faculties. An ethical teaching emerges here. "The intellect has to be ever vigilant to those enemies who wage war against the moral kingdom." (25) The enemies include anger, greed, and jealousy.

Sai Baba became well known amongst Hindu devotees for his pragmatic ethical reflections. Aspects of this approach are found in the *Notebook*, which throws light upon certain expressions not always seen in due perspective, for example, "Who are we?" (26) The latter phrase appears in the *Charters and Sayings* of Narasimhaswami, who applied a Vedantic interpretation. Narasimhaswami was unable to read the *Notebook*, although he did converse on two occasions with Abdul (via an interpreter), in 1936 and 1938.

The Shirdi *faqir* divided behaviour into four basic categories: animalistic, aggressive, satanic or evil, and angelic or divine. Man should aim for "angelic" standards by virtue of the intellect that he possesses. Yet too often man behaves like a Satan, not an angel. The intellect is neglected and abused.

Strive always to perfect your knowledge, abjure from evil deeds, wish well to all people, and keep the bad and evil-minded persons at a distance. (27)

Certain aspects of his own behaviour indicate that Sai Baba was attempting to cordon "the bad and evil-minded" from entering his mosque. He was not always welcoming. One of his devotees, Imambai Chota Khan, at first found great difficulty in being accepted by the saint. Chota Khan was a soldier, and had recently been involved in an episode of violence, of which Sai Baba showed an unexpected knowledge, while deeming the tragic event to be a serious drawback (Shepherd 2015:182–183).

A significant phrase appears in the *Notebook*. "If you realize that there is an inner Controller, then review your actions and way of living, and decide which of the four tendencies are predominant in you." (28)

The four tendencies here refer to the animalistic, aggressive, satanic, and angelic. This is evidently what Sai Baba meant by such cautionary phrases as "Who are we?" The saint was referring to a form of self-analysis, logically applicable to the "path" that so often becomes a form of fantasy and self-delusion. This was not a meditation routine, but something more immediate, and perhaps rather more demanding.

The Shirdi *faqir* emphasises a list of vices to be avoided. These include: deceiving others, embezzlement, insincerity, "producing cheap shoddy goods," destroying the faith of others, and self-deceit. This is followed by an encouragement to do better.

> If you truly discriminate—then wisdom, knowledge, learning, ingenuity, ability, good conduct, caring for the welfare of others, perseverance—all these good qualities will arise in you and will keep you company until the end of your life. (29)

There is no doubt that Sai Baba did formulate a strong ethical teaching, which he frequently administered in pithy remarks and asides to visitors. He obviously considered these ethical requisites to be more important than the extravagant paraphernalia often associated with spirituality.

The Sufi tone of the *Notebook* is not invariable. This text also contains passages referring to Hindu *avatars* or divine incarnations. Some analysts believe that certain statements are those of Abdul, including the assertion: "The present Kaliyuga *avatar* is Sai Baba." (30) That claim is followed by an apparently contradictory theme: "In this world there are always 10-20 *avatars* of similar kind living at the same time." (31)

A *qawwali* or song by Abdul is quoted. This song demonstrates a positive assessment of the saint's unorthodox Sufi role. The composition includes the line: "Sai Baba embodies the Vedas, as also *Allah*." (32) This commemoration of an inter-religious affinity is accompanied by another evocative theme: "The *darbar* (court, audience) of Sai Baba is that of a *qalandar*." (33) This signification has been contracted. (34) The *qalandar* was a type of unorthodox Sufi, represented during the medieval era by diverse mendicants. (35) Sai Baba was not a mendicant during his mature years, living for a lengthy period in Shirdi.

Afterwards, in the *Notebook*, come the lists of Sufi figures relating to *khanwadas* or orders, including the Chishti Order and earlier lineages associated with Abu Yazid al-Bistami and Junayd of Baghdad. These lists are followed by a version of the Sufi hierarchy of saints, here led by thirteen *qutubs*, the key man being the *qutub al-aqtab* (in other versions of Sufi teaching, there are only one or five *qutubs*). The basic idea is that, just as emperors rule the earth, "spiritual arrangements are entrusted to holy men" in the "management of the inner world." (36)

Sai Baba stresses renunciation and celibacy. His teaching in this respect was not emphasised to householders, with whom he adopted different tactics. Abdul was a *faqir* from an early age, and accustomed to rigours. "You should be awake day and night, remain away from women, avoid rich food, reside in the jungles and mountains." (37) However, Abdul did not have to live in the wilderness. He was permitted by Sai Baba to marry in his later years, and thereafter lived with his family at Shirdi.

Warnings are given in the *Notebook*. A Sufi poet is cited. "That Sufi who is not pure (*safi*) will earn the wrath of God." (38) Sai Baba evidently regarded some nominal Sufis as deviants. Some interesting and complex passages follow. The strong judgment is made that "some *faqirs* are so wicked that we feel like taking away their *kafni* [robe] and consigning them to the fire." (39)

The reprehensible Sufis are here called "false *pirs* and *faqirs*." They are implied as being at the "satanic" level of expression. Some regarded "the dance and song of the prostitute" (40) as being a legitimate Sufi mode of worship. These activities apparently refer to the *mahfil* (get-together) at some Sufi shrines in India, where courtesans or nautch (dance) girls were invited to perform as entertainers. The *mahfil* was a musical scenario. In earlier decades, British officers and Indian sepoys had been spectators of nautch performances at a more general level, but by the mid-nineteenth century these occurrences had stopped because of complaints made by Christian army chaplains and Muslim reformists (Green 2009:81–2). Sai Baba was clearly on the side of reformists.

According to Sai Baba, the erring Sufis were not on the path to *Allah*, but on the path leading to the blindness of Satan. In that connection, he says: "This dangerous wall of the world (separating you from God) is fleeting, and so to engross yourself in it, is truly madness." (41) Elsewhere, another reference of Sai Baba to demolishing a wall, was interpreted in terms of Vedantic teachings about body and *atman*. (42)

A major objection is expressed by the Shirdi saint. "Someone pretends to become a *pir* [adept Sufi], showing his skills, attracting and influencing people in order to fill his coffers and amass wealth." (43) He also complains that false *pirs* "boast about being *Sayyads* or *Pirzadas* or *Shaykhs*." (44) In contrast, Sai Baba did not amass wealth, and did not refer to himself as a Sufi or *pir*. Insofar as is known, he only used the word *faqir* in reference to himself. The *pirzadas* were a well known category of Sufi, being hereditary descendants of Sufi saints, and prominent as custodians of Sufi tombs (see Appendix I).

Although Sai Baba appears to be an orthodox Sufi, via his deference to the *Quran* and his acknowledgment of Sufi Orders, he is very unorthodox in other respects. He maintained the basic morality of Islamic asceticism (*faqiri*), but diverged from the ritualist approach. His approach was mystical, not formal.

> When in the *nimbar* (niche) of your heart, the Beloved is enthroned, what is the need for the *pesh-imam* (priest)? If we can achieve *ivadat* (our end) by prayer to God (*Allah*), what is the necessity to go to the *masjid* to listen to the *Kutba*? If all the time we are engrossed in devotion to God, why should we do *namaz* five times a day? (45)

His own partial performance of *namaz* (daily ritual prayer) was regarded as erratic by orthodox Muslims. His outlook converged with that of the more esoteric Sufis, who were quite often in conflict with the *ulama*. Unorthodox Sufis were frequently known by the label of *majzub*, and were derided as madmen by the *mullas*.

A strikingly radical reflection emerges in the *Notebook*:

> There are thousands of mullahs (teachers), thousands of alims (scholars), hundreds of thousands of mufti (jurists), millions

of qadis (judges). Most of these people have started taking bribes. (Warren 1999:306)

This accusation, featuring exaggerated numbers, serves to place Sai Baba firmly in the category of dissenters against corruption. Further testimony to his unorthodox religious orientation is the *Notebook* statement:

> Vishnu is equal to the *Bismillah ar-Rahim*, *Allah* the Merciful the Pardoner. Ali is equal to Brahma. Mahadev [Shiva] is equal to Mohammed and to *Malik al-maut*, the angel of death. (46)

The religious liberalism of Sai Baba was a clear demarcator from "orthodox Sufis," who demonstrated an insular attitude to Hindus. The liberalism of the Shirdi saint was a distinctive continuation of earlier trends in symbiosis between Hinduism and Sufism, events which had occurred in Maharashtra since the sixteenth century.

3. *Qalandar* and *Majzub* Trends

The *Notebook* of Abdul Baba reveals an "unorthodox Sufi" context for Sai Baba. He was not an antinomian radical in the dissolute category, but a moral and mystical radical, the ethical content of his teaching being pronounced.

Sai Baba lived as a simple *faqir*, refusing to appropriate wealth. He remained a beggar until the end of his life. Like Hazrat Babajan, he had no formal honours, and claimed no *silsila*. (47) The Arabic word *silsila* denotes a lineage or chain of spiritual descent, common to the Sufi Orders, and frequently claiming an ultimate affiliation with the Prophet Muhammad.

Sai Baba was a marginalised figure in relation to the Sufi Orders. The *Notebook* merely provides skeletal lists of revered traditional figures associated with the Orders, and does not claim any affiliation. Sai Baba emerges as an independent mystic, removed from organisations.

A song of Abdul, appearing in the *Notebook*, fleetingly refers to Sai Baba in a *qalandar* context, indicating that the saint was unorthodox. "The *darbar* (audience) of Sai Baba is that of a *qalandar*" (Warren 1999:289). This reference is significant. However, the attribution needs to be set in due context, to avoid confusions. The nonconformist tag of *qalandar* (a Persian word) had been in vogue for several centuries, and was still used in India. Sai Baba was not by any means typical of this diverse category. Abdul probably used the tag because Sai Baba was not affiliated to any Sufi Order. The independents varied substantially in their characteristics.

The subject of *qalandars* is difficult to penetrate in terms of history, as distinct from popular lore. "The term *qalandari*, to which the *Arabian Nights* has given wide currency, covers in its historical usage a wide range of dervish types. It was loosely applied in the East to any wandering *faqir*, but it was also adopted by certain groups and even distinctive orders were formed, hence the problems of defining the term" (Trimingham 1971:267).

A liberal scholar, Professor Saiyid Athar Abbas Rizvi, reflected that "the history of Sufism has been made infinitely more colourful by the role of the qalandars" (Rizvi 1978:301). The eleventh century Sufi poet Baba Tahir was active in West Iran, and is credited with an early testimony to this phenomenon, referring to himself "as a wandering dervish (*darwish-i qalandar*), with no roof over his head, sleeping with a stone for a pillow, constantly harassed by spiritual anxieties" (ibid:76).

Qalandars early gained a reputation for celibacy and aversion to owning property. Many were mendicants, and noted for a distinctive habit of shaving off the beard, hair, and eyebrows. In India, they are reported to have favoured a saffron robe in the fourteenth century, (48) although (or because) that colour was strongly associated with Hindu holy men. The *qalandar* contingent were often degenerate and exhibitionist by the nineteenth century. Some extremist *qalandars* in Qajar Iran were addicted to wine and opium. The vagaries of this category have led to such definitions of *qalandar* as: "A dervish type that disregards appearance and flouts public opinion" (Trimingham 1971:309). Their antinomian tendencies were not represented by Sai Baba.

There are also other terms which denote an unorthodox Sufi orientation. A well known designation is that of *majzub*, a Persian word deriving from Arabic. This word gained widespread usage in India from the Mughal era onwards, and generally referred to an abstracted saint, believed to be in

Qalandar and Majzub Trends

close communion with the divine. However, manifestations of the *majzub* lifestyle were diverse. For instance, the term *majzub* was applied to Sarmad, the radical *qalandar* who went naked like some Hindu holy men. This mystic aroused the pious wrath of *ulama* at the Mughal court of Aurangzeb, an event resulting in his execution. (49)

Sarmad was a highly literate *majzub*, an Islamised Jew in close association with the liberal Mughal prince Dara Shikoh, who favoured amicable relations between Muslims and Hindus. This contrasted with the fundamentalist or *jihadi* tendencies of the clerical opposition. Inclinations to liberalism at the Mughal court continued in the nineteenth century, when leading rebels of the Sepoy Rebellion selected the last Mughal emperor (Bahadur Shah II) as a figurehead.

Unfortunately, more insular tendencies were also in occurrence. During the fourteenth century, the spread of Sufism to the Deccan showed some tolerance on the part of the Chishti Order. One objective of the continuing influx was to propagate Islam.

> These [Chishti] missionaries acquired a following of non-Muslims, not all of whom were converted to Islam. Their work undoubtedly contributed towards stabilisation of Muslim rule in Maharashtra. Though at first, conversion to Islam seems to have been voluntary, later on as political power passed to Muslims, the conversion policy of missionaries and rulers perhaps assumed a comparatively aggressive form. (50)

In contrast, tolerant and independent *majzub* trends featured in Islamic milieux of North India and the Deccan. The origin of this phenomenon has been dated to the Lodi dynasty (1451–1526). One focus was Bijapur, a city of the Deccan where diverse mystics and nonconformists appeared in the seventeenth and eighteenth centuries (see Appendix I). The biographical records are only fragmentary, but the general developments indicate a widespread resistance to the insular mandate of "orthodox Sufism," which frequently militated against liberal Sufis and Hindus, the latter being regarded as underdog *kafirs* or infidels. (51)

A number of *majazib*, at Bijapur and elsewhere, were known to adopt nakedness like some Hindu *sadhus*. Sai Baba has become associated with the *majzub* category (Shepherd 2015:22–37), in an effort to penetrate his unorthodox role. He did not favour nudity, always wearing his white *kafni* and accompanying headgear. This was the recognised garb of Muslim *faqirs*, a feature which did not prevent him from gaining many Hindu devotees. During his last years, he permitted Hindu *arati* ceremonies at the mosque where he resided.

Basic misunderstandings about "unorthodox" Sufism have been in currency. For instance, a fairly frequent contemporary belief is that *majzubs* (or *majazib*) were mentally deranged. The blanket assumption has been supported by some Western academics (but not others). The proscribing *ulama* certainly wanted everyone to believe that *majzub* dissidents were madmen, and of no consequence.

Some *majzub* entities retired to the forests and jungles, lived in caves, and were careful to keep a low profile in the face of orthodox disapproval. Others are known to have been active in towns and cities. Hagiographies followed stock ideas of what occurred, and were keen to elaborate miracle events in the absence of relevant details.

The Islamic *ulama* were sometimes acting as "orthodox Sufis." These conservatives caricatured unorthodox Sufis as "madmen" (*majazib*, the plural of *majzub*). This adverse reflection basically meant that the *majazib* did not hate Hindus like the insular *mullas* did, and were not concerned with formal Islamic observances. The castigation also targeted monistic teachings, and perhaps also implied a lack of pedigree (*silsila*) on the part of unorthodox mystics distanced from any affiliation with Sufi Orders.

The orthodox Sufis became notorious, even within their own ranks, for the acquisition of royal land grants. The *khanaqah* endowments of Sufi Orders often decoded to an opulent lifestyle, in which goods could be hoarded in the Sufi retreat and storerooms. A "Sufi petty gentry" of *pirzadas* developed at Bijapur in the seventeenth century. The *pirzadas* were hereditary descendants of saints, and acted as prestigious custodians of Sufi tombs. This trend became widespread in the Deccan, and also other regions. Status and funding does not necessarily amount to spiritual achievement.

Trappings of orthodox Sufism included both the *dargah* (tomb or shrine) and the *khanaqah* (organisational centre). Sufi tombs became popular foci for legend and festival, and were believed to be repositories of the *barakat* (blessing, power) of the deceased saint.

Whatever his precise background, Sai Baba was far removed from the tendencies demonstrated by orthodox Sufism. His liberal and nonconformist attitude is reflected in numerous features of his lifestyle and disposition. For instance, he chose allusive speech in preference to any form of dogma. He is perhaps best described as an independent *faqir*.

4. Arrival at Shirdi

Sai Baba reputedly followed a *faqir* from the age of eight. The identity of this *faqir* is a blank. When he arrived in the village of Shirdi, at an uncertain date, Sai Baba initially stayed for a short while only. He is stated to have departed, returning later. The duration of absence is variously reported.

According to the *Shri Sai Satcharita*, the young "Sainath" first appeared "in the Shirdi village, under a Neem tree, at the tender age of sixteen.... In which country, which righteous family, or in which parental abode, Baba took birth, this no one knew." (52) The age given here has led to the dating of 1854 for the first arrival. However, "Baba suddenly disappeared from Shirdi, only to reappear, once again, in the company of Chand Patil [Patel]." (53) The last mentioned person was a Muslim householder.

Another event is mentioned very fleetingly, and to date lacks due context. "It is common knowledge among the villagers that [Sai] Baba sat near this *samadhi* [tomb], in meditation, observing total silence for a period of twelve years." (54)

The obscure tomb is also described as a cell. Dabholkar, the narrator, was clearly sceptical of the lore which had developed about this site. Sai Baba had reputedly told the villagers that an exhumed underground cell (paved with limestone) was the seat of his guru. "Baba dearly loved a joke. Maybe, the cell was his own dwelling." (55)

The early phase of Sai Baba's residence at Shirdi is very sparsely recorded, a fact which has led to uncertainties and divergent reconstructions.

Arrival at Shirdi

Chand Patel was the Muslim headman of distant Dhupkhed, a village situated near Aurangabad. "His wife's nephew was engaged to be married to a bride from Shirdi." (56) Yet according to Das Ganu, Patel's "wife's sister" was the relative who got married. (57) Another report refers to a girl who married Hamid, the son of Aminbhai of Shirdi. (58) The discrepancy in gender does not greatly affect the narrative, but is proof that some details became altered in transmission.

Sai Baba accompanied the marriage party to Shirdi. They travelled on horseback and in bullock carts. This company arrived at a yard or compound adjoining the Khandoba temple, on the outskirts of Shirdi. A banyan tree is mentioned. The compound (or field) belonged to Mhalsapati, the priest of the temple. This *pujari* is said to have addressed the visiting *faqir* with the Marathi words: "*Ya* [welcome] *Sai.*" According to Dabholkar, "from then onwards, that name became his proper name." (59)

The *Satcharita* does not mention the fact that Sai was a name current amongst Muslim *faqirs*, a name apparently deriving from the Arabic word *sa'ih*, which denoted an itinerant ascetic. The detail about Mhalsapati may have been an innovation created to explain the origin of the saint's name. However, there is a credible and realistic report that Mhalsapati turned Sai Baba away from the Khandoba temple, instead directing him to a mosque, in view of his Muslim appearance. (60)

Dabholkar emphasised a defensive theme in relation to the issue of religious identity:

> Indestructible and ancient that Sai is, he is neither Hindu nor Muslim. He has no caste, no descent, no family, no *gotra*. The state of self-realisation was the core of his being. (61)

Although one can appreciate the admirable religious neutrality of this statement, Dabholkar does overlook here the subject's identity as a Muslim *faqir*. Sai Baba eventually chose to live in a mosque (*masjid*), and was frequently avoided by high caste Hindus, who feared contamination through any association with him. His Hindu devotees adopted some discretionary measures, including the identification as "neither Hindu nor Muslim."

The saint was not concerned to emphasise religious identity or to preach doctrines. In this sense, he was indeed quite independent from both Islam and Hinduism.

The allusive speech of Sai Baba left his early years largely a blank for the historian. We know for certain that, in his later years, he wanted his Hindu and Muslim devotees to live in amicable association, avoiding the frictions that could arise. Eventually, the Hindus substantially outnumbered the Muslim followers, leading to what has been called a "Hinduisation" tendency in the depiction of events. (62)

The insularist tactic against Sai Baba has continued. Some fundamentalists have urged that he was a Muslim *faqir*, and should therefore not be worshipped by Hindus (see Appendix II). This stigma fails to match the praiseworthy religious liberalism of Sai Baba.

5. Intolerance and Liberality

The caste Hindus who were disconcerted by Sai Baba had little or no idea about history. They associated him with Islam, and did not understand Sufism. Even today, knowledge of complexities in Sufi history is largely obscured by generalising concepts and assumptions.

The liberalism of Sai Baba stands in stark contrast to insular tendencies of Islamic preaching in India. The "orthodox Sufi" was not always too far removed from the extremely aggressive attitudes early associated with Sayed Nuruddin Mubarak Ghaznawi (d.1234-5). This man was a disciple of the well known Shihabuddin Suhrawardi of Baghdad, inspirer of the Suhrawardi Order. Ghaznawi moved to Delhi, where he was appointed *Shaikh al-Islam* by the Turkish Sultan Iltutmish (regd 1211–36). Such a role was the means to obtain stipend and land.

According to the fourteenth century historian Ziyauddin Barani, the preaching of Ghaznawi emphasised principles for the protection of Islam. He enjoined rulers to disgrace Hindus. "They should not tolerate the sight of Hindus, and in particular they should exterminate the Brahmans, who are the leaders of heretics and disseminators of heresy. They should not allow *kafirs* (infidels) and *mushriks* [polytheists] to lead an honourable life or assign to them high office." (63)

This intolerance was apparently accompanied by the theme that Islamic philosophers should be banished, and "the teaching of philosophy prohibited in Islamic territories." (64) Shia Muslims were also to be disgraced. Such emphases persisted in later centuries on the part of Islamic conservatives.

The *Hidaya* was an early work on Sunni jurisprudence, and became influential in India. A Muslim commentator writes:

> The *Hidayah* is quite explicit about the legality of *jihad* (holy war) against infidels even when they have not taken the offensive. Verses of the Quran restricting *jihad* to certain contingencies were so interpreted as to show that a condition of war with non-Muslims was the norm. (65)

This political and military convenience became celebrated in wars fought by the Turkish Sultans of Delhi and the later Mughal emperors. The discrepancy included a factor often obscured:

> The non-Muslims of all parts of the world, whatever their situation or their attitude towards the Muslims, were identified with the *Kuffar* of Mecca and assumed to be inveterate enemies of Islam. The degree of their humiliation was the measure of the glory and prestige of the Muslims. (66)

A religious scholar initially influenced by the *Hidaya* was Maulana Fakhruddin Zarradi, who migrated to Delhi from Samana. He wanted to become an *alim* (religious scholar), and tended to despise Sufism. Zarradi spoke disparagingly of the Chishti sage Nizamuddin Awliya (d.1325), whom he had never met. Zarradi was afterwards persuaded to visit that Sufi, and there followed a discussion between them relating to the *Hidaya*. Zarradi's tutor had failed to clarify certain exegetical problems, but the Chishti *shaikh* explained these satisfactorily. Zarradi then became a pupil of Nizamuddin, even adopting a celibate lifestyle. (67)

According to a modern scholar, the free kitchen meal (*langar*) of Nizamuddin Awliya was "almost certainly . . . open to Hindus and Muslims alike." (68) The Chishtis gained a reputation for being the most liberal of the Sufi Orders. However, some critics urge that the Chishti Order was nevertheless conservative in supporting orthodox

Intolerance and Liberality

mandates of the *ulama*, who jettisoned religious tolerance and ideologically consigned *kafirs* (non-Muslims) to hell.

Chishtis, and other Sufi Orders, emphasised *silsila* or genealogical authority, sometimes described as a lineage or chain of spiritual descent. "Pride of descent is strong among Sufi masters, who carry in their heads long and complicated genealogies" (Ernst and Lawrence 2002:47). In contrast, Sai Baba did not claim any *silsila*.

Six centuries after Nizamuddin Awliya, at distant Shirdi, Sai Baba was providing free meals in a situation completely outside the Sufi Orders. For some years (perhaps two decades or so), Sai Baba prepared food on special days for his guests at the Shirdi mosque. He did the cooking himself, and could cater for a hundred people (Shepherd 2015:198–200). This culinary habit was superseded in his last years, when the inflow of visitors became substantial. Many affluent urban Hindu devotees then brought their own food as a communal gift.

In 2014, Swami Swarupananda Saraswati campaigned against worship of Sai Baba in Hindu temples, describing this activity as inappropriate, on the grounds that Sai was a Muslim *faqir*. The dismissive contention caused much offence amongst Shirdi Sai devotees. The Swami subsequently tendered an apology in a court of law (see Appendix II).

A basic point, so often neglected, is that any accusation (or denial) of Sai Baba being a Muslim is very misleading if due contextual details are not supplied. The independent *faqir* role of Sai Baba is, to date, poorly assimilated in general media. He was neither an orthodox Muslim, and nor an orthodox Sufi. His liberal outlook is distinctive in many ways, rendering invalid any stigma in terms of religious identity.

An instance of contrasting religious insularity occurred in 1909, when an orthodox *brahman* (and a medical doctor) visited Shirdi with a friend who had the prestigious role of a *mamlatdar* (revenue collector). The name of this physician escaped record. He was a devotee of Rama, and declared that he would not bow in *darshan* greeting to Sai Baba. Dabholkar states that "Sai Baba was a Muslim" (*Satcharita* 12:153). The doctor told his friend: "I cannot bring myself to make obeisance at the feet of a Muslim and therefore I have had reservations about going to Shirdi" (Dabholkar 1999:193).

The *mamlatdar* explained that nobody in Shirdi would ask the doctor to prostrate before the *faqir*, and that Sai Baba himself "expected nothing of the kind" (Kamath and Kher 1991:112). This official (unnamed) was evidently one of a substantial number of Hindus, working for the British government, who became devotees of the Shirdi *faqir*.

The medic reluctantly accompanied his friend to Shirdi. There he acted in a manner contrary to his own statements, prostrating before the saint living in the mosque. He afterwards explained to his companion that he had seen Rama (not Sai) sitting before him, and this was the reason for his act of obeisance. The doctor now reflected: "How can he [Sai] be a Muslim? No, indeed! He is a yogi, an Incarnation of God" (Dabholkar 1999:194).

The next day, this doctor vowed that he would not set foot in the mosque unless Sai Baba gave him blessing. He commenced a fast to this end, while staying at Shirdi. He was evidently attempting to coerce the saint into a favourable response. This petitioner apparently desired spiritual experiences, probably similar to his vision of Rama. The mosque was still considered alien territory.

On the fourth day of his fast, a friend from Khandesh arrived for the purpose of *darshan*. These two acquaintances had not met for nine years, and the joyful reunion caused the doctor to follow his friend into the mosque, forgetting his vow. He even prostrated before Sai Baba, along with his friend. The *faqir* was apparently aware of the fast, and made a critical comment, asking why the doctor had come into the mosque. The Rama devotee then felt remorse. "He remembered his own resolve and was filled with sadness and regret" (ibid). The medic could now see that he had acted from the wrong angle, in a state of confusion.

That night, the doctor "experienced an indescribable bliss, a state of mind that lasted for a fortnight, even after his return home" (Kamath and Kher 1991:112). The indications are that he became a devotee of Sai Baba.

This episode is probably accurate to a large extent. However, it is not generally favoured in the Sai Baba literature, probably because of the religious associations. Nevertheless, Dabholkar is explicit in his narration, and relays the sense of religious division that some devotees initially created in their minds. Such reporting surely deserves a better name than hagiography.

6. Bhakti *Sants* and Eclectic Sufis in Maharashtra

After the death of Sai Baba, an influential belief eventually emerged that he was born a Hindu in the village of Pathri, situated in the Aurangabad region of the Deccan. (69) This is not definitive history, and some dissenters believe that he was born a Muslim. Either way, his vocation demonstrates a strong assimilation of Hindu devotees, and a policy of conciliation with all creeds. Sai Baba is well known for making concessions to Hindu *arati* ritual at his mosque, and in his last years also participated in a weekly procession which has been compared to Vaishnava celebrations at Pandharpur.

Sai Baba demonstrated a clear affinity with the *bhakti* temperament of Hindus, as distinct from Vedanta or Yoga. Vaishnava devotionalism has often been compared to Sufism, and some scholars have emphasised overlapping features between the two traditions.

The Hindu *bhakti* movements were monotheistic in orientation, and opposed to caste discrimination. They are believed to have been influenced by Sufis. At the level of formal religion, Islam and Hinduism were far apart. Hinduism featured a rigid class system, while permitting much flexibility in the individual forms of worship. In Islam, the reverse tended to be operative; social organisation lacked caste rigidity, but worship was markedly standardised. (70)

Vaishnava devotionalism exercised a strong influence in Maharashtra from the thirteenth century. Traditions featuring the Vaishnava *sant* ("good man") included saints from all castes who opposed the inflexible social structure of orthodox Hinduism. There were also orthodox Vaishnava devotees.

An extension in North India exhibited some different characteristics. This trend "drew on Vaishnava *bhakti*, Sufism, and Nath Yoga, whose terminologies can be found within Sant literature." (71) Kabir and Nanak are the most famous *sant* entities in the northern vista, the latter inspiring the religion of Sikhism.

In Maharashtra, there were substantial differences between different *bhakti* traditions. One of these was the Mahanubhava *panth*, inspired by Chakradhar Swami, in the thirteenth century. This ascetic *bhakti* movement worshipped Krishna, but vigorously rejected the caste system and brahmanical ideology and ritualism. Their leaders were dissident *brahmans* who gained a following amongst low caste people. The Mahanubhava welcomed untouchables, and even created an order of ascetic women, in defiance of caste stigmas (women being generally regarded as unfit for spiritual liberation). The influence of Jainism, and even Islam, has been suggested. The Mahanubhava were afflicted by orthodox Hindu displeasure, and in response they developed a secret script for their writings. (72)

The Mahanubhava revered the names of Krishna and Dattatreya, but rejected worship of images. (73) This was a point of disagreement with the *bhaktas* committed to Vitthala. A more prominent movement in Maharashtra was the Varkari *panth*, associated with the worship of Vitthala (Vithoba), a Vaishnava deity whose famous temple at Pandharpur became a major site of pilgrimage (Dhere 2011). Varkaris were in ideological opposition to Mahanubhavs. "By many accounts, the two religious groups were bitter rivals, disparaging each other in their narrative, though the lion's share of lampooning came from the Mahanubhavs." (74)

The ascendant Varkaris reputedly included some well known *sants*, including Namdev (flourished *circa* 1300).

The historical Namdev is elusive. Legends depict him as living at Pandharpur, and also travelling widely. He was a favoured subject of later hagiographers, including the well known Mahipati (1715–90), whose chief source in this respect was Nabhadas, writing a century earlier in North India in a proto-Hindi dialect. (75) Manuscripts recording the poems of Namdev are as old as 1581; however, most of the extant songs attributed to him date from the seventeenth and eighteenth centuries. (76)

The version of Namdev's life by Mahipati commences with a "virgin birth" story, a recurring theme in accounts of other *sants*. Namdev is said to have been found floating on a shell in a river, the deity Vitthala having answered the prayers of his parents for a son. This literary device is seen to have avoided the issue of his low caste origin. In Marathi, his caste was called *shimpi* or "tailor," with associations of *shudra* status. However, Namdev was remembered by supporters as a *kshatriya*. (77)

A *bhakti* literature in Marathi developed at the hands of poets like Eknath and Tukaram. (78) There were many other *sants*, and in Maharashtra a substantial number of these were low caste people.

Mahipati relates how the fourteenth century Mahar *sant* Chokhamela was turned away from the temple of Vitthala at Pandharpur. The reason was caste discrimination against the fact of his being a Mahar or untouchable. (79) In subsequent centuries, many Mahars apparently became Varkaris, but they could only gaze at a distance upon Vitthala's temple. Mahars had to stop at the tomb of Chokhamela, located at the foot of the steps leading to the portal of the temple. Untouchables were not permitted to enter the Pandharpur temple until 1947. (80)

Eknath (d.1599) of Paithan was a highly literate *sant*, described as a master of the Hindi language, and also as a social reformer. His ideal of *bhakti* was in the mould of service to humanity, reversing the introspective attitude associated with brahmanical Vedanta. Yet he himself was a *brahman*, not a low caste Hindu.

Eknath was a proper Brahman scholar who lived in the orthodox center of Paithan, and yet he not only translated Sanskrit devotional material into Marathi but also wrote songs and poems clearly intended for the ears and the minds of the lowly. (81)

His guru was Janardhan Swami, who lived in Devagiri (Daulatabad), combining a religious role with that of a commander in the army of a local Muslim ruler, and indeed, monitoring the fort at Daulatabad. Janardhan related to the *panth* of Dattatreya, not the Varkari movement. Some scholars take seriously the strong indications that Janardhan's own guru was a Sufi. The complexities in this situation are pronounced.

Eknath's initiation by his guru Janardan came through a vision of Datta, who appeared before the two as a Muslim fakir. (82)

Chand Bodhale (alias Chandasahib Qadiri) has been described as the Sufi teacher of Janardhan Swami (1504–1575), a *brahman* who had Muslim disciples in addition to Hindu followers. Chand Bodhale is often identified as a Vaishnava, but the context is ambivalent. Janardhan evidently had strong Sufi affiliations, although becoming identified with Dattatreya. This situation is accompanied by an argument that Eknath tried to conceal non-Hindu affiliations, to prevent the hostility of orthodox *brahmans*. (83)

Eknath writes as a Vitthala *bhakta*, but is exceptional in some respects. His corpus is varied. He composed in Marathi the *Eknathi Bhagavata*, a lengthy poem of 18,000 couplets. This is a form of commentary on the eleventh *skandha* of the *Bhagavata Purana*, a major Vaishnava text. Eknath avoided certain other emphases found in the latter scripture, emphases that are strongly associated with Gaudiya (Bengal) Vaishnavism and allied themes of courtly love poetry.

It is typical of Maharashtrian *bhakti* that Eknath chose the stern morality of the eleventh *skandha* [book] over the erotic devotion of Krishna and the gopis in the tenth book of that [Bhagavata] Purana which was so important to Bengali *bhakti* and to Vallabhacharya. (84)

Eknath also composed philosophical works like the *Chatushloki Bhagavata*, a commentary on "the strictly Vedantic ninth chapter of the second *skandha* of the *Bhagavata Purana*." (85) Eknath was concerned to adapt various concepts of Vedanta, in the cause of what is known as *advaita-bhakti*, or non-dualist devotionalism, which was favoured by the Varkari *panth*. Varkari *bhaktas* assimilated Advaita in terms of a potential "oneness with the universal God, but rejected the traditional [Vedantic] idea that one had to abandon society in order to achieve God-realisation." (86)

Eknath did not advocate renunciation of the world, which he deemed to be impractical. This *sant* attitude converges with the outlook of Sai Baba, who seems to have generally discouraged devotees from becoming ascetics. Sai Baba was undoubtedly aware of basic themes in *sant* literature, although he is not known to have read these works. He did prescribe a reading of the *Eknathi Bhagavata* for his prominent devotee Hari S. Dixit, encouraging the latter, in this manner, to dissociate from the busy career of a lawyer.

In his role as a *brahman* scholar, Eknath edited the *Jnaneshwari*, an influential Varkari text dating back to the thirteenth century, and which is a Marathi commentary on the *Bhagavad Gita*. The *brahman* author Jnaneshwara has been discerned to combine Vaishnava *bhakti* with Advaita, moving at a tangent to purist Vedanta of the Swamis. Eknath also composed a Marathi version of Valmiki's *Ramayana*.

> He [Eknath] seems to have been concerned to put the philosophical tenets of Vedanta, stories from the Puranas

and the Epics, and an understanding of the strict morality of *dharma* into varied forms of Marathi prose and poetry so that all could be enlightened. (87)

The output of Eknath also included drama poems (*bharudas*) in Hindi and Marathi. These compositions project authorship in terms of his identification with untouchables, passing Muslim *faqirs*, members of unorthodox sects, women, and other marginalised groupings. About one sixth of his total of 300 *bharuds* commemorate untouchables, being written as though Eknath was a member of the untouchable Mahar community. In Maharashtra, the Mahars comprised almost ten per cent of the population, and existed in every Marathi-speaking village. (88)

"There is a clear indication of Eknath's conviction that a Mahar could be a true bhakta." (89) One legend depicts him as breaking caste rules by eating at the home of a Mahar *bhakta*. However, despite his unorthodox behaviour, Eknath retained his brahmanical status at Paithan.

Tukaram (d.1649) is described as a *shudra*. His family owned agricultural land and a trading venue at Dehu, a village near Poona (Pune). They conducted a money-lending business, normally impossible for *shudras*. One explanation is that the family was originally *kshatriya*, becoming identified with the *shudra* caste as a consequence of local vicissitudes. At that era, the *brahmans* in Maharashtra apparently referred to all non-*brahmans* as *shudras*. Tukaram was not a poor man, being described by some writers as inheriting a spacious house and maintaining his own private Vitthala temple. The family deity was Vitthala.

During 1630–32, a severe famine caused many people and cattle to die of starvation. Tukaram lost his wife, all his cattle, and also his business. One version says that criticism from local *brahmans* forced him into isolation. For a time, he lived in a mountain cave. He married a second time, and became a Vaishnava poet. Some popular episodes are based on verses whose authenticity has been doubted. The major source is Mahipati (d.1790), a hagiologist who wrote over a century after the death of Tukaram. A general impression conveyed is that Tukaram encouraged *bhakti* while opposing priestly ritual.

The *bhakti* poems or *abhangas* of Tukaram became very famous after his death, (90) being associated with the expanding Varkari *panth*. (91) Some analysts have concluded that many Tukaram poems were composed by later Vaishnava generations. Nevertheless, as with the verses of Kabir and others who fall in the same approximate category, the influential "style" poetry can merit inspection as a religious phenomenon. Despite the obscure details of his biography, "Tukaram is perhaps the most revered saint in Maharashtra, who stressed the love of the Lord as the path to liberation." (92)

Some commentators refer to a situation of low caste *sants* being influenced by liberal Sufis, who were benevolent towards low caste people. A claim has been made that "there was hardly any saint of the *Bhakti* school who had not passed some of his time in a *khanaqah*." (93) The extent of such interaction is uncertain, and there are different views on the matter. Many orthodox Sufis were perhaps more concerned with conversion to Islam than any cultural exchange; or possibly, they were simply indifferent to *kafir* activities. *Khanaqahs* were centres of the Sufi Orders, whose *shaikhs* varied in disposition. A liberal Chishti, Shah Aminuddin Ala of Bijapur, is one of the more attractive *khanaqah* entities, gaining the reputation of a *majzub* who welcomed Hindus (see Appendix I).

> The vast majority of the Indian Muslims are converts. . . . The main agency for conversion were the mystics, and most of the large scale conversions seem to have taken place in the fifteenth and sixteenth centuries. But legend and fact have become so mixed up that hardly any such event can be precisely dated. (Mujeeb 1967:21–22)

Conversion is now an issue. British colonial assumptions about missionary Sufis are today regarded with caution by specialist scholars. One deduction has been that the writings of Sufis, and biographical accounts, indicate that Sufis were not generally concerned with conversion to Islam. However, there is the contrasting theme that, in the territories formerly known as East and West Pakistan, Sufis were active in conversion programmes (East Pakistan became Bangladesh in 1971). These geographical sectors witnessed a strong increase in the Muslim population. (94)

In Maharashtra, a friction between Hindus and Muslims is evident in the output of Eknath, whose drama poem *Hindu-Turk Samvad* (*Debate between a Hindu and Muslim*) reveals the extent of religious antipathies. Hindus were regarded as idolators and upholders of caste, while Muslims were derided for animal sacrifices, worship of Sufi tombs, and the desire to convert Hindus (Ernst 1992:34).

The eighteenth century hagiographer Mahipati provides a story of the early Maratha saint Bahira Jatadeva, a *brahman* whose resolve of total detachment from the world resorted to becoming a Muslim. This *sant* wished for a life of abnegation and censure, instead of becoming a revered forest ascetic who would gain disciples. That was why Bahira changed religion, to discourage elevation of himself amongst Hindus. Bahira was afterwards criticised by Hindus for transiting to a low caste. "In this tale of conversion to Islam and apostasy, there is only the vaguest notion of Islamic religion; becoming a Muslim is primarily seen as an estrangement from one's caste group.... Typical of the *bhakti* position, the story also sees conventional religion, whether Hindu or Islamic, as a detour from the esoteric truth of the self" (Ernst 1992:35–36).

The tolerant Mughal emperor Akbar abolished the *jizya* tax in 1565, a measure resented by many of the *ulama*. Both Jains and Hindus seem to have gained increased respect via the Mughal project of translating many Sanskrit manuscripts into Persian (Truschke 2016).

Ahmad Sirhindi (d.1634) was a Naqshbandi *shaikh* of North India who called for a revival of the *jizya* tax. This was a fundamentalist (and orthodox Sufi) reaction to liberal trends in process during the reign of Akbar. In his letters, Sirhindi zealously described the execution of the Sikh Guru Arjun as a great victory for Islam. "Sirhindi's orthodoxy was epitomised in his assertion that on the Day of Judgment people would be asked about their adherence to the *sharia* rather than about their mystical affiliation" (Weissmann 2007:1-2).

Hindu critics of Islam have complained that the famous medieval Chishti Sufis were silent spectators of the marginalisation of *kafirs* (non-Muslims) in India. One accusation is that Hindu slaves were sold in the bazaars of Ghazna and other exploitive locations. The lucrative slave trade is not an attractive feature of the landscape (Lal 1994). Fabulously wealthy Islamic rulers of North India owned vast numbers of slaves and maintained extensive harems. Many less affluent people in that society also owned slaves. The predatory tradition of slavery was continued by the Marathas and European colonialists. The British had many plantations throughout their empire, and these investments were tended by slaves. Many Indians went to distant colonies as bondservants. The East India Company eventually abolished the sale of slaves via the Indian Slavery Act of 1843 (Major 2012).

The Maratha reaction to late Mughal dominance is closely associated with Shivaji, a ruler who despatched the Mughal general Afzal Khan in an episode that became legendary. The Maratha army became a formidable fighting force. A deep resentment of the emperor Aurangzeb continued into the post-Mughal era. The general tensions created a sense of religious divide in Maharashtra that still hallmarked the period during which Sai Baba lived at Shirdi. The Muslim culture of that region was by then very much the loser in areas outside the Nizam's domain. Maratha *brahmans* were often averse to the eccentric *faqir* living in an alien mosque. They feared contamination, an obsession created by priestly taboos.

In a much more positive light, a linguistic factor confirms one avenue of interaction between different religions. A sequence of Deccani Sufi poets is testimony to a process of symbiosis. Writing in Marathi, these poets demonstrate a strong degree of syncretism between Sufism and Hinduism. There are various names involved, but three are more well known.

Shaikh Muhammad (d.1660) was born at Shrigonde in the Ahmednagar district. He originally lived as a soldier, being a *havildar* at Dharur fort. He gained Hindu supporters, and extolled a formless deity, known as *Nirguni Nirakar*. He is sometimes described as a follower of Advaita Vedanta, which is misleading. His writings reveal influences from both the Vaishnava *bhakti* and unorthodox Sufi traditions. He escaped the *ulama* cordon against *kafirs*. Shaikh Muhammad criticised both Muslims and Hindus, the former for their iconoclasm, and the latter for caste discrimination and polytheism. A consensus of opinion appears to be that his teacher was Chand Bodhale, although one or two scholars phrase this matter in alternative terms.

In 1645, Shaikh Muhammad composed the *Yogasamgrama*, his major work, in a poetic format. Some verses praise Vithoba (Vitthala), the deity of Pandharpur. This makes him a very unusual Vaishnava. However, he did not advocate pilgrimage to Pandharpur, and expressed a view that pilgrimage is useless without purification of the heart. His form of monotheism tends to strongly reflect Islam (or Sufism in this instance). He describes the genuine Sufi:

> The true living Sufi is the one who has eliminated anger and lust. Constantly he remembers *Allah* even while breathing in and out. He avoids useless talk and he enjoys happiness in solitude. He does not show pride in his Sufi achievement. (Warren 1999:167)

Shaikh Muhammad employs reference to Hindu scriptures and various gods, including Vishnu and Shiva. These deities relate to a formless (*nirguna*) context; he is nevertheless cautious about the large number of gods and goddesses. Each chapter of the *Yogasamgrama* commences with an invocation to Ganesha, the elephant-headed son of Shiva. This was a conventional feature of Hindu writings in Marathi. Shaikh Muhammad did make some adaptations, however. An example of his eclectic style is: "Salute to Sri Ganesha. Allah is great and the only one" (Warren 1999:163).

The *Yoga-samgraha* is noted for an attack on brahmanical ritualism. This is consistent, in certain respects, with emphases of some Hindu *bhaktas*. The author accepts the validity of standard Hindu deities, but rejects folk deities such as Khandoba. Shaikh Muhammad opposes certain practices associated with these folk deities.

Shaikh Muhammad became portrayed as an incarnation (or reincarnation) of Kabir. According to the Marathi scholar Ramchandra Dhere (1930–2016), the works of this eclectic Muslim poet show the influence of Eknath, Kabir, and the *Swatmasukha* of Janardhan Swami (Dhere 2008; Tulpule 1979:377–378; Warren 1999:162–169).

Shah Muntoji Bahamani (died *circa* 1650), of Qadiri affiliation, was accepted by the local Lingayat community at Narayanpur. Shaikh Muhammad is also known to have gained several Hindu followers, including Mudha Pangula. This kind of situation is not generally familiar. "It was possible, therefore, in this atmosphere, for a Brahmin to accept a Muslim disciple, and vice versa, a Muslim or Sufi *pir* could accept Hindu *chelas* or students, without any formal conversion" (Warren 1999:162).

Muntoji was celebrated by hagiographers like Mahipati, who calls him Sant Bahamani. Dhere calls him Brahmini, not being certain of his origin in the Bahamani family. Muntoji composed the *Panchikarana*, in a notable attempt to prove that the teachings of Hinduism and Sufism amount to the same truth (Dhere 2008). This text is described as a dictionary, supplying linguistic equivalents in Marathi and Persian/Urdu for "significant religious and philosophical terms and concepts" (Warren 1999:160).

Some generations later, Shah Muni (1756–1807) was a Sufi who lived during the Maratha rule of the Peshwas. He adopted his second name in honour of his Hindu guru Munindra Swami, associated with Dattatreya. His eclectic book *Siddhanta Bodha* was completed near Satara in 1795. Shah Muni "became well versed in the *Vedas, Puranas* and *Dharmasastras,* but he never abandoned his Muslim allegiance." (95)

The situation of Shah Muni reflects a dramatic social change. He says: "I was born as a Muslim who is [regarded] as lower than the low *shudra* class." He laments that Muslims had destroyed Hindu temples and were prone to violence, breaking images and sacrificing cows. In this context, Shah Muni declares: "In the pit of the Muslims I was born, but I am now engaged in the love of Shri Krishna. I have taken refuge in the saints and I beg for your acceptance." (96)

This poet was asking his Hindu readers for pardon. Outside the Nizam's domain, the Muslim minority had now lost political power in Maharashtra, and were regarded as outcastes by Hindu orthodoxy. "Shah Muni sought to situate the Muslims in the spiritual history of Maharashtra, in order to legitimise Muslims in the overall scheme of things." (97)

A few generations later, Sai Baba was the recipient of orthodox Hindu stigma, but did not react with hostility. "Like the Sufi poets before him he wanted to promote the essential unity of *Sufi-bhakti* concepts." (98)

Sai Baba was a distinctive exemplar of the symbiosis that had been occurring. He permitted the ostentatious *chavadi* procession, in which Hindu devotees honoured him as a virtual *maharaja,* although he remained an austere *faqir* with no possessions.

Some of his Hindu devotees were Vitthala *bhaktas,* including Das Ganu (1868–1962) and Hari S. Dixit (1864–1926). The *Shri Sai Satcharita* records that when Das Ganu was advised by Sai Baba to observe the *bhakta* discipline of a *naam-saptah* (a week of chanting the divine name), he importuned Sai Baba, insisting that Vitthala must appear to him.

The saint responded: "Yes, yes, Vitthal will appear in form before you! Only, the devotee must have faith enough!" Sai Baba then mentioned Hindu holy places like Pandharpur and Dwaraka, and added: "Everything is in Shirdi itself. You do not have to seek it far. After all, is Vitthal going to appear from a secret place? Moved by the intense love of his devotees, he will incarnate in this very place, for you." (99)

Das Ganu is said to have gained the *Vitthal-darshan* in Shirdi. Missing here is a dimension supplied by Narasimhaswami, who informs that Das Ganu was distracted by the desire to attend Pandharpur festivals, and also doubtful of the ability of Sai Baba to grant such experiences. (100) Sai Baba did not encourage devotees to visit Pandharpur, a popular destination of pilgrims. "Everything is in Shirdi itself." He was averse to caste discrimination, which survived at Pandharpur until 1947.

On another occasion, Dixit experienced "the darshan of Vitthal," while sitting in meditation at Shirdi. He soon afterwards went to Sai Baba the same morning. The *faqir* acknowledged his vision of Vitthala, but warned: "That Vitthal is very elusive. Hold on to him fast and fix him in place, forcibly. Or else, he will give you the slip, if you are inattentive, even for a moment." (101)

Only a few pages earlier, Dabholkar informs: "Allah's name constantly on his lips, is the sign to recognise him [Sai Baba]." (102) Further, "with his great fondness for chanting God's name, [Sai] Baba repeated '*Allah Malik*' ceaselessly." (103)

This saint's ability to cross the religious divide is signified by such reminders in the *Satcharita* as: "A Hindu or a Muslim, to him both were equal." (104)

7. An Independent *Faqir*

Shirdi was an agricultural village in Maharashtra, then known as the Bombay Presidency. Most of the villagers were Hindus. When Sai Baba arrived there, only about a hundred (or less) mud-brick houses existed. A few small shops sold basic foods and commodities such as oil for lamps. Only three small temples were visible, including a Vitthala temple in the centre of the village. The Khandoba temple was located on the village outskirts. Here Sai Baba was refused admission by the priest Mhalsapati, who discriminated on the basis of his Muslim identity.

A Maruti (Hanuman) temple existed near the mosque which Sai Baba eventually inhabited. The mosque was dilapidated, and the earthen floor pitted with holes. Islamic influence in the region had declined, the nearest Muslim centre being Sangamner, over thirty miles away. The Muslim minority in Shirdi seems to have comprised poor artisans and labourers; there was also a shopkeeper amongst them. "There were just a few Muhammadan houses and the Muhammadan population was very poor." (105)

Sai Baba is described by Dabholkar as being committed to gardening work. (106) Yet he also sat under a *neem* tree, and at one time lived in the nearby forest. The chronology is missing. A reference to twelve years silence (107) is suspended in a literary vacuum of otherwise vague timeline.

Speculations about a tomb or cell have been prodigious. Supposedly located near the *neem* tree, no archaeological remains exist. The tomb was reputedly that of the *faqir's* guru, but Dabholkar evidently viewed this belief sceptically. Sai

Baba definitely did refer to a guru or teacher, but without providing any clear identity.

The laconic name of "Venkusha" was favoured by devotee Das Ganu in relation to the obscure teacher of Sai Baba. The Shirdi saint made a reference to "Venkusha" during a well known interrogation by a magistrate from the Dhulia court (Shepherd 2015:82,190,358n129). It is very difficult to pin down this allusive reference to any historical context. The poet Das Ganu associated the name Venkusha with Gopalrao Deshmukh, whom he promoted as the guru of Sai Baba. Das Ganu ventured a detailed version of the guru that has been regarded by historians as an unintentional fiction.

The legend of Gopalrao Deshmukh figures in many devotee accounts of Sai Baba. This creation of Das Ganu involves the acute discrepancy of a contrasting period in time. Gopalrao died in 1802, and cannot have been the guru of Sai Baba. Vishwas B. Kher concluded: "I find no basis whatsoever for the claim that Gopalrao was the guru of Sai Baba; it is a fiction propagated by Das Ganu." (108)

An early Muslim commentator was caught off guard in this respect. Dr. Abdul Ghani was influenced by Das Ganu in relation to Gopalrao (Ghani 1939:47-51). At that time, Das Ganu had a monolithic profile in this area of interest, second only to Dabholkar in priority, but more well known. The *sannyasin* Narasimhaswami also credited the story of Gopalrao, and subsequently with far more influence than Ghani.

Nevertheless, Sai Baba did make contact with a number of Hindu holy men in Shirdi. These persons are mentioned by Dabholkar, but there is no indication that they were teachers of Sai. In a striking and largely unplumbed episode, Sai Baba temporarily moved to Rahata in close proximity to the Sufi known as Jawahar Ali, alias Bapu Shah Jindewali (Shepherd 2015:106-110).

An Independent Faqir

At some unknown date, Sai Baba took up residence in the local mosque at Shirdi, where he innovated a *dhuni* or sacred fire. He gained the reputation of being a country doctor or herbalist, and was known as a *hakim* (a Muslim designation). The *dhuni* fire was an accessory for both Muslim *faqirs* and Nath Yogis (although believed to have originated with the latter contingent).

Diverse Vaishnava and Shaiva *sadhus* also maintain a *dhuni*, especially the Shaivas. Rites of worship (*puja*) attend the fire in such instances. There were no Vaishnava or Shaiva trappings in the case of Sai Baba. Unlike *sadhus*, he did not smear his body with ashes. To visitors, Sai Baba often gave ash (*udi*) from the *dhuni* as a token of blessing. The *udi* became credited with curative properties and miraculous qualities by devotees. In this respect, a similar situation applied with many *sadhus*. At the Shirdi mosque, there were none of the typical Shaiva auspices that are so well known elsewhere, including distinctive *mantras*. A *sadhu dhuni* is often the scene of ascetic exercises, found also in the milieu of some Muslim *faqirs*. Those accompaniments were lacking in the environment of Sai Baba.

There were numerous visiting *faqirs* at Shirdi over the years. Most of these reaped obscurity. The place of accommodation for these men was a shed known as a *taqiya*, reserved for Muslims. Sai Baba frequently visited this site, and was known to sing and dance there, until *circa* 1890 according to one theory. The Hindu villagers were not familiar with the songs, which were in a Muslim language (or languages). Marianne Warren suggested that a Chishti influence was involved in this music, no doubt a form of *qawwali*. Yet there is no known link of Sai Baba with the Chishti Order.

Sai Baba was an independent *faqir*, and keen to secure an inter-religious harmony between the Hindus and Muslims who became his devotees. He did not preach doctrines or make any attempt at conversion. In fact, he frowned upon conversion to another religion, a procedure which he described in terms of an inappropriate change of parentage. When a Hindu convert to Islam was taken to him (by a Muslim), Sai Baba became angry, slapped the convert, and remarked: "Are you not ashamed to change your father?" (109)

Instead of being doctrinaire, Sai Baba was markedly allusive in his speech. Visitors did not always understand what he was talking about, and some confusions are on record. This *faqir* was not concerned to accommodate allcomers, and could be offputting.

8. Aurangabad, Gopalrao Deshmukh, and Jindewali

Sai Baba early accompanied the marriage party of Chand Patel, which journeyed from Dhupkhed village to Shirdi. Dhupkhed is one of the links afforded with the region of Aurangabad. This city of the Deccan is strongly associated with the obscure early years of Sai Baba. Aurangabad has strong Islamic associations, the city quarter then being ruled by officials of the Nizam of Hyderabad. An emerging complication was the adjoining British cantonment. The new colonial rulers for long encountered resistance from the tenacious old regime, which favoured many customs deriving from the Mughal era. Sufism was a prominent component of this urban scene.

> Sufis from the Chishtiyya and Naqshbandiyya, the major Sufi traditions of the day in India, as well as dervishes unattached to any specific Sufi lineage (*silsila*), all gathered in considerable number in the city. (Green 2006:5)

The independent sector of Sufi life is the most relevant for Sai Baba. However, very little information is available in this respect. An early Muslim version of Sai Baba relays that he retired into a cave at a mountain near Aurangabad, where he underwent severe privations "for a number of years." (110) The Aurangabad locale is indicated as the destination of this *faqir* during the interval between the first and second arrivals at Shirdi. Meher Baba was subsequently more specific in relating the obscure cave to the pilgrimage site of Khuldabad, (111) which features shrines of Sufi saints.

Further references in the Meher Baba literature indicate a strong connection with the *majzub* Bane Miyan of Aurangabad (d.1921). "It was Sai Baba who had enabled him to realise God and stationed him at Aurangabad." (112) This detail does not appear in the "official" hagiography of Bane Miyan composed by a relative. Nor does the evocative episode in which, during 1918, Sai Baba sent a special message to the *majzub* giving a premonition of his own death. (113)

Key events were obscured by such overlay as the story of Gopalrao Deshmukh, created by the poet Das Ganu, and repeated by numerous subsequent authors who took this feature at face value. We must take more notice of V. B. Kher, who refers to "the propensity of Das Ganu to be lost in his poet's dream." (114)

Das Ganu enthused at some length about the *brahman* landowner Gopalrao in his *Bhakti Saramrit*. (115) The poet identifies Sai Baba as a reincarnation of Kabir, and Gopalrao as a reincarnation of Ramananda. Gopalrao is here located in Selu, a village near Pathri. In the Das Ganu scenario, the wife of a deceased *faqir* from Manwat arrived to consign a boy of five to Gopalrao, who took him in, subsequently giving the orphan an attention that evoked jealousy from others. The boy's mother is here said to have died when he was twelve years old. Das Ganu provided literary flourishes such as: the young Sai brought to life a dead man, by applying dust from the feet of Gopalrao.

Such stories were overtaken by the detail that Gopalrao Deshmukh was an eighteenth century figure who died in 1802. (116) His date of birth is given by Kher as 1715. The conclusion of Kher is revealing: Das Ganu mistakenly imagined the association of Gopalrao with Sai Baba, providing elaborations that comprise hagiology. (117)

More attention should be given to another figure, who was dismissed by hindsight. This entity tangibly appeared in the life of the Shirdi *faqir*, as recorded by Dabholkar and

Aurangabad, Gopalrao Deshmukh, and Jindewali

Narasimhaswami. Jawahar Ali, alias Bapu Shah Jindewali, resided at Ahmednagar, a city of the Deccan to the south of Shirdi and Aurangabad. This person was a learned *maulvi* and Sufi, and knew Sai Baba at an early date in Ahmednagar. The origins of this contact are obscure; the sequel was subject to a "Hinduising" rationale that requires caution.

Jindewali moved from Ahmednagar to Rahata at an uncertain date. The village of Rahata was a few miles south of Shirdi. Sai Baba became closely associated with him, acting as his disciple. Jindewali had liberal tendencies. He is said to have initially been on good terms with the Hindu villagers of Shirdi. Afterwards, the locals turned against him because of his influence on Sai (some analysts think that these events were too early to have involved many of the villagers; hagiological elements are suspected). Jindewali is depicted as being worsted in debate by Devidas, a local holy man. The Sufi subsequently moved away, and was interpreted by opponents as an egoist presuming to be the teacher of Sai Baba. (118)

9. Nirvikalpa Samadhi

In December 1886, Sai Baba "became restless with an attack of asthma and in order to be able to bear the physical affliction, he went into *nirvikalpa Samadhi*." (119) This episode has aroused speculation as to precisely what was involved.

According to the *Shri Sai Satcharita*, Sai Baba had informed visitors that he would go into *samadhi* for three days. Dabholkar uses Sanskrit terminology, but there is no certainty that Sai Baba himself employed the word *samadhi*. The saint is also reported to have given instruction that a tomb should be dug in a corner of the mosque courtyard. This was in the possible event of a fatal outcome. Two flags were to be erected to mark the site of the grave.

Sai Baba told the devotee Mhalsapati to take care of his body during the critical three days in prospect. One night, "as in a sudden fainting fit, his body fell down, motionless." (120) The time by the clock was ten p.m. Mhalsapati then kept constant guard over what now seemed to be a corpse. Observers gave up hope of life for the inert *faqir*. However, nobody dug the grave that had been suggested. Perhaps this was because of the vigil maintained by Mhalsapati, who did not sleep, sitting with Sai Baba's head placed on his lap.

The villagers at Shirdi are reported to have gathered around in astonishment. To all appearances, the *faqir's* breathing had ceased. Islamic entities are mentioned. Dabholkar specifies the appearance of "*Mulla, Maulavi, fakir* — all came and began discussing what was to be done next." (121) This detail tends to indicate the basically Muslim milieu of Sai Baba at that early period, and which one would expect of a mosque.

Appa Kulkarni is also mentioned. This Hindu is named as one of the earliest devotees. (122) He had apparently accepted Sai Baba as his guru several years previously. Now he concluded that the saint had died. Kulkarni therefore wanted to proceed with burial. Some others agreed with him, urging that the grave should be prepared at the spot which Sai had indicated.

There was an argument about what to do. Mhalsapati steadfastly maintained his protective vigil, and after three days, in the early morning, the apparent corpse showed signs of life. Sai Baba opened his eyes, regaining consciousness of the external world. The observing "*Maulavi* and *fakir* turned pale in the face." (123) The *maulavi*, apparently an orthodox Muslim figure, had been insistent on burial.

The 1940s adaptation of this *Satcharita* episode by Gunaji is condensed, and omits reference to the Muslim observers. Whereas Narasimhaswami, in his *Life of Sai Baba*, acknowledges Muslim (and Sufi) extensions by reporting Sai Baba as saying at the outset: "I am going to *Allah*." The same writer refers to police officers urging that the corpse should be buried. A period of 24 hours between death and burial was often regarded as the maximum allowable before decomposition occurred. (124)

Sai Baba did not explain such events. They just happened. Narasimhaswami proffers a theory about the saint's "mission." Dr. Warren suggests "a direct experience of union with God." (125)

The phrase *nirvikalpa samadhi* signifies an advanced state of "inconceptual" consciousness. In some Hindu versions, the body is said to die after three days of achieving this state.

10. No Initiation or Mantra

Sai Baba has often been compared with the contemporary guru known as Swami Samarth, alias Akkalkot Swami Maharaj (d.1878). This saint lived in the small princely state of Akkalkot from 1857. (126) Sai Baba and Swami Samarth became regarded as avatars of Dattatreya. Both of these figures were anti-caste. Swami Samarth was eccentric, and evaded the question of what caste he belonged to. (127) Shortly before his death, he is reported to have told two of his devotees to transfer their attention to Shirdi. "My avatar (spirit) will be at Shirdi in Ahmednagar District." (128)

These two saints were both averse to initiation procedures, generally believed to be mandatory for gurus. Sai Baba and Swami Samarth also "referred disparagingly to the exhibition of *siddhis* [powers] and did not set store by them." (129)

Sai Baba is noted for acting in a manner contrary to what visitors expected of gurus. *Upadesha* or instruction was customarily conceived by guru followers in terms of *mantra* and initiation. Sufi Orders were also strongly associated with initiation procedures, and likewise complex *zikr* (invocation) exercises, which included breath control or *habs-i nafs* (Rizvi 1983:302), a practice apparently borrowed from Yogis. Sai Baba parted company with all these expectations. He preferred allusive speech and pragmatic ethical enjoinders. His simple form of *zikr* (e.g., *Allah Malik*) does not evidence the regimen associated with Sufi Orders.

The Sufi vogue for initiation was pronounced. By the seventeenth century, multiple initiations were commonplace in Indian Sufism (Green 2006:6). This development entailed

No Initiation or Mantra

becoming a member of more than one Sufi Order, indeed, even several or many of them. "Multiple initiation has been noted since the early fifteenth century, when a Chishti like Ashraf Jahangir Simnani claimed initiation in 14 different orders" (Ernst and Lawrence 2002:28).

Sai Baba was evidently not inclined to believe that multiple initiation was the most effective recourse for any spiritual development. Nor did he opt to pursue the art of exorcism, which was a speciality of Simnani.

Varied reports strongly indicate that Sai Baba was distanced from Yoga, both the Patanjali and Tantric versions. He did not teach Yoga of any kind. To the contrary, he cast an explicit aspersion upon *pranayama*, alluding to the dangers involved, maintaining that the practitioner would ultimately have to come to him for remedy. This was certainly true in the notable instance of Upasani Maharaj.

According to the *Satcharita*, Sai Baba "prescribed no *Yogasanas*, no *Pranayama*, no violent suppression of the sense organs, nor *mantra*, *tantra* or *yantra pooja*. And he did not ever whisper *mantra* in the ears of his devotees." (130)

Yet less realistically, the *Satcharita* credits Sai Baba with the exotic practice of *khanda yoga*, which reputedly involves severing the limbs from the body. The advantages of that daunting exercise are not too obvious. Dabholkar relied for this detail upon the story of an unnamed spectator, who claimed to see the limbs of Sai Baba strewn about the mosque. The *Satcharita* also relays that when people "came running to see the shocking spectacle of his body thus severed into parts, what they always saw was [Sai] Baba, whole and in one piece" (Dabholkar 1999:109).

A related claim (well known in the Gunaji version) is made. On one occasion, Sai was reputedly observed to vomit out his intestines, clean them thoroughly, and place them on a tree to dry (Dabholkar 1999:109). This anecdote is associated with the *dhauti* of Hatha Yoga. Such colourful accounts have created misconceptions. (131)

Sai Baba was severe in the instance of Kusha Bhav, a Tantric Yogi (perhaps a Nath Yogi) who visited him in 1908. He told Kusha Bhav to relinquish Tantric magic, which in this case had involved the use of *mantra* spells, exorcism, and harmful intentions. Sai Baba appears to have regarded this Tantric as a dangerous man. Kusha Bhav is reported to have taken drastic recourse to *mantras* for making people slaves and to kill his opponents.

The rebuffed Yogi afterwards complied with the injunction to avoid magic, and was treated to a disciplinary phase at the mosque. Sai Baba eventually told him to get married, in an evident attempt to change his lifestyle. However, Kusha Bhav later reverted to his suspect inclinations for "miraculously" producing commodities desired by his audience. After the death of Sai Baba, the Yogi was keen to exhibit ash (*udi*) in his hands, as if this were a miracle. His questionable performance is overdue for criticism. (132) See also Chapter 27 of this book for further reference to Kusha Bhav.

Some traditional accounts relating to Sufism have caused other confusions. Medieval developments included a competition between orthodox Sufis and Nath Yogis in the exercise of powers. For instance, the Kubravi savant Sayyid Ashraf Jahangir Simnani (d.1425) became a Chishti Sufi when he moved to Bengal. There his Chishti teacher Ala ad-din instructed him to spread Chishti teachings in Jaunpur.

> The Sayyid hesitated to accept: a popular Suhrawardi saint, Sayyid Sadr ad-din *aka* Chiragh-i Hind, had already claimed that region as his *wilayah* or spiritual domain. But Ala ad-din assured Sayyid Ashraf of eventual success. He settled in Kichhauchha, a village in the district of Jaunpur renowned for its occult practitioners, yogis and exorcists. He trained himself to be a masterful exorcist, and after outmanoeuvring his Hindu rivals as well as Chiragh-i Hind, Sayyid Ashraf Jahangir Simnani became the master of Kichhauchha. (133)

No Initiation or Mantra

Sai Baba was well removed from this circuit of rivalries. The pursuit of powers and techniques so often encourages competition and loss of meaning. The medieval competition between Sufis and Yogis gained legendary proportions, and does little to impress many modern readers (Ernst 2005).

In relation to the subject of powers and miracles, many devotees of Shirdi Sai are critical of the namesake Sathya Sai Baba (d.2011), whose ashram was at Puttaparthi in Andhra. Sathya Sai strongly encouraged belief in his performance of miracles, while also claiming to be the reincarnation of Shirdi Sai. A confusion between the "two Sai Babas" has often occurred. Shirdi Sai devotees emphasise that crucial differences existed between these two figures. Sathya Sai became famous for such "miracles" as producing a Shiva *linga* from his mouth, and creating *udi* in his hand. Critics do not regard these actions as being any proof of spirituality. The "miracles" have been explained in terms of a sleight of hand and other tricks.

11. Mohiuddin Tambuli

A figure in the background of available reports is that of Mohiuddin Tambuli, a Muslim shopkeeper of Shirdi. He appears in fleeting references, the context diminished. The commentator Acharya E. Bharadwaja supplied additional information to that found in standard sources.

Tambuli was one of the minority of Muslims living at Shirdi. In his shop he sold tobacco, areca nut, and betel leaf, as Dabholkar informs. Tambuli is also strongly associated with talismans, a more occult form of merchandise and a popular interest. He apparently had some repute as a wrestler, and is described as a muscular man.

Tambuli had a son-in-law who is described as a *mantrika*. That term generally denotes a practitioner of *mantra*. The context is missing. However, we are told that a disagreement occurred with Sai Baba, apparently at an early period. This may have spilled over into the wrestling match between Sai and Tambuli that is briefly reported by Dabholkar.

This wrestling match is a rather interesting episode. Some commentators have tended to deny the report of Dabholkar, but Bharadwaja was an exception. Sai as a wrestler conveys a different image to Sai the ascetic. Moreover, Sai Baba lost to Tambuli. This realistic reporting may be nearer the truth than is sometimes credited. "Both were skilled wrestlers," says the *Satcharita*. (134)

The ability to wrestle is compatible with a soldier vocation, conceivable for the young Sai Baba because of his reported participation in the Sepoy Rebellion of 1857–8. Dabholkar does not refer to the Rebellion episode, but Narasimhaswami does. The former may be correct in stating that after Sai Baba lost the wrestling match, he "changed his entire dress; he started wearing the long *kafni*, a *langot* and a piece of cloth tied around his head." (135)

This new garb of Sai Baba was that of a *faqir*. The white *kafni* and white headgear were quite distinct from the ochre robe of the *sannyasin*. This appearance remained unchanged until his dying day, and is evident in surviving photographs.

A further complexity arises. The Bharadwaja version says that the wrestling match entailed an agreement that the loser must retreat from public visibility in Shirdi. The contest was loaded with significations of a strong antipathy to Sai on the part of Tambuli. When he lost the fight, Sai Baba had to retreat to a wasteland on the banks of the Lendi stream, leaving Tambuli as the triumphant victor in Shirdi. The Lendi wilderness was on the outskirts of the village. Neither Dabholkar nor Narasimhaswami have this detail.

The talismanic expert eventually departed from Shirdi. Tambuli opted for retirement to a Sufi shrine, and the *faqir* Sai Baba occupied (or reoccupied) the ruined mosque in the village. The relevant dates are in complete obscurity.

In 1894 (according to the reckoning of Kher), Tambuli was back on the scene in an aggressive role. He and other Muslims objected to certain recent occurrences at the mosque. This group even petitioned the *Qazi* (magistrate) of Sangamner, requesting his intervention. (136) Sangamner was about 35 miles south of Shirdi.

The grievance here was the worship (*puja*) innovated by Mhalsapati. This former priest of the Khandoba temple had become a committed devotee of Sai, and would apply sandal paste to the saint's feet (and apparently also his neck). This happened inside the mosque, and the protesting Muslims were irate. Tambuli and his gang resorted to carrying clubs, and threateningly guarded the mosque entrance. Mhalsapati was not welcome, and he dared not go inside the courtyard. Mhalsapati was a small man of meek temperament, and no match for Tambuli.

It is not clear whether the *Qazi* was actually present on this occasion, but he may have been. The hostile group had to reckon with Sai Baba, who expressed annoyance from within the mosque. Sai allowed Mhalsapati to enter, and to perform worship. The extant details are doubtless partial. Tambuli lost this time around. He thereafter disappears from the records.

12. Hindu Devotees

By the end of the 1870s, the first Hindu devotees were apparently in evidence at Shirdi. (137) These included Mhalsapati and Nanasaheb Dengle of nearby Neemgaon. Dengle was a high caste Hindu in contact with many government officials. In later decades, a substantial number of Indian officials became followers of Sai Baba, including prestigious Revenue officers.

In contrast, Mhalsapati (d.1922) was a relatively uneducated villager. He was a *sonar* (goldsmith) by caste, but later relinquished this trade. He was also the hereditary priest of the local Khandoba temple, which he guarded against intruders. He at first believed that Sai Baba was an intruder, identifying him as a Muslim and sending him elsewhere. Mhalsapati subsequently emerged as a *sevakari* (personal attendant) of the *faqir*, and was one of the most intimate devotees. He survived the saint by four years, and continued to sleep in the mosque, performing daily worship of Sai Baba and Khandoba. Mhalsapati is reported to have observed silence (*mauna*) in his last years (Williams 2004:116).

Many of Sai Baba's Hindu devotees were high caste *brahmans*, including wealthy landowners. Yet some of these visitors were disconcerted, being in a dilemma as to whether they should associate with a Muslim *faqir* who lived in a mosque.

During the 1870s and 1880s, Sai Baba was basically aloof from the outside world, and could appear dauntingly reserved and unapproachable. He gained the reputation of a "mad *faqir*." This was equivalent to a *majzub* role as found elsewhere. Neither Muslim nor Hindu householders understood him. The Shirdi saint was too far removed from their immediate horizons. Some Hindu ascetics did acknowledge his merits, however, and doubtless there were Muslim *faqirs* in a similar category (although forgotten by the predominantly Hindu reporters).

Sai Baba seems to have been living in the mosque by the start of the 1880s. An early devotee was Madhavrao Deshpande, whom Sai called Shama. This person was a schoolmaster, originally living close to the mosque. He was one of the many informants interviewed (with the aid of an interpreter) by Narasimhaswami in 1936. The resulting record was published under the title *Devotees' Experiences of Sri Sai Baba*. This is primary source material, although the contents are uneven, and prone to the accusation of including hagiology.

The same author's *Life of Sai Baba* is a longer work, and again uneven in critical estimation. Narasimhaswami did not meet Sai Baba, not appearing on the Shirdi scene until the 1930s. He expressed a high rating for certain "miracle" occurrences, including the well known story of lighting mosque lamps with water instead of oil. This episode has been attributed to 1892, and became an article of devotee belief, greatly assisted by the nationwide missionary campaign of Narasimhaswami, which lasted until the early 1950s.

Some assessors take the view that events in Sai Baba's biography do not require any complement of miracles. Sai Baba himself informed a prominent devotee (Nanasaheb Chandorkar) that he did not perform miracles (Shepherd 2015:168–170). This episode was duly reported by Narasimhaswami, who nevertheless tended to obscure the message by creating a strong interest in miracles.

Sai Baba did claim foreknowledge and a form of omnipresence. "I am in Gangapur, Pandharpur, and in all

Hindu Devotees

places." That is one of the statements found in *Charters and Sayings*, a compilation by Narasimhaswami. Many visitors to Shirdi also went to Pandharpur, a Vaishnava centre of Krishna worship. However, Sai Baba himself evidently regarded Pandharpur as a distraction.

The Vaishnava poet and singer, Das Ganu, was a long term devotee of Sai Baba. Narasimhaswami emerges as a fan of this poet's output, but lamented that Das Ganu was primarily a Vaishnava supporter of Pandharpur festivals, a disposition revealed by certain episodes on record. The *kirtankar* performances of Das Ganu, at various urban venues, are credited as the medium for arousing the interest of new devotees during Sai Baba's last years.

Narayan Govind (Nanasaheb) Chandorkar came from a wealthy *brahman* family. After graduating at university, he served as a revenue official for the British government, eventually becoming a Deputy Collector for the Ahmednagar region. He met Sai Baba in 1891, but at first resisted the saint, being influenced by his conservative father, who objected to the Muslim identity of the *faqir*. This was a typical high caste reaction to the mosque dweller at Shirdi.

Chandorkar subsequently became a devotee, making his own decision. His psychology appears to have been a mix of conservative Hinduism and university-trained reason influenced by the British educational system. He is reported to have "prided himself on his knowledge" of Vedanta and Sanskrit. (138)

A well known conversation occurred *circa* 1900-02 between Chandorkar and Sai Baba. The former was chanting, in an undertone, verse 34 of chapter 4 in the *Bhagavad-Gita*, a favourite text of this devotee. The *faqir* expressed interest in the verse, and implied that Chandorkar did not understand the meaning. This verse related to the guru-disciple relationship and the attendant teaching of *jnana* (knowledge, wisdom).

Subsequently, the conversation was widely regarded as proof of Sai Baba's intimate knowledge of the Sanskrit language. Chandorkar himself believed that Sai knew Sanskrit, and became convinced that the *faqir* "must have been a Brahmin sannyasi." (139)

More recently, Dr. Marianne Warren expressed a counter to this popular "Hinduising" argument. She emphasises that Sai Baba did not need to know Sanskrit, as he was given all the basic information necessary to decode the verse discussed. "Sai Baba first asked Nana Chandorkar to read the verse aloud slowly, then secondly to give his own interpretation and meaning, and thirdly to give the strict grammatical meaning of each word with case, mood and tense." (140)

Moreover, Sai proceeded to give a unique explanation of *Gita* 4:34, "totally different from the accepted *Advaita Bhasya* by Sankaracarya, or indeed any other Hindu commentator." (141) This novelty can feasibly be interpreted in terms of a Sufi perspective. However, the conversation was recorded by Narasimhaswami, in *Charters and Sayings*, without such indication. (142) This matter tends to underline the subtlety required in exegesis of the sources.

In relation to *Gita* 4:34, Sai Baba urged that the word *jnana* should read *ajnana*. "When you take the word '*Ajnana*' in place of '*Jnana*,' you will get the true significance." (143) A reason was supplied by the Shirdi *faqir*: "*Jnana* is not something that one can talk about. Then how can it be the subject of instruction?"

So here is a context of the guru teaching ignorance (*ajnana*). This was definitely not the meaning of traditional Vedantic commentators. According to Warren: "Sai Baba proceeded to give a very Sufistic interpretation for in Sufi thought, ignorance is associated with veils, which cover one's true self as a light is hidden by many shades which have to be torn away or removed to reveal the innate light of perfection." (144)

During the 1920s, there was still resistance to the *ajnana* interpretation amongst Hindu devotees of Sai Baba. Dabholkar felt obliged to comment on this matter, in an obvious attempt to justify the innovation. He mentions the standard interpretation of Shankara, Jnaneshvar, Anandgiri, Shridhar, and Madhusudan, in relation to the word *jnana* as found in *Gita* 4:34. Substitution by the contrasting word *ajnana* was a radical departure from tradition. "It is surprising that not all readers of the *Sai Leela* magazine appreciated that meaning [of Sai Baba] and some remained doubtful!" (145)

The *Shri Sai Leela* magazine commenced in 1923, and became the Marathi organ of the Sai Baba Sansthan at Shirdi. The traditional commentators were evidently preferred by a number of devotee readers, who were reluctant to accept the *ajnana* interpretation. The subsequent general acceptance of the innovation was probably due, in large part, to the consistent support which Dabholkar expressed for the *ajnana* theme. "I shall make yet another small attempt to justify, with some proof, the word *Ajnana*, in order to satisfy them [the doubters]." (146)

Dabholkar adds in the next sentence: "Some may even doubt as to how Baba could have had any knowledge of Sanskrit" (Dabholkar 1999:818). Sai Baba's knowledge of Sufism escaped any mention. However, Dabholkar proceeds to give an interpretation that is not typical of Hindu doctrine, for example: "So long as he [the *jnani*] is without devotion, his *Jnana* is covered up by ignorance." (147) This is discernibly a *bhakti*-oriented exegesis, offsetting the "canonical" Vedantic rationale of the debated *Gita* verse.

One may conclude that Sai Baba was warning the learned Chandorkar against the pride of scriptural knowledge. The word *ajnana* can mean "unlearned." It is not a mere doctrine (i.e., *jnana*) that is liberating, but the cognisance of what to do when *jnana* is covered up by ignorance.

13. Daily Begging Rounds

Throughout the many years he lived at Shirdi, Sai Baba maintained the ascetic lifestyle of a beggar. This *faqir* was a rigorous world renouncer. However, he did not engage in fasts, nor cultivate an emaciated appearance, contrary to the example of many other Indian ascetics.

Sai Baba was remote from the lifestyle and habits of householders. He was also quite different from the many gurus living in ashrams, whose form of lifestyle did not require begging. Sai was a beggar until his death.

When he moved to the mosque, he developed a habit of begging at the same five houses, all in the close vicinity. These were the homes of Hindu devotees. His routine was not static in this respect. Generally, Sai Baba would visit these houses several times a day. However, there were variations that are difficult to assess in terms of frequency.

He is reported to have made visits to all or any of these houses more than a dozen times a day, prior to his last years, when the number of visits was lower. On rare occasions, he would send someone else to do the begging. Another version affirms that Sai Baba initially performed eight begging rounds daily, a number that was later reduced to four. At the very end of his life, when he became frail, a further reduction occurred; he was then begging twice a day, or even once only.

Sai Baba would never enter the houses at which he begged. He would stand outside and give a distinctive call for bread. He would receive bread in the form of *bhakri*, the flat unleavened loaf typical of rural Maharashtra. This was accompanied by vegetables, including onions (to which he was very partial). Sai Baba would take these offerings back to the mosque. He had a habit of offering a pinch of food to the *dhuni* fire, without explaining his action. He would place most of the food in an earthen pot, from which any person or animal could take what they wanted. Only afterwards would he take a small amount of the food himself (although an alternative version says that he ate his portion first).

In this way, Sai Baba redistributed most of the food he begged. The contents of the food pot were consumed by many people, including low caste people. The recipients included diverse animals and birds.

The houses on his daily begging round included those of two wealthy landowners, namely Waman Gondkar Patil and Waman Sakharam Shelke. Another house belonged to Bayajibai Kote, a lady devotee who had formerly fed him in the forest. A fourth house belonged to Bayyaji Appa Kote Patil, who became a *sevakari* (personal attendant) of the saint. The fifth and last house belonged to a local moneylender, Nandaram Marwari. If the food was delayed at this house for any reason, Sai Baba would express annoyance (Williams 2004:119–122). In general, devotees did not regard his anger as being impolite, but as a reminder of expediency.

A variant list of the names of householders, featuring in the begging round, has Narayan Teli instead of Sakharam Shelke (Kamath and Kher 1991:7; Kher 2001:99). The word *teli* means oil-monger. The house of this *teli* was adjacent to the mosque. In his allusive speech, Sai Baba innovated a theme of the "oil-monger's wall" to describe an impediment afflicting perception of his own true identity. "Pull down this wall, and then we see each other clearly face to face" (Narasimhaswami 1939:19).

The version of V. B. Kher relates that, when he returned from the begging rounds, Sai Baba would eat the bread and "keep whatever was left in a corner of the masjid for anyone who needed food" (Kamath and Kher 1991:282). Such variations require flexible treatment.

Sai Baba remained a begging *faqir* without assets. He lived in a dilapidated mosque which suited his ideals of *faqiri*, meaning the *faqir* lifestyle of poverty and renunciation. He did not create any ashram or *khanaqah*. Many of his recorded utterances bear the impress of a renunciate code.

14. Memoranda of Hari S. Dixit

A relevant early document was published in 1933 by Moreshwar Pradhan, a magistrate of the Bombay High Court, who had become a devotee. Pradhan edited and translated into English the Marathi memoranda of Hari S. Dixit (d.1926), a prominent devotee of the Shirdi saint from 1909. Dixit was an eminent solicitor of Bombay (Mumbai) who chose to reside at Shirdi. His diaries dating from 1909 were for long obscure, and amongst other features, evidence a concern to record cures attributed to Sai Baba. These diaries are not the subject of the present chapter.

The compact report by Dixit, apparently dating to the early 1920s, provides mainly solid detail, with relatively few hagiological components. This work can facilitate certain conclusions of historical relevance. Lacking the poetic flourishes of Dabholkar, the Dixit coverage affords a more direct mode of reporting. Strangely enough, this document has rarely been investigated or described.

Pradhan called the Dixit report *A Sketch of the Life and Teaching of Shri Sai Baba* (or, briefly, the *Sketch*). The biographical details are more salient than teaching. A basic point is mentioned: "Whether [Sai] Baba was born a Brahmin or a Musulman cannot be authoritatively stated." During the 1920s, there was no indication of the later trend to identify the saint as being born a Hindu. That trend became evident in the 1940s, one medium for this being Swami Sai Sharan Anand (1889–1982), an author whose views became influential.

A visitor from Pathri arrived for *darshan*. Sai Baba then enquired about this distant village, evidencing to the visitor that he knew Pathri well. The narrator comments: "But this alone does not warrant that Pathri was Baba's birth place." The information is supplied that Sai Baba was familiar with several places in the territory of the Nizam, including Shelu, Manwat, Pathri, Aurangabad, and Bedar. These were "all Moglai places." The word Moglai (meaning Mughal) signifies the dominion of the Nizam of Hyderabad, a powerful Muslim ruler in that era. The indications are that some devotees were already tending to identify Pathri as the birthplace, but without sufficient evidence to convince educated persons like Dixit and Pradhan.

The *Sketch* describes Shirdi in terms of being on the trunk road for passage on foot to southern places of pilgrimage like Rameshwar and Pandharpur. This route was frequented by many holy men, who thus passed through Shirdi.

During the early years of Sai Baba at Shirdi, the Khandoba priest Mhalsapati introduced him to Kashiram Shimpi and Appa Jagale. These three Hindus were in the habit of welcoming visitors to Shirdi, especially ascetics. This trio became devotees of the *faqir* Sai Baba. Dixit describes the early days of Sai at Shirdi in terms of: "Rags to wear, he would sit where he chose, and though he appeared to be a madman, had realised the entire universe within him."

Kashiram was a cloth merchant (and apparently a tailor, as the name Shimpi implies). Kashiram made for the *faqir* a green *kafni* (robe) and cap. However, subsequently Sai preferred to wear a white *kafni*. Green is a sacred colour in Islam. Formerly, Sai Baba had worn a white or orange *kafni*, according to the *Sketch*. If this is true, then he abandoned orange in his later years. An orange, or saffron, robe is known to have been favoured by some *qalandars*, although generally being the colour for Hindu renunciate attire. White was the standard colour for Muslim *faqir* garb. Some urge that white is also a common colour worn by Hindu ascetics. It is favoured by Vaishnavas, along with yellow. There is also an argument in currency that Sai Baba may have chosen white because this colour was neutral and did not represent any particular religion.

Kashiram Shimpi was affluent. At the mosque, he would gift Sai Baba with tobacco for the *chilum* (pipe), and firewood for the *dhuni*. Kashiram often tried to give Sai money, and would even place all his cash before the *faqir*. This ascetic would only accept the paltry sum of a *pice* or two, and then only from Kashiram. The merchant would shed tears if the *faqir* refused gifts. According to Dixit, Sai Baba taught Kashiram that this attitude of donorship was vanity on his part. Circumstances conspired to make the devotee less prosperous, but afterwards his affluence returned.

In his mercantile role, Kashiram would visit other villages on market days. When returning home on one occasion, while riding a horse, he was ambushed by a gang of *dacoits* (bandits). Such robbers terrified villagers, and could be violent killers. The gang took his carts of cloth and plundered his person. One bandit had dropped a sword, and Kashiram desperately took hold of this weapon to defend himself. He killed two of the bandits, but another attacker hit him on the head with an axe. The victim fell down in a pool of blood. His situation was extremely dire. The other bandits only left him alone because they thought he was dead.

When local people found Kashiram, he implored them to take him to Shirdi, not to a hospital. His wish was granted, and he was brought into the presence of Sai Baba, who delegated Shama (Madhavrao Deshpande) to attend to him. The victim recovered, and the British Government of Bombay rewarded him with a sword for his valour in the *dacoit* episode. There is no date supplied. This event may have occurred in the 1890s or later.

Another aspect of the fraught episode is relayed by Dixit. While Kashiram was fighting the bandits, Sai Baba expressed abusive anger in Shirdi. The reason was not obvious, but devotees like Shama (Madhavrao Deshpande) felt that someone was in grave danger. In this perspective, the saint's anger was intended to avert the trouble befalling his devotee.

Shama (d.1939) was a young schoolteacher when he became a devotee. In those early days, *circa* 1880, very few people frequented the mosque. The *faqir* was regarded as eccentric by the villagers. Shama was one of the first devotees, and would prepare the tobacco pipe for Sai. Eventually, he ceased his role as a schoolmaster, his sole purpose being to serve the steadily growing number of devotee visitors. We know that Dixit was on close terms with Shama during the saint's last years. Shama was probably a major source of information about earlier events.

The *Sketch* mentions Gopalrao Gund, a revenue inspector of Kopargaon, who became a devotee. This person wanted to renovate the ruined mosque in which Sai Baba lived. The saint was very resistant, and refused to accept the proposed building materials, which he diverted elsewhere. According to Dixit, Sai "rebuilt and extended the Maruti temple and also took care of the Muslim Turbat of the place." The word *turbat* is Persian and means a tomb.

According to the *Sketch*, Sai Baba once stated that there was a *turbat* of a *pir* underneath a local neem tree (increasingly famous because of association with him). *Pir* is a Persian word, meaning a Sufi teacher. The *faqir* once told Dixit that this *turbat* was the place of his "ancestor." The meaning is not clear.

The tomb under the neem tree in Shirdi became a popular topic for devotees, although the archaeology is missing. Associations with Kabir developed, but nothing of this is mentioned by Dixit. Instead, the *Sketch* informs that Sai Baba often said his own *turbat* (tomb) would speak. In other accounts, the Islamic term for tomb disappears, and is replaced by *samadhi*, the Hindu equivalent.

Reference is made to renovation of the mosque, which occurred from 1909 onwards, and only with the reluctant permission of Sai Baba. Three carpenters were major assistants in this project. These Hindus were brothers, namely

Kondaji, Gabaji, and Tukaram. "After the construction, the management of the *masjid* [mosque] continued with these three brothers for many years." The *Sketch* informs that until the end of Sai Baba's life, Tukaram swept the mosque, cleaned the eating utensils of Sai, and heated water for the daily ablutions and mouthwash of the saint. As a rule, Sai would not allow these tasks to be performed by anyone else (Gabaji and Tukaram were still alive during the 1920s).

Hari Dixit began to stay at Shirdi *circa* 1910. He was a direct eyewitness of many events thereafter. His high caste friends at Bombay seem to have been amazed at his change of lifestyle. They informed newspapers that Dixit had become a *bua* (ascetic), and as a consequence, some people visited Shirdi to investigate Sai Baba. Dixit did not actually become an ascetic, but did modify his role from that of a wealthy metropolitan lawyer to a devotee living in a rural environment. He was able to build a house known as Dixitwada, which also served as a hostel. Elsewhere, he is reported to have maintained his career as a lawyer at the prompting of Sai Baba, while also living at Shirdi whenever he could do so.

Another new resident of Shirdi from 1910 was Bapusaheb Buti, alias Shrimant Gopalrao Mukund. This devotee is described in some sources as a millionaire, and even a multimillionaire; he was a *zamindar* or landowner of Nagpur (Kher 2001:131). The *Sketch* relates how Buti arranged for the construction of a mansion, built in black stone, and costing over a hundred thousand rupees. According to Dixit, there was no other building of such grandeur in that *taluka* (district division). The mansion was known as Butiwada, and later became the tomb of Sai Baba.

When renovation of the mosque was completed, Sai Baba had gone to the nearby village of Neemgaon. He was transported from Neemgaon in a procession featuring musicians, and then "ushered in state into the new *masjid*." No date is given. From other sources, we know that an increasing degree of ceremony was occurring, at the instigation of devotees. However, this enthusiasm was resisted to a substantial extent by Sai Baba himself, although he did not prevent these developments.

From the year 1910, many people in Bombay heard of the Shirdi saint, as a consequence of Narayan Chandorkar bringing Das Ganu to the metropolis. The *Sketch* describes Das Ganu as "one of the leading Kirtankar Varkaris of Pandharpur," and a devotee of Sai Baba. The full description is missing in some other accounts, but tends to confirm the emphasis of Narasimhaswami that Das Ganu was first and foremost a Vaishnava *bhakta,* and secondarily a Sai devotee.

Numerous devotees were influenced by Das Ganu's narration of miracle stories in his poetic *Bhakti Lilamrit* (1906), three chapters of which related to Sai Baba. Dixit mentions the miracle of lighting mosque lamps with water instead of oil, first described by Das Ganu many years earlier.

Dixit praises the example of Radhakrishna Ayi, a *brahman* widow who lived at Shirdi until her death in 1916, at the age of only thirty-five. She favoured elaborate trappings that became visible in the *chavadi* procession. Ayi also "twice swept the passages in the village through which Sai Baba walked." This reference appears to be abbreviated, and may mean twice daily. Dixit adds that she removed "every kind of rubbish" on these roads. Prior to the labours of Ayi, this work was performed by Balaji Patil Nevaskar.

Nevaskar came to Shirdi after "renouncing the world." The signification is not that of a *sannyasin*. Friends came after him in an effort to persuade him to return, but he declined. He always swept the roads and cleaned the mosque (apparently before Tukaram was allocated the latter role). Nevaskar was very retiring, and took the *darshan* (meeting) of Sai Baba "from a distance and never went near." He gifted the *faqir* with all his agricultural income, but Sai "returned almost the whole of it."

Balaji Nevaskar is here reported in terms of drinking only water closely related to the saint. He would drink the water in which Sai bathed, or water left in the *faqir's* drinking vessel. Nevaskar would also drink the *tirtha*, meaning the water used by devotees to wash the saint's feet. The *tirtha* water was frequently consumed by devotees at Shirdi, but some high caste persons were averse to this practice (being reported elsewhere to have feared contamination from the Muslim who inhabited a mosque).

After two years or so, Balaji Nevaskar was instructed by Sai Baba to go back home, and he complied. However, the devotee continued to visit Shirdi. He died some years later.

Additional information about Nevaskar is found in the *Shri Sai Satcharita*, a far more commonly used source. He lived at Nevasa with his two wives and children. His family would sometimes visit Shirdi for *darshan* of the saint. The family connection would explain why Sai Baba sent the devotee back home after some time; Sai did not generally encourage renunciation amongst householders. Nevaskar was a low caste farmer. Every year, at the time of harvest, he would bring his entire crop of grain to the mosque courtyard at Shirdi, gifting this commodity to the *faqir*. The small portion accepted by Sai was used to make bread. The bulk of the grain was given back to Nevaskar, for the use of his family. The devotee continued this harvest practice until his death (Dabholkar 1999:584–87).

According to Dabholkar and Dixit, the only water that Nevaskar would drink was "the used water that flowed out from the washing place after Baba's bath, and his washing his hands, feet, mouth" (ibid:584).

The priestly issue of contamination was given a very pointed twist by Sai Baba, a subtlety often ignored. From 1910 (and perhaps earlier), Bhagoji Shinde was a *sevakari* or personal attendant of the Shirdi *faqir*. Dixit informs that Bhagoji was "an outright leper," and yet Sai Baba associated with him as if Bhagoji were "the healthiest person."

Bhagoji would arrive at the mosque in the early morning. He would undo the bandage on Sai Baba's right hand (see Chapter 29), and apply massage to the saint's hands and body. Then Bhagoji would prepare the tobacco pipe. Sai would smoke this *chilum* and then pass it back to Bhagoji, who would also smoke the pipe. That interchange of the pipe would occur several times, and then the leper would depart.

The *Sketch* does not mention the reservation of some high caste visitors, who are known to have been in revulsion at the idea of sharing a pipe with a Muslim *faqir*. The presence of a leper would merely have confirmed to such scruples that the Shirdi mosque was to be avoided. A leper could be shunned even by low castes. Bhagoji Shinde was one of the strongest social statements ever made by Sai Baba.

The daily morning ablutions of Sai Baba are described by Dixit. "This was a sight worth to see." Using much water, the *faqir* would wash his hands, feet, mouth, and ears. Moreover, he "cleaned all these parts of the body in a very delicate manner." This washing process was not the only event in personal hygiene. "The same process Baba followed at the time of his bath." The frequency of the bath varies in different accounts. His fastidious attention to cleanliness may have contributed to the local belief (reported by Dabholkar) that Sai once cleaned his intestines in a fantastic manner (hanging them on a tree to dry).

After ablutions, Sai Baba would undertake his first begging round of the day, eating only very little when returning to the mosque. Afterwards he gave audience to visitors in what the *Sketch* calls a *darbar*, a word having connotations of a royal court, and which fits the Hindu mood of celebrating the saint in his last years.

Devotees are referred to by Dixit as *bhaktas*. At the mosque assemblies, Sai Baba "gave advice in the form of (by narrating) stories." The parables were accompanied by a more explicit mode of advice. Themes of Sai Baba included a strong faith in God, patience for the realisation of God, to love all creatures alike, not to wound the feelings of others, to be straightforward and honest in all our actions, and not to take the services of others without due payment. Such emphases fit the ethical aspect of Sai Baba's expression. Dixit makes no reference to Vedanta or Yoga.

"A very large proportion amongst the devotees of Sai Baba went to him for the fulfilment of their worldly desires." Dixit follows the view that, in this manner, the petitioners were encouraged to adopt spiritual objectives. However, the *darshan* situation was not always straightforward.

The *Sketch* reports the instance of an astrologer who arrived at Shirdi with a calculating objective. This visitor placed a manual of astrology in the saint's hands, intending to receive the book back as *prasad*. He believed that, by this procedure, he would gain the blessing of the saint, and thus be enabled to make a fortune from astrology. However, Sai Baba would not give the book back, and instead passed the volume to Bapusaheb (Gopalrao) Buti, a devotee from Nagpur who had become a resident of Shirdi. In this way, the visitor lost his manual. The astrologer had ostensibly made a gift of the book; the *faqir* was not obliged to return the gift and thereby assist the scheming strategy.

Buti was not an avid reader, but did become interested in the book. He is reported to have become a proficient amateur astrologer, giving free predictions to other devotees. Sai Baba himself is not known to have endorsed astrology (he took the view that predictions were often wrong, or only partly right). The *Sketch* interprets the event in terms of an emphasis from the Shirdi saint: any art or science is best utilised when given free of charge.

Sai Baba occasionally welcomed manual work on his own part. At some undated period, he participated with some devotees in the digging and construction of a well. The site was near a main road, at the Lendi garden.

In collaboration with Govind Dabholkar, Hari Dixit launched a Marathi journal called *Shri Sai Leela* in 1923. The *Sketch* originally appeared in the first volume of this journal. The journal project was an outcome of the Sai Baba Sansthan, created by Dixit at Shirdi after the saint's death.

15. *Shri Sai Satcharita*

Many of the books about Sai Baba draw freely upon passages found in the lengthy *Shri Sai Satcharita* of Dabholkar.

Govind R. Dabholkar (1859–1929) was a *brahman* devotee of Sai Baba from 1910. He wrote the *Shri Sai Satcharita* during the 1920s. This lengthy poetic work in Marathi has many references to early devotees of Sai Baba. The *Satcharita* has been described as a hagiography. However, many factual indicators are included in the contents.

The erudite Sai devotee, Vishwas B. Kher, concluded that the *Satcharita* is "authentic to a considerable extent," but also "inaccurate in some of the details" (Kher 2001:151). This observation was attended by a reflection that "the core of it [the *Satcharita*] is in essence a legend rather than historical truth" (ibid). In this sense, Kher described Dabholkar's work as "the *Pothi* or *Gatha* of the *leelas* of Sai Baba" (ibid). The word *pothi* means religious text, and therefore, "historical truth must be searched [for] elsewhere" (ibid). These important considerations are often overlooked. They signify that, whatever the degree of authenticity involved in the *Satcharita*, missing contextual details are needed to establish historical facts.

Dabholkar gives a list of social and religious categories who visited Shirdi during the saint's lifetime, and with the objective of gaining his *darshan* (meeting, audience). Dabholkar is here referring to the last decade of Sai Baba's life. Included in this list are astrologers, wealthy men, Vaishnava *gosavis* (ascetics), Vedanta *sannyasins*, pilgrims, and *mahars* (untouchables). There were also singers, dancers, jugglers, musicians, low caste fortune tellers, the blind, and the lame. There were also Kanphata (Nath) Yogis and "followers of Nanak," apparently meaning Sikhs. (148) We know that Muslim and Zoroastrian visitors also arrived.

The last decade of Sai Baba's life was marked by a strong influx of urban Hindus, a development which eclipsed the minority of Muslim adherents. Dabholkar himself was part of this urban wave, and initially a magistrate at Bombay.

Dabholkar viewed Sai Baba's *dhuni* (sacred fire) in the light of Vedic associations. This fire was kept burning day and night in the Shirdi mosque. Dabholkar urges: "Baba always acted according to the *Shruti* [scripture] which says, 'Till you are alive, always follow the vow of *Agnihotra* (i.e., keeping the fire, morning and evening, after offering the fire a handful of rice).' " (149)

The *Agnihotra* was an ancient Vedic fire ceremony, whereas the *dhuni* fire was common to Muslim *faqirs*, Nath Yogis, and varied *sadhus*. The *dhuni* resort of Sai Baba amounted to an ascetic commemoration of fire, in contrast to the archaic *Agnihotra*, a householder observance. Both the ancient Zoroastrian and Vedic traditions awarded esteem to fire rituals, including both hearth fire rites and more elaborate priestly programmes. It is not easy to determine exactly what significance the *dhuni* had for Sai Baba.

The *dhuni* fire was certainly very distinctive in a mosque, not being a traditional component of Islamic worship. Sai Baba is reported to have thrown into the *dhuni* a morsel of the bread and rice that he begged daily, at the time when he ate some of the food himself. His attendants would continually replenish the *dhuni* with wood, and the ash became a feature of his interchanges with visitors.

Sai Baba customarily uttered Islamic phrases at the *dhuni* and elsewhere, not Vedic texts.

[Sai] Baba would talk and laugh and move freely with all. The words "*Allah Malik*" were constantly on his lips. He disliked arguments and unprofitable wranglings. His staff (i.e., the baton) was always kept near at hand. (150)

The Islamic speech of Sai Baba, mediated via the Deccani Urdu dialect, was disconcerting to some Hindu observers. The extent of his familiarity with Marathi is uncertain. His staff was actually a short stick (*satka*), a trapping of some ascetics; this accessory is featured in a number of anecdotes.

The *udi* (ash) from the *dhuni* became invested with a strong significance by devotees. Sai Baba "took *udi* by the fistfuls from it [the *dhuni*] and gave them to the devotees when bidding them adieu." (151) The ash was regarded as *prasad* by Hindus, meaning a gift from the guru or deity. Sai would smear the ash on the forehead of a departing visitor, using his thumb for this action, and also "placing the hand on their head in benediction." (152)

The allusive speech of this *faqir* included *goshtis* (parables). Some of these were apparently reminiscences. Sai once described how, as a young boy, he secured a job as an embroiderer in metal thread. Other boys also worked with him, but his efforts transpired to be worth double that of his comrades. In gratitude, his employer gave him a new turban and scarf, but he just tied these in a bundle without wearing them. In further illustration of the point made, Sai Baba emphasised that an ordinary gift is always limited and inadequate, but "when God gives something, it has no end, even to the end of time." (153)

This reflection was transposed into his current situation at Shirdi, where visitors were so often requesting material things from him. As usual, the references of Sai Baba were interspersed with mention of the *Faqir* (capital F), meaning *Allah*:

> No one heeds my words. No one listens to me attentively! His [the Faqir's] treasury is overflowing, but no one cares to bring

the carts [to take away the treasure]. Nobody will dig, when asked to do so. No one bothers to make the effort. I say, "Dig for that wealth and carry it away by the cart-loads." (154)

This communication ended with the phrase: "As you sow, so you reap." This was a characteristic saying of Sai Baba, and part of his ethical teaching.

The saint satirised the attitude of many visitors to Shirdi:

Everyone says, "Give, give only [material things] to me." My Master [or the *Faqir*] says, "Take, O take this [material distraction] away." (155)

Sai Baba was referring here to the material gains and prospects desired by visitors coming for *darshan*. Many petitioners wanted health, cures, offspring, a better job, prosperity, and numerous other blessings of this mundane nature. A spiritual objective was largely, if not completely, foreign to their conceptions and expectations.

Sai Baba was evidently well aware of the nature of events and incongruous anticipations. His various strategies and eccentricities may need to be interpreted in this light.

16. Dakshina

Prior to 1908, Sai Baba would not ask for money, and moreover, would not even touch any gift of this nature. This attitude reflected the ideal of *faqiri* or renunciation. When he eventually changed his habit, some criticism resulted.

In his last years, Sai Baba became controversial for his habit of requesting money in fairly numerous situations. These alms he called *dakshina*, a word borrowed from the lexicon of Hinduism, and signifying a donation or gift bestowed in charity to a tutor or priest, as a token of respect. *Dakshina* is not a payment for work done or for favours granted. *Dakshina* is expected to be given according to the wealth or assets of the donor. In the case of Sai Baba, *dakshina* had nothing to do with caste status, ritual, or sacrifice. His gesture amounted to a kind of tax upon affluent devotees, most of whom were high caste Hindus.

Ascetics are also entitled to receive a *dakshina*. A general idea exists that *dakshina* is expected to be given voluntarily. However, some priests, tutors, or ascetics demand *dakshina* as their entitlement. Such a request may not be popular. The ascetic is expected to be above any preoccupation with money. Donors may grumble and complain, but refusal of the request is likely to be considered extremely improper, even if beyond the means of the person concerned.

An outstanding feature of the ascetic *dakshina* at Shirdi was that Sai Baba never kept any of the money for himself. He quickly passed on the donations, and by nightfall had nothing left. In this way, he maintained his lifestyle as an austere begging *faqir*. Sai Baba died without assets or funds.

People who viewed these events with incomplete information were liable to get the wrong ideas as to what was occurring. Many local devotees, ascetics, poor people, and yet others, benefited from the extensive redistribution of funds.

Sai Baba might request smaller or larger amounts, and would not accept money from everyone. Sometimes he would ask for all the cash that a visitor had on his person, and instances were known of people trying to conceal their return fare (that is, the cost of a railway ticket to go back home). The return fare was also demanded as *dakshina* in a number of cases.

The *dakshina* procedure commenced at the period when a substantial influx of devotees began to visit Shirdi from urban areas, especially Bombay. These people were mainly affluent, and not poor like the villagers. They brought gifts of food, which were likewise redistributed.

"Sai Baba's request for *dakshina*, though reflecting humanitarian concerns, surprised and scandalised many." (156) Asking for money ran counter to the code of the *sannyasin*, the Hindu renunciate. Muslim *faqirs* were likewise not generally associated with such practices. The innovation is memorable, reflecting an unorthodox approach. The *dakshina* tactic did not answer to any recognised mode of spiritual conduct. The fact that Sai Baba continued his daily begging rounds added to the apparent eccentricity of his role. Nevertheless, he did preserve *faqiri* in his routine and lifestyle.

The so-called "mad *faqir*" had not only become the major attraction at Shirdi, but also the most charitable agency in the region.

> It was said that his income equalled that of the Governor of a Province. Indeed, the authorities wanted to levy income tax . . . but as Sai Baba never had anything left by the end of the day it proved impossible. They did, however, levy income tax on several of his pensioners, poor followers to whom he gave a more or less regular allowance. (157)

17. Swami Somdev and the Flag

Swami Somdev (Somadeva) is described by Dabholkar as one of the *sannyasins* who visited Sai Baba. Originally living at Uttar Kashi in the north, Somdev came south to Nagpur in 1911, and there heard about the *faqir* of Shirdi. A friend gave him a letter of introduction to Sai. The Swami, accordingly, went by railway train to Kopargaon, from where he took a *tonga* (horse cab) to Shirdi.

From a distance, Swami Somdev glimpsed flags that were flying at Shirdi, and especially one at the mosque. The visitor interpreted these banners as a sign that Sai Baba wanted fame and honour, being so eager to advertise his presence. Dabholkar retrospectively describes the attitude of Somdev: "This *sadhu* ([Sai] simply flaunts his greatness by flying the flag, and this itself is a grave deficiency in his saintliness. Why should I go for the *darshan* of such a *sadhu*?" (158)

At this juncture, Somdev also heard that Sai Baba took part in a procession from the mosque to the *chavadi*, with an accompaniment of beating drums. This scenario was interpreted by the visitor as a sign of grave affectation. The fact is that Sai Baba did not ask for the *chavadi* procession to occur, and nor did he organise this popular event. Instead, he made a concession to the enthusiastic wishes and expectations of devotees. He actually resisted the procession in some ways.

On the basis of his own interpretation, Swami Somdev decided to leave without proceeding further to the mosque. A strong possibility is that caste scruples were also aroused in this instance, about taking the *darshan* of a Muslim *faqir*.

Swami Somdev and the Flag

The Swami's companions then told him that the villagers had positioned the mosque flag (and the other banners), not Sai Baba. Things now looked different. The Swami then reconsidered, and decided to continue with the objective of *darshan*. When he encountered Sai Baba, he "experienced great joy and he felt so completely at peace with himself that he felt like staying there forever." (159)

A drawback now occurred, however. Sai Baba displayed anger towards the visitor, and implied that Somdev was a hypocrite. The *faqir* is reported to have said: "Get out and be gone! And don't you dare approach my mosque again! Why take the *darshan* of one who puts up flags on the mosque? Is this any sign of a saint? Not even a moment should be wasted here!" (160)

Swami Somdev accepted the rebuke, and this time did not allow himself to be deflected. Later, he returned to the mosque courtyard, and gazed at the *faqir* from a distance, assimilating the situation in his mind. Sai Baba again made angry remarks, which actually mirrored "his [Somdev's] own thoughts, word for word." (161) The *sannyasin* was not allowed to forget his recent doubts, which were clearly discrepant.

18. Devotees Reading Books

Sai Baba himself did not read books. Many devotees were keen to gain his approval of sacred texts which they wanted to read. "If a devotee wished to read a particular book, he quite naturally felt that he should first place it in Baba's hands and then receive it back as his *'prasad'*. So that, later when he read the book, he would acquire special merit." (162)

The intermediary in this procedure was Shama (Madhavrao Deshpande), one of the earliest devotees of Sai Baba. Expectations were not readily gratified. When given books in this manner, Sai "would look through the pages cursorily; the devotees would then put out their hands to receive them [the books] back. But Baba would not give them back." (163) He would, instead, tell Shama to keep the books in the latter's own collection at home. Shama would mildly remonstrate, asking if he might give back the books to the owners. Sai Baba would reiterate that Shama should keep the books.

The saint's perspective, in these matters, did not converge with wishes of the devotees. Dabholkar, writing in the 1920s, refers to a future time when "these books will become useful." (164) Shama was still alive, and still dutifully keeping the books at that time. This is a striking testimony to the denial of devotee expectations.

Various beliefs about reading sacred books were in circulation. Sai Baba was sometimes thought to recommend certain texts. A literate lawyer devotee, M. B. Rege, witnessed an occasion when devotees brought books for Sai to bless.

Devotees Reading Books

Rege had not come with any book, and felt embarrassed. Sai Baba then told him that people expected to find God in the books, and yet confusion was the actual consequence. "If you unify head and heart, that is enough." (165) The saint appears to have regarded books with caution, as creating ideas about spirituality and conduct that were not actually relevant to the readers. He was not a believer in initiation or *mantra*, for instance.

Shama became involved in a stressful episode when Sai Baba did recommend a book. This occurred after the arrival at Shirdi of Ramdasi Bua, a follower of the *avatar* Rama. The daily routine of Bua included reading the *Adhyatma Ramayana*, (166) and also reciting the devotional text *Vishnusahasranaam*. Bua was apparently in public view when he performed these actions, and also sitting near Sai Baba.

One day, the saint (via Shama) asked Bua to go to the market and get some medicine for his (Sai's) stomach ache. Bua accordingly departed, leaving his holy books. Sai then went over to the books and picked up the *Vishnusahasranaam*. The *faqir* told Shama that this sacred text (*pothi*) was very beneficial, and instructed him to read it. Sai Baba dramatised this request by saying that he had once benefited from this *pothi* in a moment of stress. He did not say that he had read the text, only that he had "laid it on my heart just for a moment." (167)

Shama objected, saying he did not want the book, and that Ramdasi Bua would be furious with him for taking it. Bua was "wild by nature, hot-tempered, cross, and loses his head easily." (168) Moreover, he (Shama) could not even read the text, which was in Sanskrit. However, Sai Baba was insistent, and placed the book in Shama's pocket. Dabholkar eulogises the practice of "taking the name (*naam*)," closely associated with the Sanskrit text mentioned.

When Ramdasi Bua returned, a man named Anna, who "delighted in exciting quarrels," told him what had happened in his absence. Bua then commenced a tirade against Shama, accusing him of stealing the *pothi* and manipulating Sai Baba for this purpose. He even said that the stomach complaint of Sai "was only a pretence." (169)

Shama tried to pacify the wrathful holy man, but to no avail. Sai Baba then intervened, speaking in a cool tone, asking why Bua was so quarrelsome, and why he could not speak more gently. He is reported to have said:

> You read the *pothis* (sacred texts) all the time, and yet your heart is still impure. . . . You ought to be detached and desireless, in every sense of the word. But here you are, not being able to give up the attachment to that *pothi*! What can one say of this behaviour of yours? . . . Go back and sit in your place. *Pothis* you can get cheaper by the dozen, but a good person is hard to come by. (170)

What Sai Baba evidently admired was an attitude that transcended texts, not the habit of becoming attached to texts, and the attendant pride in reading them. Ramdasi Bua regarded himself as a holy man, reading sacred books as part of an elevated role. His pride in reading and recital was effectively useless.

Bua was still angry, and told Shama that he was going to take from him another book, in exchange for the one Sai Baba had placed in his pocket. The placatory Shama then offered Bua ten copies of the book now specified by the latter.

Another devotee was Bapusaheb Jog (d.1926) from Poona. A different experience with a book occurred in his case. A parcel arrived for Jog at the Shirdi post office, containing a contemporary commentary on the *Bhagavad Gita* by Bal G. (Lokamanya) Tilak. This commentary is well known for "an explicitly socio-political slant to the old notion of *karmamarga*." (171) When Jog went to the mosque that day, he inadvertently dropped the parcel. Sai Baba asked about the contents. The book was then handed to the *faqir*. Sai glanced very quickly through the pages, took out a rupee from his pocket, and placed this coin approvingly on the book. He gave both the coin and book to Jog, telling the devotee to read the book thoroughly. (172)

Sai Baba also permitted Jog to conduct regular classes in the building known as Sathewada (constructed in 1908). Proficient in Sanskrit, Jog daily read and explained the Varkari texts known as *Jnaneshwari* and *Eknathi Bhagavat*, two major *bhakta* works of the Maharashtrian tradition. This was a major concession of Sai Baba to the desire of devotees for a focus upon religious books.

Jog (Sakharam Hari) also performed *arati* and *puja* at Shirdi, but found that he did not achieve the peace of mind he desired. Sai Baba told him that he should struggle for detachment, and resort to begging. When his wife died, Jog became an ascetic, and started to beg for his food at Shirdi. He reputedly gained peace, and also established a strong link with Upasani Maharaj.

19. Mulay Shastri

Mulay Shastri of Nasik was described by Dabholkar as "a rigid ritualistic Agnihotra Brahmin." In 1915, he visited Shirdi in order to meet Gopalrao Buti, a wealthy devotee of Sai Baba. Mulay was not interested in seeing the *faqir*, and wished to return quickly to Nasik. His sole purpose was to ask Buti's permission to use the latter's property at Nasik for his own school of Vedic studies.

When Mulay Shastri was about to leave Shirdi, Buti suggested that he should meet Sai Baba and obtain permission to depart. "Shastri was an orthodox Brahmin and did not desire to be polluted by any contact with the *masjid* [mosque]" (Kher 2001:110). Buti therefore agreed to make the request for departure on behalf of Mulay.

The visitor was persuaded to accompany Buti and others to the mosque. Mulay was not only a scholar well versed in Sanskrit scriptures, but also considered an expert on astrology and palmistry. At that time of day, Sai Baba had purchased baskets of bananas and was distributing them. Mulay was "quite astonished when he saw Baba's feet," and wished to read the lines on them. He was not able to do so. Mulay did not want any bananas, but instead now desired to inspect the *faqir's* palm, his interest strongly aroused. Sai Baba did not cooperate, and ignored Mulay, who kept stretching out his hand. Mulay was frustrated when the saint placed bananas in his hand instead of the desired palm.

Mulay Shastri retired to the house where he was staying. Taking a ritual bath, and putting on a *sovala* (purified) silk *dhoti*, he commenced the Agnihotra rite. Meanwhile, Sai Baba

Mulay Shastri

took his walk to the Lendi. The saint made cryptic remarks about using an ochre chalk or dye, saying that he had to wear an ochre robe that day. Nobody could understand what he meant.

When Sai Baba returned to the mosque, Bapusaheb Jog informed Mulay that the *arati* rite was about to be performed in the mosque. Jog was the officiant at this ceremony. The guest was invited to attend, but declined, saying he would come for *darshan* later. Mulay Shastri preferred to adopt an *asana* (Yogic posture), sitting calmly and aloofly in his visitor quarters. His basic fear was about contracting pollution in a mosque. Mulay had already entered the mosque precincts, and was evidently in a confused state of mind.

The *faqir* then instructed Buti to bring *dakshina* from the guest. Mulay Shastri was resistant, doubting the validity of Sai Baba's request for money. Dabholkar interprets his train of thought in terms of "Why should I give *dakshina*? I am a pure, *Agnihotri Brahmin*" (Dabholkar 1999:190). His mind was in a state of internal conflict, but eventually he agreed to leave for the mosque, taking some money as *dakshina*.

Mulay remained at a distance in the mosque courtyard, perturbed by the fact that the mosque was *ovala*, meaning a contaminated place. If he entered the mosque, his state of ritual purity would be defiled. His recourse was to salute Sai Baba from a distance, showering flowers from his palms. According to Dabholkar, the hesitant and doubting guest then saw his deceased guru, Baba Gholap Shastri, wearing an ochre robe. Everyone else saw Sai Baba, but Mulay, instead, saw Gholap.

Everyone knew that Gholap Shastri (1825–77) had died many years earlier. Mulay's amazement was acute; he did not know whether to believe his eyes. His guru Gholap had been a Vedic scholar from Sangamner, who eventually became a *sannyasin* with the name of Advaitendra Saraswati. At one time, Gholap had stayed at Akkalkot as a disciple of Swami Samarth (Kher 2001:111).

A climax occurred. Mulay Shastri could no longer contain his intense feelings, and abandoned his priestly decorum.

> Overpowered with emotion and as if possessed, Mule [Mulay] Shastri ran up the steps of the *masjid* [mosque], caught hold of the feet of Sai Baba and cleansed them with his tears! All those gathered were astonished at the impulsive act. (Kher 2001:111)

Mulay believed that he was holding the feet of Gholap. He is reported to have uttered the name of Gholap. He joined in the *arati* of Sai Baba that was being performed, but sang as if he were addressing Gholap. Yet finally, when he rose to his feet, Gholap had disappeared, and instead there was Sai Baba, wearing the white *kafni*. The *faqir* now requested *dakshina*. This time Mulay did not react adversely. His scepticism had vanished. Instead, he gave unreservedly the rupees he had brought with him. Mulay also acknowledged Sai Baba as his guru (Dabholkar 1999:192).

Only after the *arati*, when the assembly was dispersing, did the details of Mulay Shastri's experience emerge. He then explained to Hari Dixit, a lawyer and devotee, that he had seen Gholap Swami in an ochre robe. Others then remembered the cryptic references of Sai Baba (to an ochre robe) earlier that morning. Sai Baba himself does not appear to have explained anything. He did not need to do so, because the vocal Mulay Shastri was eager to describe his experience over and over again to anyone interested (Kamath and Kher 1991:113–114).

There are sceptics who do not believe all the components of this episode as reported in the *Satcharita*. However, that account is of considerable interest. Dabholkar realistically relays the dilemma of a conservative priest whose outlook was strongly conditioned by conventional taboos. There were also other orthodox priests who were deterred by mosque precincts.

20. Marianne Warren and Sufism

The thesis of Dr. Marianne Warren (d.2004) derived support from the Urdu *Notebook* of Abdul Baba. She maintained that former treatments of Sai Baba had been afflicted by "Hinduisation," failing to perceive the Muslim Sufi context for the subject (an exception was my own early book *Gurus Rediscovered*).

There are varying forms of disagreement with Warren. Some Hindus refuse to acknowledge Sai Baba as a Muslim Sufi, while another interpretation (of the present writer) disputes the nature of his Sufi context and associations (Shepherd 2015). In my opinion, Warren made a number of relevant observations, but also some mistakes. This imbalance needs to be redressed.

> There is no way of knowing the extent of Sai Baba's familiarity with the early Sufi texts. . . . It is not being suggested here that Sai Baba studied these written texts or indeed any Sufi texts—but rather that his *murshid* guide would have imparted this knowledge by word of mouth, and thus he would be very familiar with basic Sufi precepts, being circulated orally throughout Maharashtra. (Warren 1999:60)

These reflections tend to realistically indicate a non-dependence upon classical Sufi literature. The early milieu of Sai Baba was probably that of independent Sufis, meaning those not claiming affiliation with Sufi Orders and the pedigrees favoured by establishment organisations. Such independents could be found in the diverse ranks of *faqirs*, many of whom existed at this time in India. However, Warren tends to strongly associate Sai Baba with orthodox mainline Sufism, not the independents.

The Sufi practices of Sai Baba can be shown to be much closer to the early mystical tradition of al-Sarraj and al-Hujwiri than those of the Sufis of Bijapur for example. (Warren 1999:60)

This type of emphasis ignores such characteristics as stone-throwing and the affinity with Hindus, both shared traits of earlier Deccani Sufis and the *faqir* Sai Baba. In contrast, there is no indication that Hujwiri (died *circa* 1075) was a conciliator with Hindus, despite his migration to India. (173) Quite unlike Sai Baba, Hujwiri did not accept reincarnation. The eleventh century Hanafi scholar stigmatised *tanasukh*, meaning the transmigration of souls. In that context, Hujwiri deemed heretical the sect known as Hulmaniyya (Nicholson 1936:260,264). This proscribing judgment meant that *tanasukh* was "not part of Sufism" (Karamustafa 2007:105).

Hujwiri was also condemnatory in relation to another belief found among Sufis. "He strenuously resists and pronounces heretical the doctrine that human personality can be merged and extinguished in the being of God" (Nicholson 1936:xiii). This theme relates to sublimation of the *nafs* (limiting self), a complex Sufi teaching diversely expressed and simplified.

In the composition of early manuals on Sufism, two of the major writers were strongly influenced by scholastic theology *(kalam)*. "Qushayri and Hujwiri succeeded in aligning Sufism with Shafii-Ashari and Hanafi-Maturidi scholarship" (Karamustafa 2007:106). Islamic legalism and *kalam* now imposed new formulae and boundaries upon Sufis, who were presented according to the biases of canonists and heresiologists.

Slightly earlier, in the tenth century, "it was considered important to prove to the world the perfect orthodoxy of Sufi tenets, and therefore a number of books were composed almost simultaneously in the last quarter of the tenth century" (Schimmel 1975:84). A very early work was the *Kitab al-Luma* of Sarraj (d.988), an Iranian from Tus. Sarraj "was in the first instance a scholar of Sufism rather than a Sufi master" (Karamustafa 2007:68–9).

Warren inclines to a portrayal of Sai Baba in terms of orthodox Sufism, associated with the Sufi Orders that formed from the twelfth century onwards. Yet some of her own statements are in contradiction to this preference.

> Heterodox Sufis are characterised by their often bizarre utterances and anti-social behaviour such as raging anger, which is sometimes accompanied by the throwing of stones. Sai Baba was well known for his violent outbursts and blazing temper, his eyes becoming red and fierce, all apparently without cause, but he soon calmed down to his normal self.... Due to his strange behaviour, Sai Baba was often classed as a mad *faqir* or *veda faqir*, before he was more generally understood. (Warren 1999:110–11)

Warren is here describing traits of *majazib*, as these are depicted in hagiographies. She chose to confuse the issue by asserting: "There is no evidence to support the idea that Sai Baba was a *majzub*, for Sai Baba assiduously followed the strict Sufi path" (ibid:111). A misunderstanding is here evident. The same scholar assumed that the category of *majzub* "fails to return to normal worldly consciousness," and misleadingly cited my own book (*Gurus Rediscovered*, 1986, page 19), which does not make any such statement.

The error of Warren here derived from her confusion about themes of Meher Baba, including his explanation of the *mast* ("God-intoxicated") category. Meher Baba also described the *majzub* (plural: *majazib*) in a very different context to that found in other sources. Meher Baba was not referring to the *majazib* of Bijapur, but to a far more select minority whom he did not stipulate in historical terms. His description is of substantial interest (e.g., Donkin 1948:21–22), but should not be confused with more well known presentations. The normative description is far more often what one encounters. I was not, and still am not, referring to any failure in "return to normal worldly consciousness," and nor any lack of strict discipline. Nor am I saying that Sai Baba was definitively a *majzub*, whatever the affinities he exercised in relation to that misunderstood category. I am content to call him an independent *faqir*.

A prominent scholar described *majazib* in terms of "ignoring all religious and social taboos" (Rizvi 1983:470). The same scholar stated that the most famous *majzub* was Sarmad, "an Armenian Jew who came from Kashan," a learned mystic eventually worsted at Delhi in an ideological collision with the fundamentalist *ulama* and the Mughal emperor Aurangzeb (ibid:475-479). There is no need whatever to view such persons as failing to return to normal consciousness. To the contrary, Sarmad should be credited with a strong degree of resolute courage, evidenced by his vocation as an Islamo-Jewish version of a *naga sadhu*, in confrontation with the conservative royal tutor Mulla Qawi (Shepherd 1988:133). The consequence was execution.

Warren was not a scholar of Persian or Urdu, but fluent in Marathi, which is an Indian language. Warren was an ardent devotee of Sathya Sai Baba (d.2011), and confused a number of references to Meher Baba and Shirdi Sai Baba. In this light, she misinterpreted certain aspects of my own earlier book. (174) Warren's respect for Shirdi Sai was accompanied by strong promotion of Sathya Sai, and only after publication of her book (in 1999) did she repudiate the Andhra guru, having by then learned more about events at his Puttaparthi ashram.

In the form of exegesis she constructed, Warren ignored the situation of liberal Sufis like Shah Aminuddin Ala, the Chishti *shaikh* of Bijapur who gained repute as a *majzub* in the seventeenth century. This liberal figure is reported to have been worshipped by many Hindus (Eaton 1978:249-250). We should not reduce his achievement by believing that he failed to return to normal worldly consciousness, which is the blanket judgment of Dr. Warren in relation to *majazib*.

Demonstrating such a blind spot, Warren is effectively convergent with the tactic of *ulama* Sufis like Maulana Muhammad Zubairi (d.1677), who accused the *majazib* at Bijapur of being insane heretics. This was because of disagreement on the part of *majazib* with the compromised lifestyle of orthodox Sufis, who opted for wealth and prestige. The orthodox Sufi role was keen to accept royal land endowments, and also to maintain insular religious policies against Hindus.

Warren failed to assimilate the preference for renunciation demonstrated by independent Sufis and *majazib*, such as those existing at Bijapur in the seventeenth and eighteenth centuries (see Appendix I). Orthodox Sufis diluted the "strict Sufi path" in their role as wealthy landed gentry. Warren preferred to dwell upon "Bhakti-Sufi" poetry, which is certainly relevant, but actually only the tip of the iceberg in terms of dissident Sufi events, departing from orthodox Islamic strictures upon *kafirs* (infidels, including Hindus).

Warren may have associated dissidents with the use of wine and *bhang* (an intoxicating drink made from cannabis leaves). These substances are mentioned in some early accounts and poetry relating to the Bijapur *majazib*, often very allusively. Wine had for long been a symbolic component in Persian Sufi poetry. More tangibly, wine was in favour at the royal court of Bijapur, but not with the *ulama*. In general, and nationwide, numerous Hindu *sadhus* and Muslim *faqirs* did resort to cannabis. One may conclude that there were also many ascetics in both religious camps who did not follow this trend.

Sai Baba was a rigorous ascetic, and evidently disapproved of alcohol and *bhang*. His *faqiri* involved strict celibacy and simple living. Like the *majazib*, he refused to acquire possessions and wealth; he died without assets. However, he was not concerned to fast, and remained robust until his last years, begging his food daily at village houses. He was not emaciated, in contrast to numerous other Muslim *faqirs* and Hindu holy men.

Warren is pointing out the obvious when she says that Sai Baba was not an orthodox Muslim. She does not appear to realise the implications of her own statements. "Sai Baba was distinctly unorthodox, to the point of heterodoxy" (Warren 1999:101). Unorthodox tendencies are not generally representative of the Sufi Orders, and may easily conflict with conformist idioms inherited from Hujwiri and Sarraj. Warren refers to Dabholkar's implication that Sai Baba was "spasmodic in his performance" of such orthodox Islamic practices as *namaz* (ritual prayer five times daily), confession of faith (*shahada*), and fasting.

In trying to find a background context here, Warren's reasoning was in part awkward and misleading. She opted to state: "Sai Baba did not formally align himself with any established Sufi orders, although he had a number of features in common with the Chishtiyya order" (ibid:109). The only feature she explicitly mentions is *sama*, or the use of music. She added in a peripheral footnote that Abdul's *Notebook* gives "a few hints that Sai Baba was more familiar with the Chishtiyya Order" (ibid:127n25). This opinion is derived from the *Notebook* having listed "the succession of Chishti masters in more detail than the other orders" (ibid). The difference is not particularly substantial, and no firm ground for a Chishti influence. All the *Notebook* listings of *khanwadas* are skeletal (ibid:289-293).

In this rather forced manner, Warren associated Sai Baba with the Chishti Order on the basis of musical performances at Shirdi. This theory is not convincing. She did qualify that "no definite link can be made between Sai Baba and Chishtis." However, she added: "His familiarity with Rumi's poetry and song is highly suggestive of some influence" (ibid:328). Warren was clearly meaning Chishti influence here, a deduction supported by her remark on the same page: "There is the hint that Sai Baba had some connection with Chishtis as he was so fond of music" (ibid).

This reflection was based on the report of Das Ganu that Sai Baba occasionally sang Muslim songs which the Marathi poet could not understand. Such references are not sufficient for an attribution of Chishti influence. Many Indian Muslims were familiar with Rumi poetry and Urdu mystical songs, an accomplishment which very often did not mean any Chishti influence.

Marked difficulties exist for any attempt to bracket the Shirdi *faqir* with the Chishti Order. For instance, Sai Baba did not claim any *silsila*, or chain of spiritual descent. Such genealogies can be lengthy, and frequently claim descent from the Prophet Muhammad. "Genealogical authority within Islam goes back to the pre-Muslim era, and to Arab clan kinship practices.... This trait of pre-Islamic Arabia still holds as an organising principle in Sufism" (Ernst and Lawrence 2002:47).

Sai Baba was a celibate all his life, a factor contrasting with Chishti preferences for marriage in many instances. Of the famous early Indian Chishti *shaikhs*, only two were voluntary celibates, namely Nizamuddin Awliya (d.1325) and Nasiruddin Chiragh-i-Dehli (d.1356). "Though they did not enjoin celibacy on their followers, some chose to follow their example" (ibid:66).

The facts of Chishti accommodation to Islamic norms do not fit an independent *faqir* like Sai Baba. "It is incumbent on Muslim males to marry, to produce children, and to care for a family. That obligation is hard to reconcile with the mandate to poverty, or at least restricted income, that characterised early Sufism" (ibid:65). Such details are often overlooked. An overall conclusion, in one of the most analytical surveys available of Chishti Sufism, is the following:

Hence in three critical respects (conjugal perseverance, adherence to Islamic ritual observances, and evidence of scholarly skills), the Sufi masters remained peculiarly, distinctively Islamic in India." (Ernst and Lawrence 2002:66)

The example of Sai Baba is in acute contrast. This celibate was clearly lukewarm in his adherence to Islamic ritual. He had no interest whatever in displaying scholarly skills, even though an Urdu document (Abdul's *Notebook*) indicates that he is unlikely to have been illiterate, contrary to an assumption of some commentators. Sai Baba is known to have occasionally chanted *al-Fatihah,* the short opening verse of the *Quran,* but not in any context of displaying the prowess of an *alim* (scholar skilled in religious law; the plural term is *ulama*).

An early Chishti figurehead was Sayed Muhammad Husaini Gisudaraz (d.1422). This prestigious Chishti *shaikh* from Delhi was active in Gulbarga. He departed from former Chishti patterns by learning Sanskrit for the purpose of refuting Hindu beliefs (Rizvi 1978:254). Gisudaraz participated in debates with *brahmans,* and claimed to have defeated many of them. The incentive here being that the losers in debate should convert to the religion of the winner. The losers did not comply (ibid). Even Jalaluddin Rumi was considered an enemy of Islam by this orthodox Sufi (see Appendix I). The extent of the influence of Gisudaraz is uncertain, but he was very well known in the Deccan. Sai Baba was the antithesis of such insular programmes.

Other features of Chishti belief and practice are also foreign to Sai Baba. The pursuit of multiple initiations was common by the seventeenth century, and surfaces in correspondence between two Sufis credited as leaders of a Chishti revival. The correspondents were Shah Kalimullah Jahanabadi (d.1729) and his disciple Nizamuddin Aurangabadi (d.1730). Chishtis were now in rivalry with the powerful Naqshbandi Order. Nizamuddin was sent from Delhi to Aurangabad on a mission to gain more disciples. He was "a sufferer from venereal disease" (Rizvi 1983:304), a detail which is no indication of a celibate lifestyle. Jahanabadi wanted to give the disciple a bride from his own family (ibid). The disciple apparently had two wives already.

Nizamuddin Aurangabadi was initiated into the four major Sufi orders, including the Naqshbandiyya. His correspondence with Jahanabadi evidences an awareness of the tension existing between different Orders on account of varying practices (Ernst and Lawrence 2002:28). The Naqshbandis avoided music and favoured a silent *zikr*. Aurangabadi was accordingly advised to moderate Chishti procedures.

Chishti hagiographies of the nineteenth century emphasise a project of integrating other Orders into the Chishtiyya (ibid). That means multiple initiations, which were believed to maximise the Sufi vocation. Sai Baba was completely outside this scenario, and resembles far more his contemporary Swami Samarth of Akkalkot (see Chapter 10). Competing Sufi Orders, and multiple initiations, were not necessarily the resolution for complexities of a much discussed spiritual path.

Dr. Warren is far less confusing when she refers to Dabholkar as "the very orthodox Brahmin biographer of Sai Baba" (ibid). Dabholkar "admits that he knew very little about Islam and certainly even less about the subtle nuances and fine distinctions of the mystical path of Sufism" (ibid). One may agree with Warren that the losses, with regard to Sufism, are pronounced in the *Shri Sai Satcharita*.

> Having acknowledged his [Sai Baba's] Muslim status, Dabholkar then proceeded to interpret and write about Sai Baba's sayings, actions and miracles in a totally Hindu manner. Later authors followed his lead, so that any Muslim references then tended to be regarded as anomalies. . . . There is no denying that Dabholkar's Hindu interpretation is valid in its own way and has proved to be of great spiritual benefit to many devotees – so much so that his work is now regarded as sacred literature (*pothi*). (Warren 1999:101–2)

Dabholkar commenced what Warren describes as the "Hinduising" interpretation, which became more accentuated in the later report of Swami Sai Sharan Anand. For instance, Anand communicated how high caste Hindu devotees "believe that if [Sai] Baba had donned Mohammaden garb and adopted some Mohammaden ways of worship. . . . it was for the purpose of killing or removing the wrong interpretation of the Veda" (cited in Warren 1999:34).

Anand also reported the belief that Sai Baba was "an incarnation of Shiva, Rama or Dattatreya," while "many believe that Sainath Maharaj is the tenth Nath" in a "succession of Navanaths beginning with Adinath." (175)

Nath legends of nine Nath Yogis were pervasive in Maharashtra, commemorating medieval events in Tantric Yoga. There is sufficient evidence to conclude that Sai Baba was not a Nath Yogi or Tantric Yogi. For instance, Professor Narke testified that the Shirdi saint did not teach *kundalini* or *siddhis*, while his aversion to *mantra* and *pranayama* is well known.

> The early Nath [Kanphata] yogis were associated with the erotic practices of Kaula Tantrism, and prominent in their pantheon are the feminine deities known as yoginis or female yogis. *Hatha* yoga [of the Nath yogis] has a much more complicated psycho-physical set of techniques than the classical yoga of Patanjali, and it is presented with a minimum of metaphysical explanation. Special practices include manipulation of subtle physiology including psychic centres called cakras [chakras], retention of semen, pronunciation of syllabic chants or mantras with occult efficacy, and the summoning of deities. Despite their ascetic emphasis on sexual restraint, the Kanphata yogis have become over the past millennium a recognisable caste. (Ernst 2005:22)

Warren emphasises poetry in "the Bhakti-Sufi traditions of Maharashtra." This means "the writings of Jnaneswar, Eknath, Tukaram and others, and those of Muntoji Bahamani, Shekh Mahammad and Shah Muni" (Warren 1999:385).

She finds in these Maharashtrian Bhakti and Sufi poets an indication of "Hindu-Muslim sharing of religious concepts, more specifically the mystical ideas of God-realisation" (ibid). The eclectic Sufis in this vista are far less well known than the Hindu *bhakti* poets. Shaikh Muhammad (1560–1650) "used Hindu symbols and Hindu imagery and metaphors to elucidate his Sufi messages, without compromising his Muslim faith, while Shah Muni (1756–1807) also spread his message in mainly Hindu surroundings" (ibid).

The same scholar says of Abdul's Urdu *Notebook* that Sai Baba's teachings were similar to those of Shah Muni, who equated Narayan with *Allah*, and the Vedas with the *Quran*. Sai Baba equated Brahma with Ali, and Vishnu with *Allah*. In the *Notebook*, the Hindu deities and avatars "are like the prophets of Islam; they are not Gods" (Warren 1999:385).

Shah Muni "accommodates Hindu gods to the point of saying that he and his ancestors were their followers" (ibid:385–6). The key to these diverse Muslim figures is "the process of accommodation of Hindu religious ideas without sacrificing Islamic ideals and convictions" (ibid:386).

Shaikh Muhammad is associated with the Qadiri Order, but did not operate within orthodox Sufi channels (see chapter 6). He wrote the *Yogasamgrama*, and employed Persian, Arabic, Sanskrit, and Marathi terms in an attempt at synthesis. "He was concerned with teaching the steps of the Sufi *tariqat* in terms acceptable to a Hindu *bhakta*, as well as with conveying the essential feeling and experience of a Sufi" (ibid:159).

Warren infers that Sai Baba "must have acted as a spiritual master or *pir* to a floating population of itinerant Sufis wandering around Maharashtra in the second half of the nineteenth century" (ibid:156). However, he was not acting as any kind of master prior to the 1880s.

The Muslim devotee, Imambai Chota Khan, stated that Sai Baba knew Arabic. "At this stage we have no way of knowing if Sai Baba was quoting Arabic verses from the *Quran* from memory or whether he genuinely spoke fluent Arabic" (Warren 1999:124). This dilemma arises from the fact that Arabic verses of the *Quran* are often memorised without knowing the meaning. "He [Sai] was heard to speak many languages including Arabic, Persian and Urdu" (ibid).

Warren credits that Sai Baba employed Sufi and *bhakti* terms interchangeably, for example, *guru/pir*. (176) However, he "always referred to his own guru by the Arabic term of *murshid*" (ibid:116). Narasimhaswami reported his advice in terms of: "If you are a Rama *bhakta*, keep to Rama. If you want only *Allah*, keep to *Allah*." (177)

"To the lay observer he was a strange individual in Muslim garb whose behaviour was bizarre, and speech incomprehensible" (Warren 1999:107). This liberal *faqir*, despite his attested familiarity with the *Quran*, was not a preacher of Islam. He would express parables or *goshtis* that could be difficult to interpret, and which lacked all doctrinaire accents. He adhered to the vintage ideals of *faqiri*, involving poverty and simplicity. Sai Baba lived in a ruined mosque, and "his *kafnis* [robes] were often torn and showed evidence of being repeatedly mended" (ibid:104). This *faqir* "showed great resistance to wearing new clothes donated by devotees, preferring to mend his old ones" (ibid). The *Satcharita* says that Sai "clothed himself with a *kafni*, patched in a hundred places." (178)

Dabholkar does (if rarely) use the word *faqir*, as in his verse: "Even though I have become a fakir, freeing myself from all care, without the encumbrances of a house and family and am sitting in one place, calm and still." (179)

The high caste aversion to a Muslim could be strong. For instance, when the son of a Hindu devotee (Pradhan) became seriously ill, the household priest (Madhava Bhat) blamed Sai Baba, affirming that the illness had been incurred because the family were deferring to a Muslim saint. Bhat demanded that the family should, instead, pray to Dattatreya, but Pradhan rejoined that Sai was Dattatreya. The boy recovered, and Bhat also came to believe in the identity of Sai Baba with Dattatreya. (180)

The statements of Sai Baba included: "I am *parvardigar*. I live at Shirdi and everywhere ... the universe is in me" (Warren 1999:122). These words are found in the *Charters and Sayings* (1939) compiled by Narasimhaswami. The Persian word *Parvardigar* refers to spiritual reality, and was transmitted via the Urdu language employed by the Shirdi *faqir*.

Warren compared Sai Baba to the early Sufi figures of Abu Yazid al-Bistami and Hallaj, the former being especially noted for *shathiyat* or ecstatic utterances. These mystics were active in Islamic Iran and Iraq respectively. Time had moved on, and the milieu was now Hindu Maharashtra in the British Empire phase.

21. *Chilla-i-Makus*

In chapter 32 of the *Satcharita,* Dabholkar includes a lengthy recital attributed to Sai Baba. This is longer than the *goshtis* (parables), and may have undergone elaboration in oral and poetic transmission.

Sai Baba and his companions were wandering in the forest, wishing to escape the limitations of *"pothis* and *Puranas,"* meaning sacred texts. They encountered difficulties. A guru then appeared, and promised to give guidance if his word was respected. Only Sai agreed, and the others departed.

> He [the guru] took me to a well, tied a rope to both my legs and lowered me in the well in a feet-up head-down position. (181)

The young Sai was left in this upside down position for several hours, with the consequence that he experienced bliss. Afterwards, the guru "took me to his school," where the disciple forgot his attachment to the past. The criterion of first-hand experience is stressed, in contrast to "verbal, bookish knowledge." (182)

Commentators have generally opted for the symbolic significance of this narration. An exception was Bharadwaja, who suggested that the "upside down" rigour was factual. Warren goes further, and gives a very different interpretation to the format of Dabholkar. She interprets the "school" as a Sufi school (or *madrasah*), and the upside down exercise in terms of a well known Sufi ascetic practice.

One Sufi resort was the forty day retreat or *chilla,* a seclusion spent in fasting and recollection. In India, the

Chilla-i-Makus

Chishti Order favoured this form of discipline, but *chilla* was not unique to them. The word *chilla* can also mean a cell. An extremist variant in these activities was the *chilla-i-makus*, in which the practitioner was suspended upside down while performing prayers and contemplations. (183) Another name for this exercise was *namaz-i-makus* (inverted prayer ritual). "This practice is sometimes thought to have been borrowed from Hindu ascetics, although it is recorded among Iranian Sufis before the Turkish conquests in India." (184)

The same dramatic practice is associated with Afzal Shah Biyabani (d.1856), a well known *faqir* of Qazipeth, associated with the Qadiri and Chishti orders, and also the Rifai Order (Green 2009:34,38). His biography (in Urdu) was not composed until some fifty years after his death.

Warren links the above mentioned narration of Sai Baba to the Sufi theme of repentance (*taubat*), viewing his reported experience of bliss as an introductory phase attending the Sufi path.

> Sai Baba encouraged his visitors to practise repentance, to turn away from the life they had been living. . . . He admonished his devotees to give up bad habits such as addiction to liquor. (185)

22. Muslim Devotees and Visitors

The *faqir* Abdul arrived at Shirdi in 1889, and may have been the first Muslim devotee. The Muslim followers were in the minority compared to Hindus, and very much so during the last ten years of the saint, when a heavy influx of Hindu believers arrived from the towns and cities.

An innovation at Shirdi, in 1897, was the annual *Urs* festival. This is a specifically Muslim occurrence, and common in India as a "death anniversary" of Sufi saints at their tombs (*dargahs*). Yet Sai Baba was still living, a rather exceptional context for the *Urs*. This festival was actually suggested by a Hindu, who clearly recognised Sai Baba to be a Muslim.

A few years later, a Muslim devotee, named Amir Shakkar Dalal, successfully suggested a "sandal procession" to accompany the *Urs*. Readings from the *Quran* were followed by a traditional Muslim procession in which participants carried dishes of sandalwood paste. The procession moved around the village, accompanied by a band, after which the contents of the dishes were applied by hand to the sacred niche in the mosque where Sai Baba lived. The *Urs* at Shirdi included wrestling matches and a feast for the poor. The Hindus contributed two flags, which they carried in procession and fixed to corners of the mosque. (186)

The annual *Urs* gained another extension in 1912, when the Hindu *Ramanavami* festival was incorporated. A surging increase in the number of Hindu devotees meant that the *Urs* was soon eclipsed.

Muslim Devotees and Visitors

Meanwhile, a stream of Muslim visitors to Shirdi was in evidence. One of these was Imambai Chota Khan, a soldier who came from Aurangabad. He was advised beforehand, by a Sufi, to stand behind Sai Baba and chant a Quranic text. This meeting occurred in a Shirdi street, and the performance probably looked contrived. Sai Baba was angry, and also divulged that he knew about a recent problem of violence occurring in the visitor's career.

Chota Khan was, at first, one of many visitors (both Hindu and Muslim) who found difficulty in accessing the mosque. The mosque steps could sometimes transpire to be out of bounds. Sai Baba was liable to impose limits on *darshan* petitioners. However, when he did receive visitors, he might also be insistent upon their time of departure, which could be later than conveniently assumed.

Muslim visitors came from widespread areas over the years, including the domain of the Nizam, the important Muslim regional ruler of Hyderabad State. Some Muslim admirers of Sai Baba themselves became *faqirs*, inspired by him in various ways. Yet one of them, who wanted to be a saint, became locked in an impasse of imitation. Abdul Khader copied the ways of Sai Baba for weeks, until a distinctive meeting with Sai exercised a restraining effect.

Khader afterwards stopped trying to be a saint, and instead became a *bidi* merchant, selling cigarettes. He left Shirdi and started a *bidi* shop in the close vicinity of Hazrat Babajan at Poona. (187)

There is no reliable gauge of numbers involved in the early Muslim and Hindu contingents of Sai devotees. One form of assessment indicates that Muslims may have comprised less than a tenth of the total during the last decade of the saint's life. This is speculative. Hindus were certainly the overwhelming majority during the last years of Sai Baba.

23. Unity between Hindus and Muslims

In his *Satcharita* version of religious history in Maharashtra, Dabholkar jumped from Ramdas Swami (d.1681) to Sai Baba two centuries later. The interval was vague in those days. The Hindu writer conceived of events in terms of Ramdas and Shivaji having "protected the kingdom, the Brahmins and the sacred cow from the Muslims." (188)

In this scheme of occurrence, two hundred years later, again "disorder set in and there was a divide between the Hindus and the Muslims, which [Sai] Baba tried to bridge." (189) There is some justification for this theme via the episode, provisionally dated to 1894, when local Muslims objected to the *puja* (worship) conducted at the mosque by Mhalsapati. Tambuli and others then resorted to wielding clubs (see chapter 11).

The Shirdi *faqir* definitely did attempt to span the cultural and religious gulf that existed between the two major religious communities in India. He engineered a mood of amenable tolerance, keeping the inherent frictions at bay between his Hindu and Muslim followers.

There is little doubt that Sai Baba could be stern about religious differences. He disliked bickering between devotees, and could get annoyed. He discountenanced conversion from one religion to another. Sai Baba upbraided the prominent devotee Hari S. Dixit for making a criticism of Christians; Sai angrily told Dixit to get out of the mosque, and the offender duly apologised. (190)

Misconceptions easily occurred in the ideological rift, which intensified after the *faqir's* death in 1918. For instance, it has often been claimed that Sai Baba was a vegetarian, a refrain of some Hindu writers. Dabholkar proves this idea wrong. "Eating in the company of the fakirs, he [Sai] would eat meat, or if occasion required it, would also eat fish." (191) He ate mutton and fowl, but not beef, which would have been more offensive to Hindu religious sensitivities. Hindu devotees consumed vegetarian food, and were not coerced into different dietary habits.

Sai Baba evidently wanted followers from both of these religions to be present at the mosque where he resided. The Muslim followers were increasingly a minority. They are reported to have accepted the food offerings distributed at the mosque by Hindu *bhaktas*. Homage was not totally foreign to Muslim devotees—they would bring to the mosque flowers, sugar lumps, and coconuts as offerings. They would recite the Quranic *surah* known as *Al-Fatihah*, a chant in which Sai Baba would sometimes join. (192)

Dabholkar fleetingly records some details of significance in this context. Giving no date, he says that Sai Baba deferred to the *Ramanavami* festival by allowing a Rama cradle to be worshipped in the mosque courtyard via the *Ram-kirtan*. On the same night, the *faqir* would patronise the Islamic "sandal procession," which was busy "collecting together as many Muslims as possible." (193)

These references evidently apply to the saint's last years. Sai Baba was then "greatly interested in arranging wrestling events and would be delighted in giving away horses, *todas* and turbans as prizes." (194) A *toda* was a ring made of precious metal (gold or silver), and worn on the wrist or ankle. These items were apparently gifted by devotees, becoming part of the saint's bounty in redistribution. Wrestling matches were strongly associated with the Islamic *Urs* festival at Shirdi, which became overshadowed by *Ramanavami* as the Hindu following substantially increased in numbers.

The *Satcharita* also reports that one year, when the Islamic *Muharram* festival was drawing near, some Muslims came to the mosque with a request for a *tabut* to be made and taken in procession through the village. Sai Baba gave permission, and the *tabut* was kept for four days at the mosque. (195) Another commentator is a little more detailed, saying that Sai Baba eventually dragged the *tabut* out into the courtyard and consigned this object to a fire. (196) He was annoyed by what he called the "corpse," evidently disdaining the effigy.

The word *tabut* signifies a replica of the tomb of Husayn at Karbala. The rites of *Muharram* were celebrated with great enthusiasm amongst different Islamic communities (both Sunni and Shia) in metropolitan Bombay. The rural version at Shirdi is very sparsely documented; we only have the bare outline of this obscure episode.

The *Muharram* event at Shirdi is undated, but can be interpreted in terms of Sai Baba's aversion to formal ritual. He would go so far with orthodox observances, but no further, ultimately maintaining his independence as a renunciate *faqir* (and unorthodox Sufi).

We do not know his precise attitude to such festivals as *Muharram*. Sai Baba was probably very critical of the more exuberant urban manifestations, which offended Protestant Christians in the colonial sphere during the mid-nineteenth century. "The Muharram processions of the Deccan, in which groups of men dressed as tigers, bears and women, and in which large numbers of revellers enjoyed the intoxicating pleasures of *bhang* and toddy, seemed to embody the state of decline into which Islam had fallen in India." (197)

24. The Shirdi Mosque and *Chavadi*

The setting for these diverse events was a dilapidated rural mosque (*masjid*), which was in a chronic state of disrepair by the opening years of the twentieth century. In December 1909, devotees prevailed upon the old *faqir* to sleep alternate nights at the local *chavadi*, a village hall. Only in this way could renovation be accomplished at the mosque. Sai Baba was averse to improvements, evidently regarding the ruined building as a fitting background for his ascetic lifestyle.

This situation was remarkable in a number of respects. To some extent perhaps, Sai Baba represented centuries of *faqiri* in the Indian environment. His asceticism may be the key to his lifestyle, and far more relevant than miracle stories. When rainwater flooded into his mosque after a storm, there was no longer any place for him to sleep. However, Sai Baba refused to move out, despite pleas from devotees. Eventually, some of the devotees boldly lifted up the *faqir* and forcibly carried him out of the mosque. There was no other way to remove him from the danger zone. In this manner, he transited to dry quarters at the *chavadi* (Shepherd 2015:140).

Even after the mosque renovation project commenced, Sai Baba constantly interfered, delaying the repairs. Eventually, by 1912, the mosque courtyard was also upgraded, gaining a new roof as a protection against the sun and rain. These changes coincided with the new influx of urban devotees from places like Bombay. This influx was a major feature of the saint's last decade. These devotees were predominantly Hindu, and many of them were affluent. Events changed contour as a consequence.

The new wave of devotees were keen to implement an evening procession, accompanying Sai Baba when he walked from the mosque to the *chavadi* (at the time of the saint's regular removal to the *chavadi*). This event became known as *chavadi utsav*, a phrase found in the Sai Baba literature, e.g., Williams 2004:66–70, 148, defining the word *utsav* as meaning both procession and festival; elsewhere, *utsav* denotes a festival. The procession was only a part of the entire festive activities at Shirdi. The celebration had undeniable Hindu features, associated with the worship of Vishnu (Hari).

The format of the procession evolved gradually, and was at first relatively simple. In 1915, some influential devotees wanted the saint to be paraded in a palanquin (*palki*), but he refused. Sai Baba continued to participate in the procession, but walked behind the palanquin. Only his picture and sandals were allowed to be carried in the palanquin. Some Muslim devotees also joined this procession, which was, however, largely a Hindu event.

Being averse to any show of finery, Sai Baba became the awkward recipient of costly jewellery, which he was asked to wear temporarily at the *chavadi* on these occasions of worship and procession. Necklaces of gold and pearls were not in the *faqir* taste. Sai Baba was not always in a good mood over these developments, and resisted some improvisations, including a chariot that was used only once in the procession.

Certain influential devotees, like Radhakrishna Ayi (d.1916) and Raghuvir B. Purandhare, wished for a Shirdi version of the Vaishnava festivities at Pandharpur, a famous pilgrimage site devoted to Vitthala (Vithoba). Ayi was partial to silver adornments in the procession and at the *chavadi*. Yet "all this pomp [Sai] Baba despised." (198)

The *chavadi* procession apparently became a weekly event. A prominent commentator reports that the procession day was a Thursday. (199) Another writer informs:

The Shirdi Mosque and Chavadi

In Shirdi, Thursday is considered to be the day dedicated to one's *guru* and now it has become especially sacred to Sai Baba. Coincidentally or not, in the Sufi folk tradition Thursday is recognised as the day set aside to visit shrines. (200)

The *chavadi utsav* was not the only innovation. Performances of *arati* now occurred at both the mosque and the *chavadi*. The worship rite of *arati* involved the waving of a tray containing lighted camphor, in a predetermined motion, to the accompaniment of hymns in praise of the saint.

Sai Baba would only allow the more diluted *arati* ceremonies at the mosque. The details have been presented by an informed Hindu commentator, namely Sainathuni Sarath Babuji, who says that the *arati* developments did not commence before 1910. Performed at the mosque were the noon and evening *aratis*, being of a simple hymnal nature. In contrast, two other performances were reserved for the *chavadi*, probably because these related to temple services, and were therefore less compatible with Islam and the mosque environment (Babuji 1996).

25. Affinity with *Bhakti*

In relation to Hinduism, the major affinity of Sai Baba was the *bhakti* tradition. A number of passages in the *Shri Sai Satcharita* tend to confirm this factor. The commentary of Dabholkar includes the reflection:

> To the rigidly ritualistic, there is the binding of injunction and prohibition; to the *Jnani* there is ego in his superior knowledge; and to the yogi the shortcoming of being a hypocrite. Thus nothing will really work here, except firm faith. The learned pundits are blinded by arrogance. They are the very image of Pride. The *Jnani* runs away at their very sight and does not keep their company. The *Jnani* says can there be any god other than myself? Myself being enriched with true Knowledge, I am myself, the supreme consciousness. By virtue of his own loving devotion, a devotee [*bhakta*] will never boast of his knowledge. (201)

This was how Dabholkar interpreted a basic facet of Sai Baba's impact. The Shirdi milieux of *arati* and *chavadi utsav* were very much in the spirit of *bhakti*.

An excessive enthusiasm arose when devotees conceived of *bhakti* in terms of outward regalia such as the palanquin shunned by Sai Baba (in respect of his personal use), the chariot which he rejected, and also the necklaces of gold and pearls appearing at the time of the *chavadi* procession (or rather, at the close of this event). Such adornments were discrepant with his own preferred lifestyle of simplicity and a patched robe.

Sai Baba did not act like a Yogi. Moreover, his frequently allusive teaching was not that of Vedanta (often interpreted

Affinity with Bhakti

as the path of the *jnani*). In his well known commentary on the *Gita* verse 4:34, Sai Baba preferred to interpret *jnana* (knowledge) in terms of *ajnana*, contrary to the format found in the works of traditional Vedantic commentators. In his version, the guru cannot teach *jnana*, only the means to this transcendent knowledge, which occurs via a process of ignorance (*ajnana*) limited to words and cultural conditioning. Even some devotees resisted this interpretation, contrary to Dabholkar, who notably championed the unorthodox emphasis of Sai Baba (see Chapter 12). Indeed, Dabholkar pressed a *bhakti*-oriented interpretation of the contested verse, including the phrase: "So long as he [the *jnani*] is without devotion, his *Jnana* is covered up by ignorance" (Dabholkar 1999:820).

26. Professor Narke on What Sai Baba Taught

An academic devotee of Sai Baba was Professor Ganpatrao G. Narke of Poona (Pune). He was in contact with the saint from 1913. His assessment of the Shirdi *faqir* was relayed in an interview of 1936 as mediated by Narasimhaswami. More than most other devotees, Narke took the role of an observer. One of his conclusions was:

> Sai Baba never lectured, nor discoursed systematically as others do. He gave hints — very pregnant hints. A word or a sentence or two at a time was all he cared to utter. (202)

Narke emphasised that Sai Baba did not prescribe Raja Yoga, Karma Yoga, or Jnana Yoga (meaning Vedanta). In contrast, Bhakti was a factor, in terms of serving and loving the guru and God. (203) Yet some commentators have mistakenly opted to depict Sai as an exponent of Vedanta. Confusions with Yoga have also occurred. Narke reports that this *faqir* was not partial to *pranayama, siddhis,* and *kundalini,* these being teachings and practices inseparable from the subject of Yoga (and Tantric Yoga).

Although a renunciate himself, Sai Baba did not advocate *sannyas* (renunciation). He was evidently content with the fact that most of his visitors were householders, and not ascetics.

Narke relays that Sai Baba's "usual, almost invariable role" was that of a devotee of *Allah* and, at the same time, someone entrusted with powers to carry out what *Allah* ("the Faqir") directed. This *faqir* was constantly uttering Islamic phrases, mediated by Narasimhaswami as "*Allah Malik*" (God is Owner) and *"Allah Bhale Karega"* (God will do good). Sai Baba was also fond of expressing a phrase translated as: "I am the slave of *Allah*." (204)

Narke refers to allusive speech of the saint. However, Sai Baba also expressed moral tales and terse personal instructions. The theme underlying many of his stories, or parables, was an ethical cue: "We must sow good results in this life and the next." That reference was not merely to the hereafter, but to reincarnation. (205)

The Professor also stressed paranormal abilities of the saint. Narke credited Sai Baba with the power to travel in an invisible body to distant parts of the world. Another commentator (Dabholkar) refers to telepathic communication.

> At present, we send messages, day and night, on the wireless and flaunt our achievement, being filled with pride. For this, we have to set up wireless stations, for which unlimited money is spent. But the saints do not require such means; they send messages through their minds. (206)

27. Kusha Bhav, the Yogi

The instance of Kusha Bhav has been recounted in different versions. Two basic sources are Bharadwaja and Narasimhaswami (Shepherd 2015:241–243). I will follow the Bharadwaja version here.

In his early years, Kusha Bhav followed a Yogi whose identity survives as Datta Maharaj. In this milieu, *mantras* and *siddhis* (occult powers) were highly rated. Kusha Bhav claimed the ability to materialise objects at will. More specifically, he was believed to materialise sweetmeats, which he would distribute as *prasad* to devotees. In addition to admirers who believed in his feats, this Yogi also gained critics who accused him of being a charlatan.

To counteract his enemies, Kusha Bhav desired to learn techniques of black magic. Accordingly, he petitioned his guru to give him the *mantras* believed to exercise devastating effects. This is the field of Tantric Yoga. Datta Maharaj may have been a Nath Yogi. In an interview of 1936, Kusha Bhav reported that Datta Maharaj "very unwillingly imparted the mantras to me." Whatever happened after that, the guru is depicted as wishing to withdraw from his disciple. Datta Maharaj retired to the Himalayas, advising Kusha Bhav to seek guidance from Sai Baba.

The Tantric magician did eventually visit Shirdi (apparently in 1908). He was very disconcerted by the negative response of Sai Baba. The *faqir* was wrathful, viewing the career of Kusha Bhav as a contradiction to spirituality. Sai would not permit the visitor to enter the mosque. He derided the supposed achievements of *siddhis*, and said that

Kusha Bhav, the Yogi

the "materialised" sweetmeats were not "created" by the Yogi, as gullible devotees believed. Sai Baba's assessment of the situation was sternly reproving. He affirmed that the supposed "materialisation" amounted to cheating. The sweetmeats had not been materialised, but instead appropriated from other persons.

Kusha Bhav was deceiving himself by his subscription to beliefs in *siddhis*. The Yogi had evidently encouraged the popular belief in his own miracles, but Sai Baba was now effectively supporting the critics. Kusha Bhav had been claiming to materialise sweetmeats by the power of *mantra*. The gist of Sai Baba's repudiation was apparently that the followers who believed in Kusha Bhav were being misled as a consequence of their reverence for *siddhis*. These deceived people would be side-tracked from the due pursuit of a spiritual enlightenment. Like Kusha Bhav, the followers were in danger of elevating cheap occult powers.

Sai Baba was adamant that Kusha Bhav must relinquish the *mantras* and attendant practices. The Yogi resisted, not desiring to be humiliated. For a period of uncertain duration, Kusha Bhav vacillated in his attitude. He finally capitulated, and went to the sacred Godavari river, where he threw away the iron bangle that he wore on his right wrist. That bangle represented the power of *mantras*. As Sai Baba had directed, the Yogi now vowed to give up his practice of *mantra*. This report was derived from Kusha Bhav, who said in retrospect, that "he could no longer produce such material objects by a wave of his hand." Kusha Bhav was not admitting to any deception here.

The Yogi was afterwards permitted to visit the Shirdi mosque. The account is fragmentary. The *faqir* was still liable to be stern with Kusha Bhav. A belief developed that Sai instructed the Yogi to read the *Shree Guru Charitra* no less than 108 times. This Marathi text, of Dattatreya association, became popular amongst devotees at Shirdi (Bharadwaja 1987).

An interview in 1936, conducted by Narasimhaswami, gives strong indication that Kusha Bhav had not completely overcome the inclination to claim a form of "materialisation" (Shepherd 2015:242–243).

28. Reincarnation and Hari S. Dixit

Sai Baba clearly believed in reincarnation, and more specifically, transmigration through diverse species. Although a cardinal belief in Hinduism, a minority of Muslims had also subscribed to reincarnation (or *tanasukh*) over the centuries. This belief is also associated, in variants, with the ancient Greeks, with Jewish Kabbalah, with Buddhism, and with Jainism. The belief is regarded as fantastic by materialists, and is dismissed by some monotheistic religions, but remains a prospect for consideration.

Professor Narke relays that Sai Baba frequently referred to the past lives of devotees, and also occasionally mentioned future incarnations. (207)

> Sai Baba intimated to a number of devotees that he had known them for many lifetimes or *janmas*. This special prenatal connection he termed *rinanubanda*, and it was as if he had followed their careers throughout a series of lifetimes. (208)

Some devotee writers have speculated about *rinanubandha*, a word deriving from the Sanskrit lexicon. More factually, an early source described the appearance in Shirdi of Hari Sitaram Dixit, alias Kakasaheb (1864–1926), a *brahman* of Khandwa who became a prominent devotee (Shepherd 2015:176–179).

Dabholkar attributes the first encounter of Dixit with Sai Baba as being a consequence of his "preordained link" or *rinanubandha*. "His preordained link with Shirdi and his close and steadfast connection with Sai, was responsible for this event" (Dabholkar 1999:835). The Sanskrit word refers to a bond (*bandha*) resulting from karmic debt (*rina*), a factor at the root of consecutive incarnations. This theme entails an obligation to settle the accumulated karmic debt (resulting from past lives and continuing in the present life). If the deficit is not settled, the residual debt will be carried forward to the next incarnation. The karmic debt is also interpreted in terms of connections or links with other souls, meaning that any problem in those connections has to be resolved sooner or later.

Dixit was a friend of Narayan G. Chandorkar, the long-established Sai devotee of a high social standing. Dixit was, likewise, a wealthy person. He had a house in Ville Parle, Bombay. As a lawyer, Dixit travelled to London, and there injured his leg while climbing into a public transport vehicle. In 1909, Chandorkar visited Dixit at his bungalow in Lonavla, and suggested that the lawyer should go to Shirdi for the *darshan* of Sai Baba.

Chandorkar relayed here what seems to have been a favoured assertion of Sai: "My man, however far away he may be from me — even beyond the seven seas, I will at once, draw him to me, as a sparrow is pulled with a string tied to her." (209)

In the discussion with Chandorkar, the possibility of healing Dixit's lame leg was mentioned. Dixit is said to have dismissed this option, preferring an entreaty "to remove the lameness of my mind."

At that time, Dixit was meeting acquaintances in order to gather public support for his role as a candidate for the Legislative Council. In this connection, he visited Ahmednagar, staying with the Sai devotee Kakasaheb Mirikar. Dixit encountered there Shama (Madhavrao Deshpande), a conspicuous Sai devotee who lived at Shirdi. Dixit happened to see a photograph of Sai Baba, which exerted upon him a strong fascination. He left by train for

Shirdi, being accompanied by Shama. They had second class tickets, but the carriage was full. However, the railway guard knew Dixit, and arranged for the travellers to sit comfortably in the first class compartment. The poor could only travel third class.

Dixit and Shama alighted from the train at Kopargaon, where they met up with Chandorkar, who was also intending to visit Sai Baba. The three travellers took a *tonga* (horse cab) for Shirdi. This was in November 1909. When Dixit met the saint, the latter said to him: "I too, waited for you and then sent Shama straight to Nagar to meet you." (210)

Dixit became a devotee, and afterwards chose to reside at Shirdi, creating the commodious building known as Dixitwada. Sai Baba is reported to have promised him: "I will take you away in an aeroplane." (211) This reference was clearly allusive; Sai Baba never travelled by aeroplane, which was a rare mode of transport during his lifetime. Another version (in the *Diary of Dixit*) translates the words of Sai Baba more directly as: "I will take you in *vimana* (heavenly vehicle)."

The Sanskrit word *vimana* is used in the Epics to describe a celestial chariot. In the *Ramayana*, after winning a battle, Rama supposedly travelled from Lanka to his capital in a *vimana*. In some modern Indian languages, this word *vimana* gained the meaning of aeroplane, which is very unlikely to have been the signification intended by Sai Baba.

In 1912, Dixit was enjoined by the *faqir* to read *bhakti* texts of Eknath while living at Dixitwada. This phase is sometimes described as a "retreat"; however, Dixit was not completely secluded in the way that Upasani Maharaj experienced during the same period at the Khandoba temple. The reported intention of Sai Baba was to focus the interest of Dixit away from his legal career, which had taken up most of his attention for many years. Dixit was permitted to give explanations of the *Bhavartha Ramayana* to other devotees, although Sai Baba was guarded in relation to any pundit tendency, which he considered undesirable.

Some years after the saint's death, Dixit died suddenly in a railway train, while resting his head on the shoulder of Dabholkar. "While walking and talking normally, the body [of Dixit] just became still and lifeless, in front of everyone." (212) Dabholkar interpreted this event in terms of: "He seemed to have been quickly lifted up in an aeroplane" (Dabholkar 1999:842). The comment is also made: "You may call it death or that an aeroplane came for him" (ibid:843). The *vimana* (heavenly vehicle) remains elusive in terms of precise occurrence.

29. Bhagoji Shinde

The devotee Bhagoji Shinde suffered from leprosy. Despite the affliction, Bhagoji was allowed by Sai Baba to become a *sevakari* or personal attendant. The major source of this information is the *Shri Sai Satcharita*. "His body was full of bleeding sores, yet he was the foremost among the attendants." (213)

Bhagoji would go every morning to the mosque and massage the limbs of Sai Baba, who would sit leaning against a pillar near the *dhuni*. On the daily walk to the Lendi, Bhagoji would carry the *chattra* (umbrella) intended to shield Sai from the sun. He apparently also accompanied the *faqir* on some of the daily begging rounds. A well known photograph, taken in a Shirdi lane, is testimony to this service. One explanation is that Sai Baba was rescuing Bhagoji from the acute social discrimination which applied to lepers. The close association as a *sevakari* may have commenced in 1910, when a dramatic incident occurred in the mosque at the time of the *Diwali* festival.

Sai Baba was sitting inside the mosque near the *dhuni*, placing logs on the fire and increasing the flames. His attendant Madhav Fasle was alarmed when the saint thrust his hand into the fire. Sai Baba seemed oblivious of his action. Shama ran to the spot, and with some difficulty, pulled him away from the fire. "Baba at once came back to the waking state (from super-consciousness)." The *faqir* gave the explanation that he had saved a child who had fallen into the furnace of a blacksmith at a distant village (Dabholkar 1999:111). Shama was concerned about the scorched hand.

The injury was severe, and the *faqir* was now aware of the pain. Shama wrote a letter to Nanasaheb Chandorkar, a prominent devotee in government service. (214)

Chandorkar quickly arrived at Shirdi with a renowned doctor called Paramanand, who came from Bombay, equipped with various medicines. The medic was puzzled by the situation he found at the mosque. He tried to persuade Sai Baba to take off the bandages so that he could inspect the injured hand. The *faqir* was not compliant, and continually postponed the inspection. This went on for days, with Sai Baba repeatedly asserting: "Allah is our *Vaidya* [doctor]." The inspection did not occur, and the medicines of Paramanand were never used in this instance. (215) The independence of the Shirdi saint, in relation to medical treatment, is reminiscent of a similar attitude in the case of Hazrat Babajan (Shepherd 2014:80).

The only person whom Sai allowed to tend his injured hand was Bhagoji Shinde, who applied a bandage daily. At the saint's instruction, Bhagoji massaged the hand with *ghee* (clarified butter). The hand healed after some time. Without there being any need to do so, Bhagoji thereafter continued to massage the hand with *ghee*, at the request of the saint. The ritual of bandaging and massaging continued for eight years until the death of Sai Baba. In this manner, the leper gained importance and honour in Shirdi. He was permitted to prepare the tobacco pipe for Sai in the early morning, and also reputedly gave *udi* (*dhuni* ash) to visiting devotees at the saint's injunction.

This instance is a striking example of Sai Baba's egalitarian tendency to counter social degradation. A leper was normally shunned by everyone, especially high caste people.

30. Khaparde and Tilak

An unusual and prestigious visitor in December 1910 was Ganesh S. Khaparde (1854–1938), a wealthy lawyer and politician from Amraoti (Amravati). He returned to Shirdi a year later, and stayed there for over three months, along with his wife Lakshmibai. His *Shirdi Diary* is a record of events during that period, and a very early source. This document includes close-up references to the saint.

At Shirdi, Khaparde conducted a Vedanta study group, which read texts like the *Panchadashi* of Vidyaranya. Yet when he visited the mosque, this savant would become silent in the presence of the saint.

> Khaparde was not an ordinary person. He was a superior personage – very learned. But before Sai, he would stand with folded hands and his head lowered respectfully. (Dabholkar 1999:445)

Dabholkar adds that there were only two other devotees who would maintain silence in this manner, namely Gopalrao Buti and Tatyasaheb Noolkar. In contrast, "all the others used to speak out; some even argued with [Sai] Baba, without any reverence, fear, or awe" (ibid:445).

The saint would refer to Khaparde as Dadasaheb. The visitor would regularly go to meet the *faqir* at the mosque and *chavadi*. In his diary, Khaparde atypically refers to Sai Baba as Sayin Maharaj. The diarist describes varying moods of the *faqir*, and also his allusive speech.

In December 1911, the local people sent a deputation to Sai Baba, the purpose being to counter the plague which had struck the area. In very practical terms, the saint advised the assembly to clean the roads, to sweep the tombs and burial *ghats*, and to feed the poor.

Khaparde was a close colleague of Bal Gangadhar (Lokamanya) Tilak (1856–1920), the nationalist politician. In 1908, Tilak was imprisoned by the British for six years, on charges of sedition. That same year, Khaparde moved to London, but failed to secure the release of Tilak. Shortly after his return to India, he visited Shirdi for a week in December 1910. He returned a year afterwards, staying until March 15, 1912.

Khaparde had a genuine regard for Sai Baba, but did not anticipate remaining at Shirdi for so long. He soon wished to depart, being accustomed to a very busy schedule and a large household of many people. He was losing income at this fraught time. The *faqir* was not obliging in respect of giving permission for departure.

On December 29, 1911, Sai Baba emphasised to Khaparde that he would have to stay in Shirdi for another two months. The eminent guest accepted this dictate. The following month, while in an expansive mood, the saint cast "yogic glances" at Khaparde, who reports that as a consequence, he passed the whole day in a blissful state.

The *Shirdi Diary* of Khaparde was subsequently published, and given space by the *Shri Sai Leela* journal (of Shirdi) in 1924-5. However, some relevant details did not emerge until many years later, in 1962, when Khaparde's son Balkrishna (also a lawyer) produced a life sketch of his father, in Marathi.

The British government considered many public speeches of Khaparde to be seditious. He was in danger of prosecution accordingly. In late December 1911, the British sent a spy to Shirdi for the purpose of investigating Khaparde's situation. The Indian spy was a CID detective named Natekar, also known as Swami. Natekar successfully posed as an "initiate" who had travelled in the Himalayas and met a *mahatma*. In

Shirdi he talked with many local people, including the lady devotee Radhakrishna Ayi, always with the intention of gaining information about the man he was tracking.

Although suspicious of spies, Khaparde was not fully aware of developments, and made his own plans for the future. He wanted to leave Shirdi, but Sai Baba enjoined him to stay. In late February, 1912, Natekar urged Khaparde (by letter) to return home to Amraoti. Khaparde and his wife took the bait, but the ruse was blocked by Sai Baba. Soon after Natekar's letter, Shama (Madhavrao Deshpande) interceded with Sai on behalf of Khaparde. Shama asked permission for Khaparde's return to Amraoti. The saint responded firmly that the time was not favourable for this return, and that Khaparde would have to remain in Shirdi for some while.

Meanwhile, Natekar had gained access to Khaparde's home, and stolen some of his diaries. The prolonged stay at Shirdi resulted in rumours, spreading to Bombay and other places, that Khaparde had become mentally unbalanced in his obsession with the eccentric *faqir* Sai Baba. He had given up his practice as a lawyer, thereby losing substantial income. His political career had apparently ceased. The British Government accordingly decided not to proceed with prosecution of Khaparde. No incriminating material could be found in the diaries acquired by Natekar.

It is very difficult to avoid the conclusion that Khaparde's sojourn at Shirdi saved him from a lengthy jail sentence.

Khaparde did not return to Shirdi for nearly four years. His third visit occurred in December 1915, when he stayed for three days. Khaparde evidently had a high regard for Sai Baba. He visited on two further occasions, the most famous one dating to 1917, when he accompanied Tilak. Much less well known is his last visit in 1918, of uncertain duration, when Khaparde is believed to have sought the saint's advice about participating in a Congress deputation to England for demanding Home Rule. The response of Sai Baba is not on record.

Bal Gangadhar Tilak visited Sai Baba at Shirdi on May 19, 1917. Khaparde was also present on that occasion, and recorded the event in his diary. Tilak's party arrived by motor car from Sangamner in the morning, and went to the Dixitwada. Shama, Bapusaheb Jog, Balasaheb Bhate, and Gopalrao Buti were amongst the devotees present. They afterwards went to the mosque. Khaparde comments about the saint: "I never saw him so much pleased before." Sai made a predictable request for *dakshina*, and the guests complied.

Sai Baba told Tilak: "People are bad, keep yourself to yourself" (Kamath and Kher 1991:287). According to Bapusaheb Jog, the saint remarked to Tilak: "You have done a lot for people, but now devote yourself to your own welfare" (ibid:287).

Khaparde records that the party wished to proceed to Yeola. On their behalf, Shama accordingly asked permission for departure from Sai. The *faqir* responded with advice to avoid the heat, to take food in Shirdi, and then depart in the cool of the afternoon. He told Shama to feed the guests. So Khaparde, Tilak, and the others left to eat a meal, and afterwards returned to the mosque. They found Sai Baba "lying down as if sleeping." Evidently not wishing to interrupt him, they visited the *chavadi* (village hall) nearby, and then went back to the mosque. Sai Baba was now sitting up; he gave the guests *udi*, and also permission to leave.

A very different account exists by Narasimha Chintaman (Tatyasaheb) Kelkar, an associate of Tilak, who was also present on this occasion. Kelkar apparently resisted going to Shirdi, and says that Tilak would not have visited "Sai Maharaj" unless Khaparde had been at Shirdi. Yet Khaparde informs that he himself came with Tilak's party from Sangamner to Shirdi. Kelkar was writing some ten years later, and his memory may have blurred. V. B. Kher suggests a stronger reason for the element of dismissal in Kelkar's report. "Kelkar believed that Sai Baba was a Muslim and it seems that, therefore, he had prejudice or hostility against him." (216)

The account (in Marathi) by Kelkar can certainly be interpreted as hostile. Kelkar has none of the background detail afforded by Khaparde. He says that Sai Baba asked for *dakshina* from Tilak, but does not mention that the other guests were also in this category. Kelkar is clearly critical in relaying how Tilak gave less than the amount requested, and Sai then asked for the remainder. Tilak had to borrow money from one of his associates. No detail is given of the amount requested. A fairly common event at Shirdi was a guest not having sufficient money on their person for *dakshina*. Sai Baba was quite capable of testing the mood and receptivity of eminent visitors.

Kelkar does not mention the consideration of the *faqir* in arranging for the guests to be fed. Instead, he says that "somebody applied *udi* [ash] to him [Tilak] and gave him a coconut as *prasad*." Tilak accepted, but there followed "an embarrassing situation" for him, in the words of Kelkar (Kher 2001:126). This apparently refers to the third visit to the mosque, when Tilak was about to depart.

Sai Baba asked for water, being thirsty. "Someone handed to him a Muslim style *lota* with a spout from which he drank water" (ibid). An unnamed devotee then acted in the belief that "the water tasted by Sai Baba should be distributed as *tirtha* [holy water] to all" (ibid). This devotee then poured a small amount of the water into the palms of all those present. Kelkar says that Tilak looked embarrassed, but swallowed the water without showing any displeasure. We are not told what Kelkar did. The report of Kelkar is negative in referring to a "travesty" of an "old time-honoured practice" (ibid:127). This aspersion apparently means the request for *dakshina*.

Kelkar does not mention anything about the redistribution of *dakshina* monies which occurred at the Shirdi mosque. The cash was levied by Sai Baba from affluent visitors with varied agendas.

Tilak was not a sceptic of religion. He wrote an innovative commentary on the *Bhagavad Gita*, (217) to which Sai Baba awarded a gesture of approval (Chapter 18). Tilak has been described as a very religious man, "though 'using' religion for his political goals, as in his campaigns all over Maharashtra for the popularisation of Ganesha's cult." (218) Speculation has attended his unknown reason for visiting Shirdi. One suggestion has been: "The curiosity of meeting the *faqir* whom so many people marvelled about." (219)

By allowing his famous guests to visit him, and by feeding them, Sai Baba was getting himself into trouble. Decades later, certain details emerged more clearly. After Tilak had departed from the mosque, the District Collector of Ahmednagar arranged for a CID officer to infiltrate Shirdi. This measure was for the purpose of monitoring activities of the *faqir*. Tilak was considered a danger man by the British Raj, and a priority was given to confidential reports about any of his connections, who became suspect.

Some believe that the contact between Tilak and Sai Baba was politically significant, inferring that the latter's covert message to the former amounted to: Indian Independence would only be gained through non-violent action, not by violent measures.

Sai Baba remained aloof from the political scene, and did not agitate in any way against the British rule. Shirdi was a small and insignificant village at that time, becoming famous after his death solely due to his presence there.

Shirdi Sai Baba

Sai Baba at the Shirdi mosque

The Shirdi Mosque (Dwarakamai)
circa 1930

Sai Baba's *dhuni*

l to r: Mhalsapati, Sai Baba, Shama

Sai Baba in 1906

On the mosque steps with devotees (Sai Baba is far right)

Sai Baba with devotees

Sai Baba with garland

Dixitwada

Abdul Baba and the *Quran*

Govind R. Dabholkar

The *chavadi* at Shirdi

Gopalrao Buti

Nanasaheb Chandorkar

Ganesh S. Khaparde

B. V. Narasimhaswami

Bapusaheb Jog

Sai Baba scrutinising a book by Tukaram

Bal Gangadhar Tilak

Meher Baba, 1933

Meher Baba with Gadge Maharaj, 1954

Upasani Maharaj

Butiwada, 1920s

31. Shirdi Diary

Analysis of Khaparde's *Shirdi Diary* has varied, and is often neglected. Some of the names mentioned are obscure, and descriptions of events are frequently very brief. Nevertheless, this diary is revealing.

Khaparde arrived in Shirdi on December 5, 1910, and stayed at Sathewada, a building where devotees congregated. With Bapusaheb Jog and others, he visited the mosque to see the *faqir* (whom he calls Sayin Saheb or Sayin Maharaj). According to the diarist, Sai Baba said that he had not been well for the last two years and more, that he was eating only barley cake, and taking a little water. The *faqir* explained that he found no rest because people were always trying to see him.

The statements of Sai Baba, as reported in the diary, do not evidence any Vedantic complexion. The day after Khaparde's arrival, Sai kept repeating that there were "very high officers of God" who were "very powerful." He requested the guests to withdraw after he had distributed food. Lunch was not served until the afternoon, and they did not see the *faqir* again until the evening, when he emerged from the mosque for his regular walk to the Lendi. His routine of subsequent years appears to have become more fixed, but the standard descriptions of a timetable are probably misleading for all daily occurrences.

In the evening of December 6, Khaparde witnessed the *chavadi* procession, still formative at that time, and including a festive umbrella and a silver stick. At the *chavadi*, the *bhakta* Radhakrishna Ayi emerged, and Khaparde saw her from a distance. This lady was influential behind the scenes, and reputed for her beauty.

Varying moods of Sai Baba emerge. On one occasion, he "spoke with such wonderful sweetness, and he smiled so often and with such extraordinary grace, that the conversation will always remain engraved in my memory." The mistaken idea in some quarters, that Sai was generally irascible, has no actual basis. This conversation comprised an explanation of why he had earlier cried out "Do not beat, do not beat." Sai Baba now said that he cried out because the Patil family were quarrelling (and apparently on the verge of blows).

Khaparde encountered Balasaheb Bhate, the former sceptic and retired *mamlatdar*. "He has been staying here for some time, and has a peculiar kind of calm on his face."

In the afternoon of December 7, at an assembly in the mosque, Sai turned to Khaparde and said (translated into English):

> This world is funny. All are my subjects. I look upon all equally, but some have become thieves and what can I do for them? People who are themselves very near death, [they] desire and make preparations for the death of others. They offended me a great deal. They hurt me a good deal but I said nothing. I kept quiet. God is very great and has his officers everywhere. They are all powerful. One must be content with the state in which God keeps him. But I am very powerful. I was here eight or ten thousand years ago.

The next day, Khaparde and others visited the mosque in the afternoon, but had to depart because Sai was washing his feet and did not want to converse. They returned later, but he soon dismissed them. "He appeared very much engaged in thinking out something." This abstraction of the *faqir* was often observed, but seldom comprehended. Sometimes even when he spoke, Sai was not understood. Khaparde admits, in relation to an occasion of December 9: "Sayin Maharaj was in a very pleasant mood, and said many pleasant things, but I am afraid, I did not understand him."

A more well known conversation is described by the diarist as "exceedingly pleasant." This was the occasion at the mosque on December 10, 1910, when Sai remarked that "he was Kabir before and used to spin yarn." This disclosure was accompanied by a rather enigmatic story about the former incarnation of a young girl, who was playing with him in the mosque.

Khaparde describes a subsequent event that day, when visitors went to Sai in the afternoon, and he "treated them the same way as he treats everybody." This open-handed procedure now comprised allusions to the Teli and Marwadi, followed by reference to new buildings that were under construction. Then he added further allusive words: "The world is gone mad. Every man has acquired a peculiarity of evil thinking. I never put myself on an equality with any of them. So I never listen to what they say. No, I never reply." He then distributed *udi* (sacred ash), and told his guests to return to Sathewada for the night.

Such idioms of Sai Baba apparently referred to psychological vacillations in the world at large, and also in those around him. Shortly afterwards, two episodes of friction occurred. Some devotees went to visit Radhakrishna Ayi at her cottage nearby, but some mishap proved disruptive, one of the visitors feeling that he was not treated by the host as he deserved to be. Moreover, the wife of Bapusaheb Jog unexpectedly produced a form of negative reaction. She had been ill, and now said that she wanted to leave Shirdi. Her despairing husband (a prominent devotee) agreed that she could depart. Sai Baba then took a close interest in her case, making repeated enquiries about when she was leaving. In the evening, Bapusaheb Jog resolved to ask the formal permission of Sai Baba for his wife's departure. The lady then said that she felt better and did not wish to go away. "We wondered," comments Khaparde.

When the diarist returned to Shirdi a year later, on his first visit to Sai Baba (in the company of Shama), he could only salute from a distance, as the *faqir* was washing his hands and feet. Daily ablutions were fastidiously conducted by Sai. Later, the visitor was able to sit near Sai Baba in the mosque, and listen to a parable about a *faqir*. This was anything but the customary fare of ashram discourses found elsewhere.

Khaparde now stayed at the new Dixitwada, and mentions that he talked to Thosar (Tozer), who later became known as Swami Narayan. "Thosar is a very pleasant companion." Many years later, Swami Narayan contributed a distinctive report, in an interview, about some events at Shirdi (Shepherd 2015:238–240).

On December 9, 1911, the diarist went to the mosque, and found Sai in "a pleasant mood." The *faqir* consented to smoke the *huqqa* (water-pipe) which Khaparde proffered. "He looked wonderfully beautiful at *arti* time, but dismissed every one very soon after."

The next day, Khaparde found that Nanasaheb Chandorkar wished to tell him about instructions received from Sai, "but people gathered and the thing could not be disclosed to the view of all." Sai Baba may have felt the same way in his habit of guarded and intricate allusions. Later, the diarist "made two attempts to see Sayin Maharaj in the afternoon, but he was not in the mood to see anybody." The situation was obviously not one of mere social contacts, even though Khaparde was an eminent person.

On December 11, 1911, the diarist learned that Sai was cleaning the mosque, and prudently refrained from visiting. A deputation of local people arrived with a request for Sai to eliminate an afflicting plague. He responded by telling them to clean the roads, sweep the tombs, duly attend to the burning and burial *ghats*, and to feed the poor. The next day, Sai "was in a very good mood and sat chatting and laughing."

That same month, an old Muslim from Kalyan was present in Shirdi. This person was variously known as Dervish Saheb, Haji Saheb, Haji Siddiq Falke, and Dervish Haji Muhammad Siddiq. He had travelled to Baghdad, Constantinople, Mecca, and other places. "His conversation is very pleasant and instructive; Sayin Maharaj likes him very much, sends him food, and otherwise treats him with great consideration." At an earlier date, however, the Haji had received a rather more severe treatment (Shepherd 2015:149–150). This Muslim was celebrated in the *Shri Sai Satcharita*, his memory preserved quite strongly amongst Hindu devotees. According to Khaparde, "he [Haji Saheb] is a Karma Margi as we should call him in Hinduism, and has numerous anecdotes to tell." The Haji can also be viewed as a type of Sufi.

When the Haji departed on December 23, Sai accompanied him to the gate in the mosque courtyard. This was a very rare gesture, and evoked from Khaparde the suggestion that the departee was spiritually advanced. The diarist added: "I miss him (Haji) very much as we used to have long talks."

Khaparde frequently refers to Sai Baba as being in a good mood. For instance, on December 17, 1911, "he [Sai] was in a very good mood, and we enjoyed very much the jokes made by him." This first-hand report was much later contradicted by some dour Western preferences, of a more recent era, mistakenly affirming that the *faqir* insulted his visitors with abusive and harsh behaviour.

On December 18, at the mosque, Sai remarked to Khaparde that the latter had filled his bucket and was enjoying the cool breezes, whereas he (Sai) "was enduring all manner of trouble and had no sleep." Despite this occupational hazard, the Shirdi *faqir* "was in a very pleased mood and many people came to worship."

The next day, the diarist again "found him in a very pleasant mood." Sai proceeded to relate a parable, but one of the devotees interrupted, and so "the story ran in a different channel." In the afternoon, Sai Baba was invited to the nearby village of Neemgaon. Many devotees accompanied him there with musical instruments. The diarist adds that Radhakrishna Ayi came to greet Sai near Dixitwada, and "I saw her for the first time without the big veil on." Various brief references leave some uncertainty about the precise degree of contact between the *faqir* and this distinctive female *bhakta* (Shepherd 2015:218–220).

On December 20, Sai left the *chavadi* "without any audible remark except that *Allah* is the lord of all." The complete absence of Vedantic accents in the diary is food for thought. We may, by now, anticipate the diarist report that Sai Baba "was in a very pleased mood" that day.

Khaparde's sojourn occurred at the juncture when the newly created *arati* ceremonies gained much attention from devotees. The diarist daily attended the morning *kakad arati*, but Sai would not allow this rite in the mosque. This event occurred at the *chavadi* (or the Sathewada, where Sai was not present). It is evident that Sai Baba had a frequent tendency to curtail his periods of association with devotees. At this time, there were also complications caused by police detectives who were active in Shirdi. These men were suspicious of Khaparde, because of his association with the radical political party of Tilak.

On December 26, 1911, when descending the steps of the *chavadi*, Sai Baba was observed to be in an agitated mood, tapping his stick (*satka*) on the ground, and using "violent language" (some said that whenever Sai tapped his stick, he was giving a warning about danger or intrusions). However, in the afternoon, he was "very gracious." The *faqir* told Khaparde's son Balvant to remain and sit down in the mosque, even after he had dismissed the assembly. Sai told this young man not to admit any guests to the mosque that evening.

The next day, one of the detectives positioned himself near Sai, while another followed Khaparde. Even the chief constable of Kopargaon arrived, taking his seat in the room of Khaparde at Dixitwada. Later that day, these investigators withdrew. "In the afternoon, many people attempted to go and see Sayin Maharaj, but he was not inclined to speak and dismissed them soon."

Everyone saw Sai at dusk that day, when he emerged for his walk to the Lendi, and then again during the nocturnal *shej arati* at the *chavadi*. While Sai stayed the night at the *chavadi*, the devotees enjoyed their regular get-together at Dixitwada, where Bhishma gave a *bhajan* performance and Dixit read from the *Bhavartha Ramayana*.

On December 28, Sai Baba would not permit anyone to sit at the mosque in the afternoon, but instead dismissed the optimistic visitors by giving them *udi*. The next morning, he was in a "very good mood," and commenced a "very instructive" parable. Unfortunately, a devotee named Trimbak Rao "interrupted most foolishly," with the consequence that Sai stopped, and then changed the subject. Trimbak Rao (Maruti) had been subject to a strong mood of anger the previous day; he did not attend the *arati* "and was very sulky." The reason is not clear. However, one may deduce that mere devotion was not sufficient to win the day; other factors were necessary, including due attention.

Sai Baba now said that Khaparde had to stay at Shirdi for another two months. The wife of Khaparde was also staying at the village, and the *faqir* told her of a struggle in which he defeated the "Governor," achieving a conciliation. "The language is highly figurative and therefore difficult to interpret." This communication was subsequently believed to be a reference to government officials who were suspicious of Khaparde. Nearing dusk on December 30, the diarist visited Sai, who "treated me very kindly, called me by name, and told a small tale calculated to impress the virtue of patience."

On January 3, 1912, Sai Baba was "in a very pleased mood and laughed and abused in one and the same breath." No indication is given as to the context of abuse. The next day, Khaparde went to the mosque after five p.m., and found the *faqir* "walking about in the compound." Khaparde's wife was also present, and likewise Hari Dixit and his wife. Sai related to them a complex parable about a princess. Close attention was required for such stories, which were quite distinctive. No religious doctrine was involved, although Khaparde deduced that divine justice was vindicated in this particular parable.

On the evening of January 6, during the *arati* at the *chavadi*, Sai "was in an exceptionally pleased mood, made mystic signs to Megha [Shyam], and did what are known as 'Drishtipata' in yog[a]." The word *drishtipath* means a look of grace. Reference to Yoga is very associative in this situation. No particular religious complexion was involved here, either Hindu or Muslim. The next morning, at the *kakad arati*, Sai "looked exceedingly pleased and gave yogic glances; I passed the whole day in a sort of ecstasy." The reference to "yogic glances" has led some readers to mistakenly assume that Sai Baba was a Yogi. Khaparde was trying to describe the phenomenon by using terms well known in his milieu. Two sentences later, he refers to a situation in which Sai "sat talking with the young Mohamedans that come to the masjid."

On January 8, Sai Baba suddenly exhibited a strong mood of anger, expressing verbal abuse. Khaparde gives the interpretation that the *faqir* was here endeavouring to prevent the reappearance of plague, so greatly feared by the villagers. Three days later, Radhakrishna Ayi installed a phonograph (or gramophone), apparently in the mosque courtyard. Sai reacted to the noise made by this Western invention. "Sayin Maharaj got very angry and used hard words." However, the following day, he did permit music and dance in the courtyard of the mosque.

On January 12, Sai Baba repeatedly allowed Khaparde to smoke his *chilum* or tobacco pipe. The diarist says that many of his doubts were then resolved. The *faqir* was in a different mood the next day. "Sayin Maharaj did not say a word today and did not even throw the glances which he usually does."

A further complexity is mentioned. When the saint commenced his walk, "his mood was changed and one would think that he was angry, which he really was not."

An attitude of patience emerges. On January 15, Sai Baba asked Khaparde "how I spent the morning, which was a mild rebuke for not having read and contemplated. I went to see him again when he returned and he was very kind. He commenced a long story and kept on as if speaking to me, but I felt sleepy all the time and did not understand anything."

The next day, during the *shej arati* performed in the *chavadi*, Sai "was particularly gracious . . . and sent out wonderful currents of joy and instruction." On January 17, at the *kakad arati*, Sai "smiled most benignly; it is worthwhile spending years here to see it even once. I was overjoyed and stood gazing like mad." This well known testimony stands in acute contrast to misleading portrayals of the irascible and unsociable ascetic.

The following day, when Khaparde visited the mosque, he was treated kindly by Sai, who commenced to tell him parables. One of these included a theme of reincarnation, a topic by no means foreign to *goshtis* of Sai. However, by the time Sai Baba started on the third story, another visitor proved difficult. An unknown *faqir* had arrived for *darshan*, and touched the feet of Sai. This man (unnamed) did not want to leave, and prolonged his act of veneration. Sai Baba expressed annoyance at the interruption, but the stranger was persistent. The mood of *darshan* has a major drawback: creating a greed for the spiritual benefit believed to be acquired in this procedure of contacting a saint.

Sai Baba surely had a right to object to what was basically a selfish action. He was certainly vigorous in his demonstration of resistance. He picked up the *arati* utensils and threw them away. He did the same with plates of food. The obdurate *darshan* seeker now moved out of the compound, and stood outside the mosque precincts. By then, the commotion inside the courtyard appears to have been pronounced. Sai Baba lifted the devotee, Ram Maruti Bua, off the ground. This feat of strength did not hurt the devotee, who afterwards reported that he "felt very happy," as if elevated "to higher regions." The Shirdi *faqir* may have exercised some skill as a wrestler in earlier years, if certain accounts are to be credited.

The *arati* had apparently recommenced. Martand, the son of Mhalsapati, "showed great presence of mind," directing that the *arati* "should be finished where it was begun." Sai Baba had moved out of his usual place, causing confusion to the worshippers. He eventually resumed his customary seat, and the occasion ended with decorum, although *udi* was "distributed wholesale and not individually."

This dramatic event was interpreted by Khaparde in terms of *leela*. The resident *faqir* may have taken the opportunity to upset the increasingly rigid *arati* routine, in which *udi* distribution was one feature. Khaparde reports that Sai expressed a "torrent of hard words" on this occasion, during which he repeatedly exclaimed that he had saved Balvant (the son of Khaparde), and also prevented the death of Khaparde himself. At that time, Balvant suffered an illness while staying in Shirdi, and for three weeks was unable to visit the mosque. Khaparde apparently feared harassment from the British Raj.

The words of Sai Baba in relation to Khaparde are here reported by the diarist as: "Fakir wished to kill Dadasaheb [Khaparde] but I would not permit it." This enigmatic statement poses difficulties of interpretation. The diary refers to the intruding ascetic as "the Fakir." This may not be relevant, because on some occasions Sai Baba employed the same word "Faqir" to designate *Allah*, as recorded by Narasimhaswami in his *Charters and Sayings*. For instance, Sai stated that he requested *dakshina* "only from those whom 'The Fakir' points out to me" (Narasimhaswami 1942:17). The diarist Khaparde adds that Sai Baba also mentioned one more name on the dramatic occasion described, but this he could not afterwards recall.

The next day, January 19, Megha Shyam died in the early hours of the morning. Khaparde informs that Sai had foretold the demise three days earlier, emphasising, "This is the last *arati* of Megha." The Shaiva devotee (and *arati* officiant) knew that he was dying. After his decease, Sai Baba was very withdrawn during the *kakad arati*, and later appeared when the corpse was being brought outside for cremation. The saint touched the corpse of Megha and loudly lamented the decease. "His voice was so touching that [it] brought tears to every eye." When the corpse was consigned to the flames, Sai Baba could be heard lamenting at a distance. "He was seen waving his hands and swaying as if in *arati* to say goodbye."

Khaparde records that after the cremation, the devotees "ought to have sat praying but Bapusaheb Jog came and I [Khaparde] sat talking with him. When later I went to see Sayin Baba, he asked me how I spent the afternoon. I was very sorry to confess that I had wasted it in talking. This was a lesson to me."

Jog now replaced Megha as the *arati* officiant. Jog also attended daily sessions of the Vedanta study group undertaken by the literate Khaparde, involving readings from sacred texts. Krishnashastri Bhishma and Upasani Shastri (later Maharaj) also attended these Vedanta gatherings (which did not occur at the mosque or the *chavadi*, being a separate activity). A new attendee on January 22 was Lakshmibai Kaulgi, an aunt of Radhakrishna Ayi. This *brahman* lady "appeared to be well informed in Vedanta." She went to the mosque and saluted Sai Baba.

Subsequently, Sai called Kaulgi his mother-in-law, and also joked about her action of saluting him. Khaparde remarks: "This gave me the idea that she has been accepted by him as a disciple." Khaparde apparently regarded himself as a disciple, despite some later beliefs (of Narasimhaswami and others) that he was an outsider.

Sai Baba sometimes demonstrated that he was substantially aware of events in relation to visitors. In the evening of January 25, at the time of his walk to the Lendi, Sai related to Khaparde "nearly the whole previous history of Mrs. Lakshmi Bai Kaulgi." The diarist adds that he knew this recounting "to be correct as I knew the facts."

The reference to Kaulgi as "mother-in-law" implies a marital association. Her niece was certainly a major participant in Shirdi events, and yet obscured by vestigial references. On January 27, Radhakrishna Ayi washed the clothes of Sai, and he expressed anger with her for doing this. This mention in the diary is only fleeting. Although some commentators have concluded that Sai Baba kept Ayi at a distance, there may be grounds for believing that she was in closer proximity to the saint. She regarded Sai as Krishna, and in this respect had the attitude of a *gopi*.

Kaulgi chose to stay on at Shirdi. On February 5, 1912, Sai gave Kaulgi a piece of bread, and told her to go and eat with Radhakrishna Ayi, apparently at the latter's nearby cottage in Shirdi. Khaparde remarks: "This is great good fortune; she [Kaulgi] will be happy hereafter." This sparse reference indicates the esteem in which Ayi was held. Sai Baba is reported to have regularly gifted Ayi with bread and vegetables as *prasad*.

The next day, Khaparde was at the mosque with Shama and Dixit. Sai appears to have been more explicit than usual, and said he had been "considering long and thinking day and night." The purport was: "All were thieves, but we had to deal with them." He added that he had prayed to God night and day for their "improvement or removal but God delays." There was a recurring theme that he would not go to the *teli* or *vani*, and "never beg of them." People were not "good and devoted," but instead "unsettled in mind." This abstruse declaration of independence spotlighted the allusive merchants and thieves who interfered with a spiritual orientation.

On February 10, Khaparde found Sai "in a very pleasant mood" at the mosque. Yet the *faqir* talked allusively, commenting that "his body had been severed from his legs," and that "he had a fight with the Teli." The *teli* or oil vendor was a familiar theme to those who knew Sai well, and apparently signified aberrant or clumsy tendencies in the community at large (and not just oil vendors). Oil vendors sometimes wanted too much for their wares. The refrain of Sai Baba amounted to a pun on the expectations of a high price or dividend, comprising a distraction. *Darshan* visitors were not always to his liking, seeking spiritual and mundane profits from saintly contact. From this perspective, the intrusive *faqir* who caused a commotion on January 18 was a manifestation of the Teli complex.

On February 10, the pleasant mood of Sai Baba continued until towards the end of the noon *arati*, when he "began to exhibit signs of impatience." The indications are that he was not always keen on a routine performance of *arati*. He did not ask for this performance, but merely acceded to the wishes of devotees.

The next day, when visiting the mosque, the diarist "found many men sitting there," who were "mostly strangers." There is perhaps no need for wonder that Sai Baba chose to be allusive in the midst of people who did not know him. What were they likely to ask? He had no interest in preaching doctrines, and did not confer initiations. So many visitors wanted cures and material benefits. How could they learn his own priorities? How long would that take?

The following day, on February 12, Khaparde noticed at Dixitwada a visitor who "showed signs of being in a frenzy." This man twitched, glared, and threw shoes at Khaparde and Shivanand Shastri. "At one time we thought him drunk." Subsequently, devotees grasped that this visitor was merely feigning a "religious frenzy," with the motivation of gaining fame as a holy man. Khaparde took this pretender to the mosque, but Sai Baba ordered him to leave. The calculating "Teli" was now obliged to depart.

On February 17, Sai "was in a very pleasant mood and made jokes." After the morning *kakad arati* at the *chavadi*, he would usually utter "hard words against the internal enemies." Khaparde does not explain the significance. Sai Baba evidently felt that something more was required than *arati* singing. His allusive "hard words" ostensibly referred to *teli* merchants and to devotees like Waman Tatya and Appa Kote.

The next day, towards the end of the noon *arati*, Sai became impatient, and told the assembly to quickly vacate the mosque. Nanasaheb Chandorkar arrived in Shirdi, bringing an "artificial garden with a big moon, such as we have on marriage occasions." This item had been commissioned by Radhakrishna Ayi, who was evidently keen to install it at the *chavadi*. On February 19, this decoration featured for the first time in the *shej arati*, attracting a large crowd. The diarist says that Sai Baba did not appear to dislike the innovation.

The following day, when leaving the *chavadi*, Sai did not express any of his accustomed "hard words" after the *kakad arati*. He returned to the mosque, saying only what the diarist translated as: "God [Allah] is the greatest of all." The original phrase used was apparently "*Allah Malik*," the most favoured *zikr* of Sai Baba. In this austere mood, he objected to the ostrich eggs which Ayi had hung up at the spot where he generally sat in the mosque. "He had them pulled down and thrown away."

On February 23, 1912, Sai told Shama that Khaparde would have to remain in Shirdi for longer, the "times being very unfavourable" for him. This was a response to a request for departure made on the basis of a letter from Natekar, which raised the hopes of Khaparde's wife about a return to Amraoti. In December, Khaparde had encountered Natekar, alias Hamsa, in Shirdi. The diarist had then believed that Natekar was an "initiate" whose conversation was edifying. He had subsequently discovered that Natekar's claim to have travelled in the Himalayas was a fabrication. Natekar was in fact a CID (Criminal Investigation Department) detective working for the British.

On February 29, Khaparde found signs of tension when he arrived at the mosque just before the *chavadi* procession. Sai Baba was annoyed with some devotees who had climbed on to the mosque roof to light lamps. When the procession started, he threw his stick (*satka*) at Jog and his wife. Arriving at the *chavadi*, he was angry with Jog, demanding to know why the *arati* was being performed. Jog was now the *arati* officiant, replacing the deceased Megha Shyam. In recent years, the devotees had been successful with their plans for a daily routine of *arati* performances. However, these rites did not occur at the instruction of Sai Baba, but merely gained his assent, at times very reluctantly.

Khaparde writes of this occasion: "I thought he [Sai] would beat Bapusaheb." However, this did not happen. Instead, the *faqir* turned on Bala Shimpi and Trimbak Rao. Both received a blow from the *satka*. Shimpi ran away, but Trimbak Rao prostrated at the saint's feet. Khaparde did not view this scene with apprehension, believing that there was some meaning involved. "I think he [Trimbak Rao] received a full measure of favour and got ahead by at least a stage."

The next day, Sai Baba "seemed to be in a very good mood but looked very much tired." Trimbak Rao was now hostile to the Muslim ascetic Bade Baba ("Fakir Baba"), and "came very much near to abusing Fakir Baba for what appeared to me to be a very trifling matter." Trimbak Rao had earlier caused one or two known problems at Shirdi by his attitude and lack of due attention (as reported by Khaparde).

On March 3, Sai Baba "looked pleased" after the *kakad arati* at the *chavadi*. He did not express any "hard words," and moved quietly back to the mosque. There his attendant Abdul tried to remove a hanging lamp, and as a consequence, the lamp fell to the ground and shattered. Khaparde looked on, thinking the costly damage might anger Sai Baba. However, the *faqir* ignored this incident. The next day, Khaparde's wife was late in visiting Sai at the mosque, "but he very kindly desisted from his meal and let her worship him."

On March 7, 1912, Sai Baba "was in a very pleased mood and danced as he left the *chavadi*," on his way back to the mosque. He continued to relate various parables to Khaparde. Two days later, "he blessed as usual by saying that God was higher than all." The original phrase is not supplied. The same passage indicates that Sai Baba rarely kept on his person the cumbersome garlands placed around his neck by visitors. When he went for a walk at dusk, "he was in a pleased mood but said that he did not care for buntings," apparently meaning decorations that were in evidence near the mosque.

On March 10, the saint told Khaparde: "Look here, be careful. Some guests will come; do not admit them." The diarist was soon after assailed by news from his acquaintances at Amraoti (Amravati) that they were short of money. Two days later, Baba Palekar arrived from Amraoti to stay with Khaparde in Shirdi. This man was keen to get permission from Sai Baba for Khaparde to depart. At first the time of departure was unresolved, but soon crystallised as a result of Palekar's persistence.

On the day of his departure, March 15, Khaparde attended the *kakad arati*, and then went to the mosque with

Shirdi Diary

Palekar and Dixit. He learned that a Rohilla follower was in a belligerent mood and hostile towards Butya. The Rohilla is not identified by name, but is described as molesting Butya. Sai Baba "was pacifying the Rohilla and Butya," an indication of religious divisions that he was at times confronted with. The *faqir* wanted goodwill between Muslims and Hindus, not aggression (see also Shepherd 2015:154–155).

After the meal, Khaparde and Palekar were given *udi* by Sai. He told them to start off, "blessing our journey with the words '*Allah Bhala Karega.*' " The diarist then said farewell to Bhate, Dada Kelkar, Nanasaheb Chandorkar, Upasani Shastri, Mrs. Kaulgi, and others.

The diary of Khaparde is free of preoccupation with miracles. He was a highly literate person, continually reading and writing letters while staying in Shirdi. Perhaps only Chandorkar, Upasani, and Jog could seriously rival him for Sanskrit learning. The orientation of Khaparde was later criticised by the ascetic Narasimhaswami for a lack of devotional commitment, but Vishwas Kher has contradicted this assessment (Shepherd 2015:261–262). We know that, after returning to Amraoti, Khaparde wrote on March 16: "I sat talking with them [visitors] about my stay at Shiradi [Shirdi], the mode of life there, and the spiritual greatness of Sayin Saheb [Sai Baba] who is constantly present to my mind."

Nearly four years later, Khaparde returned to Shirdi, in late December 1915, for three days. Shortly beforehand, he had a long talk about Sai Baba with Ganpatrao Narke (later a Professor). Khaparde affirms in his diary that Sai "is a great living saint." At the Shirdi mosque, he found that the saint's health was "very poor; he is much bothered by cough." This is evidently a reference to the asthma afflicting Sai Baba. Yet Khaparde relates of the occasion, as a whole, that "I am exceedingly happy." He also encountered his old friends Shama, Dixit, Jog, Bhate, and others.

The next day, December 30, 1915, Khaparde sat talking with Bade Baba (alias Fakir Baba), "who has advanced wonderfully and appears to be on the point of being permanently admitted to the spiritual hierarchy." No further details are supplied. This is an attractive variant of the Hindu-Muslim goodwill relations which Sai encouraged. Bade was a Muslim ascetic who had been living in and near Shirdi for several years.

The diarist records that about a hundred people were invited that day to breakfast, which was served very late. Khaparde reports that the new stone house (*wada*) of Gopalrao (Bapusaheb) Buti was progressing well. This sturdy building was later to become the tomb of Sai Baba.

On the day of his departure (December 31), Khaparde encountered Hari V. Sathe. This eminent devotee convened a meeting at Sathewada, where Khaparde found "some eight gentlemen" assembled. That party were making arrangements for a new Sansthan at Shirdi, a development now afflicted by some degree of obscurity. They approved the advice of Khaparde not to collect money from those in receipt of incoming funds distributed by Sai Baba. Sathe was the leader of this group, and subsequently encountered serious difficulty in furthering the Sansthan project (Shepherd 2015:249–251).

32. Bhishma and the *Trikalajnani*

In 1911, Ganesh Khaparde asked Krishnashastri J. Bhishma to accompany him to Shirdi. The latter agreed, and there is, accordingly, some reference to Bhishma in the *Shirdi Diary* of Khaparde.

Bhishma was a *brahman* landowner from a village in the Nagpur district, living on the income from his farms. An adherent of Vitthala worship at Pandharpur, he was a well known *kirtankar* or singer/reciter. In 1908, this Vaishnava had a dream which impressed him. Bhishma saw in his dream a Vaishnava holy man with a *tripundra* daubed on his forehead, sandalwood paste on his body, and *puja* (worship) being conducted at his feet. Bhishma asked this person his identity, but the holy man would not reply, instead pointing to a newspaper on which the sacred phrase Sat-Chit-Ananda appeared in bold letters.

When he arrived in Shirdi with Khaparde, in early December 1911, Bhishma was still apprehensive about meeting a Muslim *faqir* in a mosque. In particular, Sai Baba was well known for offering his tobacco pipe to visitors. Orthodox Hindus like Bhishma regarded such participation in terms of pollution, smoking a pipe contaminated by the lips of a person lacking caste status.

When Bhishma went to the mosque assembly, Sai Baba greeted him with folded hands, exclaiming: "Jaya Sat-Chit-Ananda." The visitor was puzzled, wondering if Sai Baba was the Vaishnava holy man he had seen in a dream. Sai Baba appeared to be a Muslim, although the daily *puja* in the mosque resembled Vaishnava worship, with sandal paste being applied to his feet and neck.

The *brahman* devotees of this *faqir* were in the habit of drinking the *tirtha* or holy water used to wash his feet during *puja*. This was done at their own wish, not at the request of Sai Baba. Bhishma scrupulously refrained from this observance, his attitude again reflecting an aversion to caste contamination. Such reservations seem to have been fairly common amongst high caste visitors who were not devotees. Even some devotees like Das Ganu were averse to *tirtha*.

For some days, Sai Baba would not offer the pipe to Bhishma, evidently sensitive to his caste scruples. This situation changed when the saint expressed a parable that engrossed Bhishma's attention. A devotee was preparing the pipe and gave this to Sai, who passed the pipe unexpectedly to Bhishma. The latter was caught off guard and took a puff of the pipe.

Sai Baba then made remarks reported as: "Look here, I move about everywhere – hills and mountains, Bombay, Pune, Satara, Nagpur – it is Rama who dwells in all these places."

The most well known component of this episode followed. The saint requested that Bhishma should give him five *laddus*, a type of popular confectionary. The wording was allusive, making no sense to a literal interpretation.

The attitude of Bhishma was changing fast. He now identified the holy man in his dream as Sai Baba. He placed his head in obeisance on the saint's feet, and asked a *sevakari* (attendant) for *tirtha*. He was no longer concerned with the caste bias against a Muslim living in a mosque. "Sai Baba put his palm on Bhishma's head for [a] full two minutes; Bhishma went into ecstasy" (Kher 2001:149).

The guest afterwards spent a day reflecting on the possible meaning of five *laddus*. When he awoke the next

Bhishma and the Trikalajnani

morning, Bhishma composed a stanza in praise of Sai. Then he produced four more stanzas in this idiom, and gave these to the *faqir*. Sai Baba asked him to recite these five verses, and again applied his palm to the poet's head. "Bhishma felt exalted" (ibid:150). Subsequently, the poet composed more verses, eventually producing nine *arati* songs while he was in Shirdi. Bhishma was thus able to prepare the booklet *Shri Sainath Sagunopasana*, which was published via funding from Khaparde. Bhishma's effort created a format for what later became known as the *Book of Shirdi Aratis* (Babuji 1996).

Khaparde and Bhishma apparently had a similar problem in relation to dispelling doubts. One day at the mosque, in January 1912, Sai Baba repeatedly allowed Khaparde to smoke his tobacco pipe. Khaparde wrote in the *Shirdi Diary* that this event solved many of his problems, giving him understanding. However, his case was different from Bhishma, in that Khaparde appears to have been far less concerned about caste matters, and did not react to Muslims.

Bhishma came to describe Sai Baba as a *trikalajnani*, meaning one who has knowledge of the past, the present, and the future.

33. The Amiable and Angry Saint

Sai Baba gained the reputation of having angry moods, in which he was capable of using abusive language. However, the complaining words seem to have been largely unintelligible to listeners, in conformity with his strong tendencies to allusion. Generalising assertions have been made, failing to recognise indications that Sai Baba adapted his mode of expression with different devotees.

In some more dramatic instances, the *faqir* of Shirdi is reported to have hit miscreants with his *satka* (stick), an ascetic emblem and utility item. Abdul Baba and Bapusaheb Jog (Sakharam Hari), both experienced this treatment, which they accepted as a blessing, not an affliction. Abdul was one of the devotees who did not object to stern treatment from the saint, in a mood of the latter sometimes described as *jalal* (angry majesty).

Ramachandra Atmaram (Babasaheb) Tarkhad was a devotee of the Shirdi saint in his last years. Tarkhad gained a Western education, and also a managerial position in a flourishing mill-owning company (Makanji Khatau Mills Ltd) in Bombay. His criteria were science, technology, and turnover. His monthly salary was very high by the standards of his time. Tarkhad belonged to a wealthy and prestigious family, who acquired two motor cars. However, Tarkhad knew that something was lacking in his lifestyle.

A follower of the Prarthana Samaj, Tarkhad did not believe in image worship, and was not enthusiastic about visiting saints. His own ideal of spirituality envisaged the

The Amiable and Angry Saint

guru or *satpurush* in terms of tranquillity and gracious decorum.

Tarkhad made his first visit to Shirdi in September 1910. (220) He was disconcerted when two other visitors kept asking him questions, as if they were at a loss to understand things. Sai Baba told Shama to give him advice, which transpired to be: "Even in the midst of turmoil and anxiety, you should direct your mind constantly toward God" (Kamath and Kher 1991:263).

According to his own account, Tarkhad felt happy about that occasion, but also had a lingering doubt because of some reports he heard about abusive language and beating on the part of Sai Baba. He does not say whether these reports came from critics or devotees. His account continues:

> That a *satpurush* should abuse was not possible and the writer had resolved in his mind that, if ever Sai Baba used bad words, whether they were addressed to him or anyone else, or if he witnessed Sai Baba hitting anyone, in his own presence, he would that very moment, leave Shirdi never to return. (Kher 2001:128, citing *Shri Sai Leela*, 1932)

Tarkhad goes on to relate that he had visited Shirdi a number of times. This is not an exaggeration, because he visited on many occasions, and was well known to the resident devotees. "But never even once did Sai utter any bad word or hit anyone while he [Tarkhad] was with him" (ibid). These words are part of Tarkhad's own testimony.

Circa 1915, Tarkhad was once reprimanded by Sai Baba in a rather sophisticated manner. The devotee became involved in "fighting for a seat with a police constable" on a crowded railway train at Manmad. When Tarkhad arrived at Shirdi later that day, Sai made polite but pointed remarks to him. "We should not engage in contest with such people! Who are we? This we must inquire into" (Narasimhaswami 1939, entry 120).

This caution was interpreted many years later, by the ascetic Narasimhaswami, as a Vedantic theme relating to metaphysics. However, the issue was evidently rather more pragmatic, befitting the role of a householder averse to violence of any kind. Saints must be gentle and amiable, and devotees must not fight policemen. Due warnings must sometimes be given, and perhaps even admonitions.

If we compare Tarkhad with Abdul and Jog, some differences emerge. Abdul was a world-renouncing *faqir* from an early age, one who lived a simple life revolving around instructions from Sai Baba. Abdul was accustomed to hard work and self-abnegation. He also removed the snakes which were so common in Shirdi, and some of which were very poisonous. The cane, or rather the *satka*, was not difficult for him to accept in situations of rebuke. There were bonuses. Abdul was the only person whom Sai Baba allowed to accompany him inside the Lendi garden. All other devotees had to stop at the Lendi entrance on this daily expedition.

Bapusaheb Jog (d.1926) possessed a more complex temperament than some of the other devotees. A learned *brahman* proficient in Sanskrit, he was permitted by Sai Baba to hold "classes" at Shirdi, meaning to give readings from well known scriptures (Dixit and Deo also participated, but to a lesser extent). Jog was also the major *arati* officiant at Shirdi for several years, at times risking displeasure from Sai in this role of worship. On one occasion when Sai Baba asked him for *dakshina*, Jog became angry, primarily because he did not have any money with him at the time. The *faqir* then told him not to lose his temper. Eventually Jog became an ascetic, at the encouragement of Sai Baba (who did not generally advocate this lifestyle). Jog was also familiar with the unusual example of Upasani Maharaj, to whom he transferred his worship after Sai Baba's decease.

34. Death and Burial

The saint's health deteriorated during his final two or three years. He was subject to asthma, and often needed to be assisted. During his evening round of begging, he would go out on foot, accompanied by Gopalrao Buti and Nanasaheb Nimonkar. These two men would sometimes carry him in his weakened condition. Yet he maintained his rugged *faqir* lifestyle to the end, living in austere simplicity.

During the daytime, his company "was open to all and for the most part, nobody was prohibited; but during the night, the restrictions were severe" (Dabholkar 1999:698). When Sai Baba returned from his evening round of begging, devotees went back to their homes. There were rare exceptions like Mhalsapati and the lady Lakshmibai Shinde. The latter was a resident of Shirdi, and had been a devotee for many years. She was the only woman allowed into the mosque when the curtain (comprising the door) was down. Sai Baba gave her four rupees daily (Williams 2004:114). Every day she now prepared food for him, meaning bread (*bhakri*) and vegetables.

This feeding habit apparently commenced on the undated occasion, years earlier, when Sai Baba complained of feeling hungry. Lakshmibai had then brought bread and vegetables. The saint disconcertingly picked up the plate of food and placed this before a dog. He made a comment indicating his sense of empathy with the dog. "All living creatures experience the same hunger. Though he [the dog] is dumb and I am vocal, is there any difference in the hunger?" (221)

An episode concerning another animal occurred only a week before the death of Sai Baba. Three Muslim mendicants, described as *dervishes*, arrived at Shirdi with a bullock cart containing a tiger bound with iron chains. This beast was their means of livelihood, being exhibited by them at villages for entertainment. This was not the original *dervish* vocation, but a derivative popular in India. The tiger had contracted a disease, and the visitors apparently hoped for a cure. The *dervishes* described to Sai Baba the condition of this animal, and he gave them permission to bring the tiger into his presence. The tiger then appeared in chains, but fell dead, apparently in the mosque courtyard, or on the mosque steps. The saint gave directions for the animal to be buried at a local Shiva temple. (222)

At the end of September 1918, Sai Baba contracted fever. This apparently subsided after a few days, but he would not take food and grew weaker. He was still ill, and would groan and moan occasionally. (223) He would sit for most of the time, and lie down for a short while on a mattress. In mid-October, he ceased the morning and evening begging rounds. After the noon *arati* on October 15, he sent away a number of devotees present in the mosque for their meal, including Gopalrao Buti and Hari S. Dixit.

His death occurred shortly afterwards that same day. Sai Baba remained sitting and was conscious until the last. The group remaining with him are named as Lakshmibai Shinde, Bhagoji Shinde, Lakshman Bala Shimpi, Bayaji Kote, Nanasaheb Nimonkar, "and some other local people." Shama sat a little further away on the mosque steps. The breathing of the *faqir* became slower, and Nimonkar desperately poured some water into his mouth, only to find that this spilled out. Nimonkar then cried out "Deva!" In a weak voice, Sai then uttered "Ah!" He died leaning against Bayaji Kote at 2.35 p.m.

His last words are said to have been: "Take me to the *wada*; I will feel better there." (224) The *wada* was a stone edifice recently constructed in Shirdi by the wealthy devotee Gopalrao Buti. This building was known as the Butiwada.

Death and Burial

Extra detail is afforded by Dabholkar, who says that the saint sent away the devotees to have their meal, "but two or three villagers wanted to stay." Some devotees insisted that they should not be asked to leave. However, Sai Baba "hurriedly sent everyone away." He told Dixit and others: "Go to the *wada* and come after your meal" (225). This group obeyed and departed for the *wada*. Subsequently they were urgently called back, but "missed the last meeting." They found the corpse of Sai "on the lap of Bayaji Kote." (226)

After the death of Sai Baba, a substantial disagreement occurred between the Muslim and Hindu followers. (227) The Muslims said that the corpse should be taken for burial to the local cemetery. However, the majority of devotees were Hindus; a number of them urged that the saint had expressed his wish to be buried in the Butiwada.

On October 16, 1918, the *mamlatdar* (revenue officer) of Kopargaon arrived, and encountered a large gathering of devotees. He found that about two hundred Hindus favoured burial in the Butiwada, while a hundred persons were against. There are different versions of events. The *mamlatdar* was not satisfied by the lack of unanimity, and suggested referring this matter to the revenue collector of Ahmednagar. The Hindu devotee Hari S. Dixit then contacted that eminent official. One version reads:

> The Muslims were aware that Kakasaheb Dixit was highly regarded and respected by one and all and commanded great influence in the Government circles. The outcome of the controversy was, therefore, in no doubt and would be according to his opinion. As such many felt that there was no use opposing him. So at last the dissenters decided to give conditional consent to the interring of the body in Buti Wada. The condition was that just as the Muslims had free access to the *masjid* [mosque] during the lifetime of Sai Baba, they should enjoy the same freedom to visit the *masjid* and the wada. To that the Hindus gladly agreed. (228)

According to this report, on the evening of October 16, the saint's corpse was taken in procession to the Butiwada for burial. (229) However, another version awards emphasis to a missing event, described by Bappa Baba (an old devotee living at Shirdi). According to him, the corpse of Sai Baba was kept on a plank inside the *chavadi* for three days before burial. This was apparently for the purpose of assisting an inspection by the revenue collector of Ahmednagar, who arrived at the end of that interim period.

The visiting official decided the religious issue by concluding that Sai Baba could not be a Muslim but only a Hindu, on the basis of the undergarment known as *langoti*. This has been considered a very arbitrary verdict. "The *langoti* is a common item of clothing among all Indians, Hindu and Muslim, and it is known to be worn by Sufis as well." (230)

The Butiwada afterwards became known as the *samadhi mandir*, this site undergoing extensive changes with the passing of time. Shirdi became a famous pilgrimage venue, the old village disappearing.

35. Bane Miyan of Aurangabad

In 1918, four months before his death, Sai Baba sent two Muslim emissaries to Aurangabad for the purpose of contacting two Sufi entities in that city, namely Hazrat Shamsuddin Miyan and Bane Miyan. (231) Kasim (son of Bade Baba) was a stranger to Aurangabad, and as a consequence, Sai requested Imambai Chota Khan to accompany him. Chota Khan had formerly been a soldier in the service of the Nizam of Hyderabad, and was familiar with the Aurangabad region.

Sufism had a strong presence in Aurangabad. At the popular level, the famous shrines of Nizamuddin Aurangabadi (d.1729) and Ahmad Gujarati Shattari were clearly visible. Less saliently, Shamsuddin Miyan appears to have been a decorous and convivial entity with the repute of a *faqir*. He was known to Chota Khan, and came especially to meet the two emissaries at the railway station. He asked: "Who are the guests who have come from Faqir Sai?" The visitors duly informed him of their identity and the nature of their mission. Shamsuddin Miyan afterwards "repeated Sai Baba's instructions to them word for word." (232) He was evidently intent upon what Sai Baba had communicated.

Shamsuddin Miyan then took Kasim and Chota Khan back to his home, where he quickly arranged for everything specified by the *faqir* of Shirdi. The instructions of Sai Baba entailed a musical performance of *qawwali* and *moulu*, alongside the charity of *langar* (preparation and distribution of food). Sai Baba gifted Shamsuddin with 250 rupees for the purpose of feeding a large number of poor people.

The next day, Kasim and Chota Khan arrived at the home of Bane Miyan, a very different kind of *faqir* to Shamsuddin. He had the reputation of being a *majzub*. The two visitors found Bane Miyan standing with one arm raised in the air. He had maintained this discipline for what was apparently a lengthy period; the austere exercise is generally associated with Hindu holy men. Bane Miyan was not a welcoming entity like Shamsuddin, instead being totally abstracted from his surroundings and public life.

Bane Miyan led a very retiring existence. He was looked after by assistants who are described by Chota Khan as Arabs, which can be accepted literally, in view of the strong Islamic migration to the Deccan from countries like Arabia. These Arab attendants warned the visitors not to come too close, in case Bane Miyan became angry and beat them. This unusual *faqir* was averse to interruption, and extremely uncommunicative. He was the antithesis of any preaching role. The misconceptions that were created about him require some patience to understand.

Chota Khan was an ex-soldier, a strong and vigorous man. After waiting for an hour in evident trepidation, he boldly moved forward and placed around Bane Miyan's neck the garland of *sevanti* flowers despatched by Sai Baba. The *majzub* then lowered his raised arm, and was not threatening, as some had feared. Chota Khan then uttered the message which Sai had communicated for Bane Miyan. The recipient listened quietly and stared at the sky, tears rolling down his cheeks.

The message was brief and enigmatic. "Ninth day. *Allah* himself takes away the lamp which *Allah* has placed. Such is *Allah's* mercy" (Narasimhaswami 2002:605). An alternative translation is: "On the ninth day of the ninth month, *Allah* would take away the life (literally his fire). Such is *Allah's* wish." (233)

Sai Baba died four months later, on the ninth day of the ninth month of the Islamic calendar. The nature of his link with Bane Miyan remains obscure. Sources markedly diverge on this point. One version describes Sai as the teacher of this *majzub*, (234) while another affirms that Sai was his disciple. (235)

Both Shamsuddin Miyan and Bane Miyan (d.1921) were celebrated after their death via the shrines which appeared in their name. The domed shrine (*dargah*) of Bane Miyan was constructed in 1932 by his relatives, and gained a popular Urs festival. An imperative necessity is to penetrate the legends which accumulated around this *majzub*, as he came to be known. A misleading Urdu hagiography was composed by a nephew of Bane Miyan. This writer exercised a very different disposition to that of his uncle, acquiring wealth and status in his career as an orthodox Sufi. Here we are presented with a discrepant role, and one which has caused considerable confusion via the attendant preferences of description.

Bane Miyan was not interested in human contact, far less, wealth and status. He did not seek disciples or admirers, and did not read books. Unlike his brothers, he never married and had no offspring. His life was spent in an indrawn state of focus, accompanied by an austerity that was effortless to him. His basic lifestyle was so simple and aloof that fantastic and discrepant stories developed as a "miracle" substitute, created by promoters who desired a more sensational profile. Bane Miyan was described as a *majzub* in the hagiography, but that word was very loosely used, and is easily confused with the degenerate standards of lesser *faqirs* and their followers.

Originally a soldier in the British commanded regiments of Hyderabad State (an army funded by the Nizam), Bane Miyan (Muhammad Azam Khan) moved to Aurangabad at an uncertain date, possibly in the 1850s, or maybe later. He reputedly sat under a tree for some years, and lived naked like a Hindu *sadhu*, with only a blanket and a bucket as possessions. The hagiography contains anecdotes referring to customs of the time, and these do not reflect Bane Miyan's own lifestyle or orientation. Bane Miyan was reputedly 105 years old at his death, which may be an exaggeration.

An American historian has caricatured Bane Miyan as spending his days "lazing and raving" around the Aurangabad cantonment, (236) a verdict which can evoke disagreement. That assessment is based on a hagiography of doubtful relevance in many respects. The hagiography has also encouraged a description of Bane Miyan as "a cannabis-smoking miracle-worker who regularly harangued the British in Aurangabad from the gutters as they passed." (237)

Attempts to penetrate the history are frustrated by various discrepancies. Bane Miyan's date of birth is variously given as 1808, 1816, and 1819, with a more recent tendency to contract this to a period over thirty years later. (238) More reliable is the detail that his family had migrated to Hyderabad from the Punjab during the lifetime of his grandfather. Migration of Muslims to Hyderabad from distant regions was pronounced. The father of Bane Miyan served in a cavalry regiment of the Hyderabad Contingent. The oral tradition of his life has been considered more accurate than the written lore, but the former derives from a nephew (Muinuddin Khan) who was only 16 years old when Bane Miyan died. This source gives the information that Bane Miyan served as a sergeant (*havildar*) in the Contingent army, prior to becoming a *faqir*.

In contrast to the oral traditions, the military background is missing from the hagiography entitled *Azam al-Karamat*, composed *circa* 1921 by Muhammad Ismail Khan (d.1956), a nephew of Bane Miyan. This extravagant document, appearing at the *faqir's* death, opted to present the early life of Bane Miyan in the mould of "an infant recluse and miracle-worker." (239) While this discrepancy is all too obvious, the overall format of the "biography" is also misleading, because of the elaborations and imaginations imposed. The miracle stories are too accentuated for sober acceptance. Bane Miyan did not give autobiographical reminiscences; the supposed events were created by hindsight, by relatives and devotees who came to believe in them.

The move to Aurangabad is an obscure event. The text hagiography is silent about this, while the oral version assumes that Bane Miyan travelled to this city after leaving the army, on the death of Afzal Shah Biyabani in 1856. Bane Miyan arrived with his two brothers, who were both also *sepoys*, a detail which has led to the theory that this trio (or one of them) were posted to Aurangabad on military duty.

In relation to the "biography" as a whole, "the only certain date available is found in surviving official documents kept by Bane Miyan's family dating to the 1920s." (240) This refers to the year 1891, when the Nizam, namely Mahbub Ali Khan, granted an income of 15 rupees per month for the food and drink of Bane Miyan. The latter was evidently famous by that time, and may have been living as a *faqir* for many years prior.

Hagiological flourishes were easy to add in the absence of historical details. The *Azam al-Karamat* includes encounters with persons from different ethnic groups, for instance, an Arab savant from Medina called Madani Saheb. The *faqir* is credited with miraculously assisting this man to escape the local police. The contact may well have existed, but is distorted and obscured by the popular resort to supernatural lore. In more general terms, the British Raj are a target of the hagiology. "The cantonment's [British] masters are shown as jittery and unnerved, perplexed by Bane Miyan's constant ability to thwart them through the miracles he directed to his friends." (241)

One episode depicts Bane Miyan calling out in the cantonment bazaar to a *sepoy*, referring to him as a person of much higher rank. The common soldier here points out the mistake made in ranking, but found later the same day that he was promoted by a British officer. This reference has been decoded to mean Colonel Harry Ross. The latter was the chief officer at Ahmednagar, which became the administrative centre for Aurangabad cantonment in 1902. Ross visited Aurangabad many times between 1902 and 1918. A relevant deduction is that the author of *Azam al-Karamat* here played on the recent memory of Ross "to add to Bane Miyan's reputation." (242) We should not regard such stories as being, in any way, factual.

Professor Nile Green allocates the events described in the same hagiography to the period 1900–1920, and especially the final phase, "with a concentration on the years between 1915 and 1920." (243) This theory states: "In the last decade of his life he [Bane Miyan] was compelled by his mania to prowl the streets of the same [Aurangabad] cantonment." (244) That version does not tally with the report found in the Sai Baba literature (which is not mentioned by Green), where Bane Miyan appears as a recluse, resistant to visitors even in his own home.

This retiring career was far removed from any role as a disruptive agent of "mania" and anti-British sentiment in the streets and cantonment bazaar. Yet the seditious role is what we find in the *Azam al-Karamat*, where numerous episodes are attributed to the regimental bazaar, "which Bane Miyan liked to frequent in his bullock cart so as to call out to passing soldiers and occasionally harangue the otherwise orderly district's administrators." (245)

One may doubt whether this *faqir* actually possessed a bullock cart. The analyst may also hold in strong question the idea that the introverted *majzub* harangued British administrators. However, this is what the audience for hagiology probably wanted to hear. Bane Miyan was too retiring for the tastes of miraculisers, who created the portrait of an aggressive anti-British reactionary. Muslim relatives of the *faqir* were no doubt resentful of the missionary

Bane Miyan of Aurangabad

activities on the part of such Christian evangelists as Henry Smith (d.1938), who preached in the cantonment bazaar between 1902 and 1918, attempting to convert the Muslims of Aurangabad.

In this way, the abstracted Bane Miyan became projected as a foil to evangelists and administrators of the Raj, as a dissident incendiary who reflected the mood of a resentful local populace. He was certainly unsociable, but that is not equivalent to being a political agitator. The latter role was becoming widely favoured at this period of national "non-cooperation" against the British, a trend which probably influenced the author of *Azam al-Karamat*.

The hagiography refers to a hereditary religious role of *shaikh*, the family of Bane Miyan having been noted for "learned Friday sermons back in their Punjabi homeland before they turned sepoy." (246) Some admirers would probably have preferred Bane Miyan to be a preacher of Islam. In reality, he was a silent and non-discoursing saint, who went naked like Hindu holy men, and who appealed to an interreligious audience that was diminished by hagiology. (247) His followers included Hindus and Zoroastrians, and even "Britons" (British).

The oral tradition relays that, while still a soldier, Bane Miyan experienced an ecstatic state of attraction (*jazb*) towards *Allah*. British military officers believed that he had become insane, and he was accordingly placed in an asylum. This recourse is by no means impossible; the colonial system consigned many Indians to asylums. However, the legend has to be duly analysed. Bane Miyan was reputedly confined in a "mad-house" (*pagalkhana*) at Jalna, a cantonment town about sixty miles east of Aurangabad. (248) The date is unknown, and even the destination is very much in question. (249) Caution is required in any interpretation of these events.

According to *Azam al-Karamat*, the British cantonment magistrate of Aurangabad instructed soldiers to take the "mad *sepoy*" to the asylum, the mode of transport being a bullock cart. Yet after sunset the same day, the madman was seen entering the shop of an opium dealer in the Aurangabad bazaar. This "miracle" purportedly happened more than once. An obvious intention of the author is to depict the British "bazaar master" expressing his eventual recognition of Bane Miyan's greatness as a "Muslim padre." (250)

This report cannot be taken at face value. The entire scenario can be questioned. Jalna was a long distance away, and could scarcely be reached so quickly via the laborious mode of travel represented by bullock carts, which could not compete with horses for speed. Opium shops were known to sepoys in urban areas; these shops usually sold cannabis. The hagiography has been construed by some Westerners to mean that the "mad *sepoy*" was a cannabis addict. He was reputedly given a *chilum* pipe, associated with cannabis, a substance generally admixed with tobacco by consumers. In one anecdote, this pipe is said to cure snakebite; the miracle story is no guarantee of any factual occurrence.

The Sufi state of *jazb* was reducible to drugs amongst the *faqir* imitators of a *majzub* role. There were apparently many of these indulgents, a virtual fashion having been created by extremist *qalandars*, and thought by some to originate within the ranks of Hindu ascetics. *Majzub* types were often *faqirs*, substantially (but not always) existing outside the Sufi Orders representing orthodoxy. There were marked differences amongst them, but simplification has abounded in diverse reports, not least because some European and American assessors classify such phenomena in terms of madness.

The introduction to *Azam al-Karamat* emphasises that Bane Miyan was a *majzub*, and not merely mad (*pagal*). The disconcerting phrase has emerged, in a commentary, that Bane Miyan "was divinely licensed to do as he pleased." (251) The Aurangabad *faqir* does not appear to have made any such claim; the attributions were created by supporters. The

Bane Miyan of Aurangabad

recent tag of "holy fool for the colonial era" (252) is based on hagiology, viewing the psychology of Bane Miyan in terms of clinical madness, and through the lens of Western biases compatible with British Raj reductionism.

In a contrasting perspective, Bane Miyan moved at a tangent to the degenerate world of mediocre *faqirs*, only to be conflated with them by hagiography and establishment Sufism. An American commentator assumes a "regular use of the drug" cannabis on the part of the supposedly mad Aurangabad *faqir*. (253) The basis for that deduction is unreliable hagiology. (254)

A few photographs of Bane Miyan have survived. These reveal him as a naked man with a white beard; however, in one image he wears a gold-embroidered cloak. A recent commentator describes these photos as showing him "naked and bewildered." (255) The precise psychology of the subject is unknown, and is not determined by the assumptions about madness and drug usage.

Very significant is the development emerging amongst supporters at the end of this *faqir's* life. In 1917, a formal certificate in Persian was being used to promote the hagiographer Ismail Khan (the *faqir's* nephew) as the *khalifa* (deputy, successor) of Bane Miyan. Being indifferent to texts and documents, Bane Miyan was evidently not the originator of this *sanad-e-khilafat*. Ismail Khan was by now managing the donations from affluent and prestigious well-wishers. The officious document bore the seals and signatures of several eminent locals, including the hereditary Sufi representatives (*pirzadas*) of the Mughal era saints Shah Sokhta Miyan and Nizamuddin Aurangabadi.

These eminent and living orthodox Sufis bore the title of *sajjada nashin*. This Persian term means "master of the prayer mat," and designated the current leader of an established Sufi grouping. As a consequence of his new *khalifa* status, Ismail Khan himself became a *sajjada nashin*. (256) This exalted role was far removed from the disposition of Bane Miyan, instead representing membership of a religious class, ascendant in the realm of the Nizam. In other words, we are discussing establishment Sufism, which could gain material benefits via the ownership of land and property.

The divide between the unorthodox *majzubs* and the orthodox Sufis was a recurring phenomenon. Rigorous *faqirs* like Sai Baba and Bane Miyan did not seek land or property. The assimilation to religious orthodoxy was resisted by the "poor" Sufis, a category often obscured and misrepresented by wealthy elites in diverse guises.

Ismail Khan also gained the prerogative to direct popular *Urs* festivals, or death anniversaries, of the figures now being claimed in Bane Miyan's Sufi lineage. These entities included the renowned Abdul Qadir Jilani (d.1166), associated with the presumed spiritual ancestry of the *faqir's* early patron, Afzal Shah Biyabani. The *Urs* of Jilani had achieved the status of a public holiday in Hyderabad.

The formal certificate of honour included a prerogative for Ismail Khan to appoint disciples or deputies of his own. In the past, *majazib* had reacted to such formal insignia, deeming these procedures and displays to be an entirely artificial creation of the orthodox Sufi establishment patronised by the *ulama*.

The prestigious organisation of *Urs* festivals, by Ismail Khan, links with the topic of "*sepoy* recreation," involving themes that were projected into the hagiography of Bane Miyan composed by the same nephew. (257) The *Azam al-Karamat* includes a scenario associated with popular entertainments of soldiers, which Bane Miyan had renounced when he became a *faqir*. Ismail Khan was not a renouncing *faqir*, and blurred the difference between contrasting approaches and priorities. Many hagiographies reflect predilections and limitations of the authors, not the supposed subject. (258)

Bane Miyan of Aurangabad

The funeral of Bane Miyan, occurring in 1921, was attended by a very large crowd of Hindus and Muslims. This event lasted all day; the shops in the bazaars were all closed in mourning. The Muslim mourners at Aurangabad filled the Friday mosque built by the Mughal emperor Aurangzeb. This assembly overflowed into the ruins of that ruler's former palace known as Qila Arak. (259)

The introverted *majzub* Bane Miyan had maintained an arduous ascetic practice strongly associated with Hindu holy men. He also went naked like Hindu *sadhus*. Although he came from an orthodox Muslim military family, Bane Miyan did not discriminate against Hindus, and gained many Hindu followers. At his funeral, Hindu supporters had a substantial presence. Such an instance surely deserves a higher rating than the accusation of insanity, a British Raj stigma that is best avoided.

36. Gadge Maharaj

An unusual holy man associated with Sai Baba was Gadge Maharaj (1876–1956), also known as Debuji Zhingraji Janorkar. He was born at Shedgaon village, in the Amravati (Amraoti) district of Maharashtra. He was a *shudra* of the *dhobi* (washerman) caste. In his early years he apparently worked in a field, but lost his land. Gadge was reputedly inspired by a *sadhu* to adopt a renunciate life as a mendicant, his only possession being a mud pot.

After some years, this low caste ascetic emerged as a social reformer in the villages of Maharashtra. He would always carry a broom; upon entering a village, he would commence to sweep and clean the streets and gutters. This was lowly "sweeper" work associated with untouchables. Gadge gained well-wishers and donations, using the money to build hospitals, schools, and animal shelters.

Amongst his admirers was Dr. B. R. Ambedkar, an important leader of the untouchables. Gadge was in strong sympathy with the *harijans* (untouchables), and built *dharmashalas* for them at Pandharpur, Nasik, Poona, and other places. He also worked to assist lepers, being keen to promote hygiene and sanitation. The versatile Gadge Maharaj campaigned against alcohol consumption and other problems in society.

The teaching of Gadge was frequently given in the form of *kirtans*, a popular media for discourse, in which he included critique of ritualism. He opposed animal sacrifice, especially that of cows; this practice was prevalent amongst low caste people. His ideals were hard work and selfless service to the poor and animals. Gadge might be described as a role model for Karma Yoga. His rugged practicality was far removed from pursuits of Raja Yoga and Tantric Yoga.

While building a *dharmashala* at Nasik, his incoming funds stopped. At that juncture, Gadge visited Sai Baba at Shirdi. However, when the visitor climbed the steps of the mosque, Sai greeted him with verbal abuse. Gadge was not deterred by the onslaught, knowing that Sai Baba was a complex entity. Instead of complaining, the visitor broke into laughter. The *faqir* responded by joining in the laughter.

Devotee interpretation of this well known episode has tended to be that the anger of Sai targeted the bad luck recently suffered by Gadge in relation to funds. Gadge was now convinced that his work would prosper. Soon afterwards, more donations were obtained, and the Nasik *dharmashala* was completed.

This event occurred during the last years of Sai Baba. It is possible that an earlier, and obscured, contact occurred between Gadge and the saint of Shirdi. A version of Gadge and Sai was supplied by Bharadwaja, who, however, attributed the first contact to a very early date that is difficult to believe (Shepherd 2015:50–51). If the account is credited to any extent, then some adaptation and elaboration must be allowed for. Gadge is reported to have divulged biographical details (relating to his contact with Sai Baba) when he visited the home of Nanasaheb Rasane, the son of Sai devotee Damodar Rasane.

More reliable is the record of contact between Gadge and Meher Baba in the former's last years. Gadge greatly esteemed Meher Baba, and invited him to Pandharpur in 1954. The resulting interchange was so strong, and essentially inspiring, that Gadge told the visitor: "I am too old now to do any more work; if you keep me with you, I will not be a burden to you. One *bhakri* [loaf of bread] and one *kafni* [robe] are all that I need" (Kalchuri 1998:4577).

Gadge Maharaj remained independent, but died only two years later. He is now widely regarded as one of the most impressive saints of Maharashtra.

37. Zoroastrian Visitors

In accord with his policy of religious liberalism, Sai Baba welcomed Zoroastrian visitors to Shirdi. These included both Parsis and Iranis, the two Zoroastrian population sectors found in India.

About 1915, two Parsi Zoroastrians visited Shirdi. Cursetji Shapurji Peston Jamas was a railway worker and the foreman of a reclamation yard. He and his brother-in-law stayed for a few days. They boarded at Dixitwada, the large house in Shirdi constructed by Hari S. Dixit a few years earlier. They found that only wealthy people (including mine owners) were accommodated upstairs. The two Parsis were left downstairs; these men felt that they were being relegated as strangers of no consequence. They complained of this situation to Sai Baba when they saw him at the mosque. Their version of Dixitwada was to the effect of: "rich people enjoying comforts above and poor people left downstairs to suffer inconvenience."

The *faqir* told someone present to give these Parsi visitors due accommodation upstairs at the Dixitwada. It is apparent that a sense of social exclusiveness was in operation, however indirectly this was exerted. Many of the devotees were high caste Hindus, including Dixit himself. When the two Parsis subsequently departed from the village, Sai came out of the mosque and "graciously waved his hand." (260)

Another Parsi visitor was Gustad N. Hansotia (1890–1958), who eventually became a resident of Shirdi during the last months of Sai Baba's life. Gustad visited the saint from 1910 onwards, and became familiar with the methods of Sai

Baba. In 1918 he gave up his job in Bombay, and stayed in close proximity to the Shirdi *faqir* for six months.

Sai Baba seems to have encouraged the move of Gustad to Shirdi. Yet when the Parsi arrived, the *faqir* ignored him. Gustad accepted this lack of acknowledgment, sitting unobtrusively at the back of the daily gatherings occurring in the mosque. The new resident lived a very simple life. His accommodation was limited to a veranda. His only possessions were a bedding roll and a trunk (or suitcase).

Sai ignored Gustad for two months, giving attention to other devotees. Then one morning when Gustad bowed to Sai in respect, before taking his seat at the mosque, the *faqir* unexpectedly acknowledged his presence. At the end of the gathering, Sai Baba spoke with Gustad in private, asking if he could arrange to obtain 500 rupees as *dakshina*. Requests for *dakshina* could be unsparing. Gustad had brought with him to Shirdi a sum of 500 rupees, which he had not disclosed to anyone. This money he kept in his trunk. He had so far spent 50 rupees on living expenses.

The Parsi devotee quickly fetched the existing money from his trunk, and gave this to Sai, who commented that the *dakshina* was fifty rupees short. Gustad rose to the occasion, and said that he would obtain the remainder by some means or other. He felt that the whole episode was an opportunity which he should meet. His very scanty possessions included a new blanket, which he mentioned. A wealthy devotee then offered him fifty rupees, more than the blanket was worth. So Gustad parted with the blanket. Sai Baba then expressed his appreciation of Gustad's commitment, which was total. In contrast, many other devotees only gave a fraction of their overall assets.

As a consequence, Gustad achieved more intimacy with the saint. Yet this process involved a degree of notable hardship. Afterwards, Gustad found that his trunk and bedding roll had disappeared from the veranda he inhabited.

He was unable to discover who had taken these items. Gustad was the only Zoroastrian living at Shirdi, and he found himself effectively an outsider to both the Hindu and Muslim residents. He moved from the veranda and commenced to live under a tree, like one of the ascetics.

Every day, Gustad attended the gatherings at the mosque, and reputedly became a personal attendant (*sevakari*) of the enigmatic *faqir*. Yet he frequently went hungry, to the extent that his body became emaciated. His clothes were now ragged. His poverty was total. Many of the devotees were wealthy, but ignored his plight. One evening Sai Baba made remarks associated with Karma Yoga, emphasising that there was no action better than feeding a hungry brother. Some Hindu devotees responded to this message, and gave Gustad some much needed food. However, they did not follow up afterwards, with the consequence that Gustad was again left to starve.

This exacting novitiate ended with the death of Sai. Gustad may have been one of the persons present with the saint when he died at the Shirdi mosque in October 1918. (261) The Parsi was certainly one of the coffin bearers at the subsequent funeral, when the corpse of the *faqir* was interred at the Butiwada. Gustad was neutral to the argument, then occurring between Muslim and Hindu devotees, about the place of burial.

Gustad Hansotia is one of the most fascinating instances of interaction with Sai Baba. At a much later date, his reminiscences were filtered through the speech and fragmented reports of others. He himself became silent during the 1920s, and did not produce written memoirs. (262)

An Irani Zoroastrian visitor to Shirdi was Meher Baba (1894–1969), whose original name was Merwan S. Irani. This young man arrived in December 1915, during a phase of his career when he visited various entities of spiritual repute. Merwan was urged to visit Sai Baba by Hazrat Babajan of Poona, who insisted that Sai possessed a "key" which Merwan needed. The reference was very allusive.

After some setbacks, Merwan Irani encountered Sai Baba when the latter was returning from the Lendi garden to the mosque. Merwan prostrated before him. Sai then uttered the unusual greeting of *"Parvardigar!"* This Persian (and Urdu) word has the literal meaning of "sustainer" or "nourisher," and is used in reference to *Khuda* (God) or *Allah*. Sai Baba's employment of this term was entirely consonant with his use of Urdu. However, the precise meaning he awarded the word in this situation is not clear. The episode does not appear in the Sai Baba sources, but in the Meher Baba literature, where the word *Parvardigar* likewise has a metaphysical significance. (263)

On a completely different occasion, Sai Baba is reported to have made a first person statement featuring the Persian word. *Charters and Sayings* relays: "I am *Parvardigar*. I live at Shirdi and everywhere" (Narasimhaswami 1942:10). The Hindu compiler here translated the unfamiliar word to mean God. A factor of omnipresence is indicated.

Sai Baba is also known to have used the word *Parvardigar* in a very allusive conversation with a magistrate who visited Shirdi. When asked his caste or race, Sai responded: *"Parvardigar"* (Shepherd 2015:190). The rejoinder is obviously not literal, but again indicates a mystical form of identity.

Merwan Irani thereafter made return visits to Shirdi and again encountered Sai Baba, the details being obscure. In later years, Meher Baba made many respectful remarks about Sai Baba, describing him as the leading spiritual master of his time. (264) The reminiscences of Meher Baba are still largely unplumbed. (265)

Meher Baba became a disciple of Upasani Maharaj, and eventually established the Meherabad ashram, near Ahmednagar. He gained many Hindu and Zoroastrian followers, and also some Muslim supporters. He observed strict silence from 1925, and supported the cause of untouchables. Unlike Sai and Upasani, he visited Iran and Western countries. His parents were both immigrants from Central Iran, and in 1929, he visited his ancestral location on the Yazd plain. Irani Zoroastrians are sometimes mistakenly confused with Parsis, who are a different (but related) ethnic grouping of the same religion.

The misconception is sometimes encountered that, because Meher Baba was a Zoroastrian by birth, therefore he must have taught Zoroastrian doctrines and sponsored Zoroastrian rituals. This is a very erroneous assumption. Meher Baba avoided those doctrines and rituals, and was, instead, independent. His liberal teaching did make reference to Vedantic and Sufi themes, but he would not identify with either of those traditions.

38. Upasani Maharaj

The most evocative and disputed disciple of Sai Baba was Upasani Maharaj (1870–1941), who became an independent saint, living at nearby Sakori. His case history has frequently been neglected, with a resulting loss in detail, and attendant confusions about what actually happened at Shirdi. Only a brief summary can be afforded here (from an unpublished work attempting to rectify the lacunae).

Kashinath Govind Upasani Shastri was a *brahman* born at Satana, near Nasik. His grandfather was a well known pundit. Upasani became attracted to the renunciate life at an early age. Reacting to the unwanted pressures of an arranged marriage, he left home in his teens to live as a mendicant. His subsequent adventures included an ascetic vigil at a cave on Bhorgad mountain, near Nasik. As a consequence of this *sadhana*, he became emaciated, and needed a period of recovery before returning home.

There followed a lengthy phase as a householder. Upasani was married a third time by his relatives. Not wishing to become a pundit, he chose Ayurvedic medicine as a profession. Moving to Amraoti, he became a successful *vaidh* (doctor), and later developed an ambition to become a landowner. However, he became very disillusioned by difficulties he encountered on his estate. He lost both his land and his money.

In 1910, he contracted a serious breathing ailment caused by the Yogic practice of *pranayama*. He became desperate for relief, and consulted doctors. They could not cure him. This failure made him seek the advice of a Yogi at Rahuri. That practitioner advised him to visit Sai Baba, but Upasani was disconcerted by the Muslim identity of the Shirdi saint. Only with reluctance, and after some delay, did he subsequently visit Sai Baba. A change of attitude resulted.

The breathing ailment was overcome. Upasani lived for some time at an isolated temple of Khandoba, located on the outskirts of Shirdi. He was now under the instructions of Sai Baba, whom he considered a surpassing mystic. This phase, dating to 1911–14, is detailed in some basic sources, although generally obscure elsewhere. Acute and transcendent experiences transformed Upasani into a "knower of *Brahman*," at first with a tendency to disorientation. There is some evidence that Sai Baba closely monitored the progress of his disciple.

This period includes the participation of Upasani in the study group that Ganesh Khaparde conducted at Shirdi during the latter's sojourn in early 1912 (and which is mentioned in the *Shirdi Diary*). Upasani was introduced to the *Panchadashi*, apparently at the instigation of Sai Baba. This famous text of Advaita was at first difficult for Upasani to interpret, as he had previously been reared to the conceptualism of Vishishtadvaita Vedanta.

The subsequent phase at the Khandoba temple evidences some bizarre characteristics. Upasani had to endure the presence of snakes and scorpions, and also harassment from undiscerning persons. Two medical doctors intervened, arranging for his removal to Shinde in 1914. Upasani needed to recuperate and to eat regularly. The emaciated ascetic had contracted constipation and an ailment of piles. The situation was not comprehended by his detractors at Shirdi, who chose to view Upasani as a rival of Sai Baba, and a threat to their own prestige as devotees of the Shirdi saint.

Upasani became famous when he sojourned at Kharagpur in 1915. This town in West Bengal had a very mixed ethnic and linguistic population. He gained many *brahman* devotees, but concentrated upon assisting *bhangis* or "untouchable" sweepers, in whose colony he chose to live, amidst conditions of squalor. His own role as a sweeper is remarkable for a tendency to break the caste divide. This was not the lifestyle of a typical guru, and far removed from his ancestral roots in punditry.

Moving south to other places, Upasani was celebrated in various cities like Nagpur and Bombay. He returned to Shirdi a number of times during this itinerary, but again met with opposition from conservative devotees of Sai Baba (despite the glowing recommendations of Upasani from Sai himself). Upasani settled at the village of Sakori (Sakuri) in 1917. Here an ashram developed, and new temples appeared. However, Upasani continued to be resistant to devotee worship of his own person.

Upasani Maharaj was a rigorous renunciate. He did not wear the ochre robe of a *sannyasin*, but instead favoured a common gunny cloth (or "sackcloth"). He was not a member of any religious sect. Upasani was unpredictable in his behaviour, but consistent in providing distinctive discourses, many of which were recorded in the 1920s.

Eventually, he created a community of nuns, known as the Upasani Kanya Kumari Sthan. During the 1930s, his forthright innovations created strong opposition from the brahmanical establishment, who did not approve of women taking a role in Sanskrit learning and religious ritual performances. The conservative campaign of stigma was vigorous and influential, but ultimately failed. After his death, the community of nuns survived at Sakori. Their code of simple and austere living was indebted to Upasani. The nuns gained celebrity, and the detractors were proven wrong. The leader of these women was Godavari Mataji (1914–1990), a disciple of Upasani since the 1920s. She became a famous saint of Maharashtra. (266)

Appendix I

Sufis and *Majazib* of Bijapur

In his book entitled *The Sufis of Bijapur*, the historian Richard M. Eaton revealed dimensions in the history of Indian Sufism that were formerly largely unknown. He deduced that, by the seventeenth century, "the institutionalised vow of [Sufi] allegiance had begun carrying with it an increasing amount of ritual and a diminishing amount of mystical knowledge" (Eaton 1978:xxvii).

This is a reference to the vow known as *bai'at*, generally involving affiliation with a Sufi *shaikh*, who might ultimately claim a spiritual pedigree deriving from the Prophet Muhammad. The lack of "mystical knowledge" was camouflaged by the fact that "people who took the vow considered themselves Sufis and were considered as such by their contemporaries" (ibid). One should be duly analytical of events in the field of "Sufism."

A reviewer of Eaton made a significant observation about the situation in the Deccan:

> Some Sufis, particularly foreign immigrants, were very orthodox, almost indistinguishable from the *ulema* [*ulama*] at court, eschewed contact with the Hindus and use of their language, and were vigorous "Arabizers," critical of Sultans deemed insufficiently unbending in their Islamic orthodoxy. (Lehmann 1980:387)

Appendix I: Sufis and Majazib of Bijapur

Eaton emphasised that analysis of such phenomena, in terms of the Sufi Orders alone, was not sufficiently comprehensive. Some Sufis belonged to two or more Orders simultaneously, while Sufis belonging to the same Order could exhibit markedly different tendencies. There were also independent Sufis who belonged to no Order at all. Eaton proposed a form of assessment that could more successfully accommodate the variations in role. He urged "an understanding of the socio-historical milieu in which they [Sufis] lived." This means that "only by understanding the nature of the historical context and how it changed," are we able to comprehend the response of Sufis to their environment (Eaton 1978:xxxi–ii).

Trends and dispositions within Sufi Orders could change substantially. A graphic example is afforded by the instance of Sayed Muhammad Husaini Bandanavaz Gisudaraz (d.1422), who apparently became leader of the Chishti Order in the Deccan (Ernst 1992:138). His activity indicates the extent to which some Chishti ideals were compromised in fifteenth century Gulbarga, to where Gisudaraz moved, south from Delhi. His predecessors had scrupulously avoided involvement with the court and distractions created by patronage, whereas Gisudaraz apparently accepted several villages as tax-free land from Sultan Firuz Shah Bahmani (1397–1422).

Moreover, the Sultan's brother Ahmad Bahmani "lavished great sums of money" on the *khanaqah* of Gisudaraz (Eaton 1978:52). When Ahmad succeeded to the throne in 1422, he gifted Gisudaraz and his circle with more towns and villages in the Gulbarga region.

> It was a normal pattern in the history of Indian Sufism that, as a Sufi's political sympathies merged with those of the court, his doctrinal position generally became more orthodox. This was certainly true in the case of Gisudaraz. (Eaton 1978:52)

Contrasting with the Chishtis of Delhi, Gisudaraz sided with the *ulama* (the Islamic equivalent of clergy). His position emerges as very orthodox. Gisudaraz declared the "supremacy of Islamic law (*shariat*) over all Sufi stages" (ibid), and mounted a "tirade" against the *wahdat al-wujud* teaching of Ibn al-Arabi (d.1240). He also fulminated against the liberal Persian Sufi poets Fariduddin Attar and Jalaluddin Rumi (d.1273). These three figures were denounced by Gisudaraz "as enemies of Islam" (ibid). The situation was insular. "By contrast with prevailing Chishti custom, Gisu Daraz learnt Sanskrit and acquired a knowledge of the Hindu epics in an attempt to refute the religious beliefs in Hinduism" (Rizvi 1978:254). On Gisudaraz, see further Eaton 2005:33ff.

A very similar outlook was demonstrated earlier by an orthodox Sufi *shaikh* of the Kubravi Order, namely Ala ad-Dawla Simnani (1261–1336). His conservative attitude opposed the *wujudi* teaching of the gnostic Ibn al-Arabi (d.1240). When Simnani encountered the Sufi mystic Haji-yi Amuli, he "ascertained the true nature of Amuli's heterodox and pantheistic beliefs, and tried to convince his Turkish attendant to kill him; under threat of death, Amuli renounced his beliefs" (Elias 1995:26).

The family of Simnani came from the landed aristocracy of Khurasan (ibid:15). Simnani declared that Sufis were wrong to live in poverty, believing that denial meant a rejection of divine bounty (Rizvi 1978:249). Simnani possessed large areas of land, using the revenue to finance "pious enterprises" (Elias 1995:25). Even though he gave away some of his wealth, it was not difficult for him to build a *khanaqah* or Sufi centre. "Simnani gives the distinct impression that he gave away all his worldly possessions and adopted the life of a penniless ascetic" (ibid:24–25). He is reported to have gained an annual 90,000 *dirhams* from his land (ibid:25). "In his old age he often lamented having resigned his official court position, affirming that high government status enabled Sufis to crush the theological innovators and heretics" (Rizvi 1978:249).

This orthodox Sufi of Iran was influential via his followers in India. However, the monistic Ibn al-Arabi remained popular in the subcontinent. "For Simnani there is no possibility of union with the divine" (Elias 1995:98). Instead, he firmly believed in *jihad*, notably including the exoteric sense of holy war on the battlefield (ibid:55). The outlook of Simnani can be read, at least in part, in terms of his support for "annihilation of the Buddhists," a cause furthered by the Ilkhanid dynasty. Simnani apparently feared that this project was "likely to be undermined because the *Wujudi* ideas could be accommodated with the particular brand of Buddhism in Iran" (Rizvi 1978:250).

Simnani was prominent amongst an orthodox Sufi group of "militant proselytisers." These zealous pietists favoured "a campaign of ruthless persecution of Buddhists" conducted by Ghazan Khan Mahmud, a Mongol ruler in Iran converted to Islam (Rizvi 1978:249). The losers have been described in terms of Irani Buddhism, a form of Mahayanist syncretism evolved by monks who wrote lost works in Arabic (ibid:248). The Buddhist monks were also involved in missionary activity. Some of their practices are obscure, but we do know that Simnani had been initiated into "a special type of *zikr* in which the head moved rapidly in all directions, resulting in strong flashes of light, believed to be mystical" (ibid:249).

The result of these developments was an insular trend further afield. "In India Simnani's missionaries exhorted Sufis to convert the Brahmans and become active proselytisers of Islam" (ibid:250).

From the fifteenth century onwards, leadership of Sufi Orders and groupings, especially in India, "became mainly hereditary as blood replaced merit as the chief criterion of succession." The *barakat* (spiritual power) of a saint was believed to be transmitted to his descendants and to his tomb. The popular appeal of Sufism became extensive via the tomb cults. The majority of subscribers were not interested in mystical achievement, but in mundane relief or acquisition, supposedly gained via the *barakat*. In general, this situation facilitated the introduction of astrology, magic, and belief in talismans and charms, as a "means of preserving the flow of *barakat* from the [deceased] saint" (Eaton 1978:xxx–xxxi).

At Bijapur, this trend related to more than one Sufi Order, primarily the Qadiriyya and Shattariya. In the seventeenth century, numerous Sufis at Bijapur gained royal land grants. The *pirzada* was the custodian of a *dargah* (tomb); this category gained hereditary prestige. The full term is *in'amdar-pirzada*, meaning a land grant Sufi and shrine guardian. The word *pirzada* means "born of a *pir*," being evocative of hereditary lineage. The word *in'amdar* referred to wealthy people, usually (but not necessarily) with land, who received a part of their wealth from the ruler. The word *inam*, or reward, could mean land, money, horses, elephants, gold, and so forth.

At Bijapur, the *pirzadas* collected stipends, like courtiers. They dressed like noblemen, and were carried everywhere in palanquins, in much the same manner as aristocrats. "Living in the lustre of a fortunate ancestry, the landed Sufis, though perhaps ignorant of Sufism, filled a need in the spiritual lives of the common devotees who attended the *dargahs*" (Eaton 1978:237). This is a clement judgment. The dissenting *majazib* evidently detested the *pirzadas* as spurious Sufi entities whose real status amounted to that of parasites.

One of those who chose the palanquin existence was Habib Allah (d.1632), a Shattari and prominent deputy of the reformist Shah Sibghat Allah. The latter did not compromise with the indulgences of courtiers, and was expelled to Arabia. In the wake of this event, Habib Allah became one of the landed Sufis, thus securing prestige (ibid:236). He subsequently criticised his son for rejecting the role of a landed Sufi. The offspring became a *majzub*, a word which can gain different meanings according to the context bestowed. The plural is *majazib*. At that period, the basic meaning of the term *majzub* was resistance to the ways of landed Sufis and orthodox Islamic Sufi doctrine.

The orthodox Sufi, Maulana Muhammad Zubairi (d.1677), applied the stigma of atheist to anyone who neglected *namaz*, the daily Islamic prayer ritual (ibid:278). This was apparently

Appendix I: Sufis and Majazib of Bijapur

a reference to his contemporary Shah Aminuddin Ala, who gained fame as a *majzub*. Shah Aminuddin and other *majazib* were not atheists at all, but this is how the *ulama* liked to portray them.

The conflict between Shah Aminuddin and his orthodox Sufi opponents does reveal the extensive gulf separating landed Sufis from the *majazib*. These were "the two Sufi types most characteristic of late seventeenth century Bijapur" (ibid:255). The explanation is provided:

> While the one had become thoroughly absorbed into the social and religious world of the *ulama*, the other had just as resolutely turned his back on that world while adopting unorthodox doctrines and practices. (Eaton 1978:255–6)

The nature of the doctrines and practices has caused some confusion and disagreement, not merely due to lack of detailed information, but also because of the substantial variation in practices. However, some basic features of the situation are reasonably clear. For instance, "Amin al-Din evidently borrowed his cosmology from a Hindu philosophical system" (ibid:255). Such a recourse would have been quite sufficient to gain censure from the *pirzada* Sufis, who zealously maintained the *ulama* attitude that Hindus were *kafirs* (infidels) of no consequence. This negation involved a belief that *kafirs* were grossly inferior in every way, and lacking any worthwhile skill or knowledge.

Like his father, Shah Aminuddin Ala was *sajjada nashin* (hereditary director) of a Sufi *khanaqah* (centre), located at Shahpur Hillock. However, this Chishti Sufi reversed the meaning which elsewhere attached to the role of *sajjada nashin*, in terms of a *pirzada* Sufi disposition to conservative dogma. One of his disciples, Muhammad Muazzam, related that Aminuddin was worshipped by *lakhs* of Hindus (ibid:249). This would literally mean hundreds of thousands. "After all due account is made for hagiographical exaggeration, the passage nonetheless indicates the Sufi's receptive attitude toward non-Muslims" (ibid:250).

At Bijapur, Hindus were the local Kannada-speaking population. Eaton mentions "the possibility that Lingayats formed a significant component of the outer circle of devotees attached to seventeenth century Shahpur Hillock" (ibid). Lingayats were Virashaivas. They wore a *linga* around their necks, but rejected temple worship and resisted caste barriers.

Many *majazib* existed at Bijapur, in reaction to the *pirzada* Sufis. Unfortunately, very little is known about most of them. The sources reflect hagiological conventions and poetic overlay. There is a current tendency to assume that these dissidents resorted to wine and drugs, but caution is needed on this point. One may easily believe that "their bizarre display of contempt for the outward observances of Islam led some to rank charlatanism" (ibid:281). Imitators are not the best guide to events, and so frequently attend occurrences like the ideological conflict at Bijapur.

The hagiology of wine emerges in such instances as Nuruddin Ishaq Qadiri (d.1687-8), a *majzub* of Nilanga. The legend portrays him as favouring the presence of dancing women, and also being in the habit of requesting wine from visitors. When placing the cup to his mouth, the wine would merely pour through his beard and spill onto the floor. "Although it was believed that he [Nuruddin] was fond of wine, in truth he was pouring the forbidden drink to the floor" (ibid:269). Such reports are discernibly manipulating stock allusions that substituted for the lack of information about the *majazib*.

A poet who made many allusions was Mahmud Bahri (d.1717-18). A sympathiser with the *majzub* tradition, Bahri had links with the Chishti Order. Originating in the town of Gogi, he moved to Bijapur during the reign of Sultan Sikandar Adil Shahi (1672–86). After the collapse of the Adil Shahi dynasty, caused by the militant campaign of Aurangzeb, Bahri moved to Hyderabad. Meanwhile, at Bijapur he became an anti-establishment poet. Much of his output reflects what Eaton calls the outlook of an "ecstatic Sufi." The metaphor is quite pronounced.

Bahri contributed to a folk literature written in Dakhni, often read by women. In this local language, he wrote a poem which he translated into Persian as *Arus-i Irfan*. That work includes anecdotes and stories. Evident is the poet's disdain of the *pirzada* Sufis, "citing their low literary standards, their concern merely with expanding their circles of Sufi clients, and their compromises with the court" (Eaton 1988 and online). A concession of Bahri to Hinduism appears in his reference to the "intoxicated" Sufi (or *majzub*) as a *sadhu*, and to Allah as Hari Ram (Eaton 1978:261).

This radical poet eulogised the substance known as *bhang*, which featured in his Dakhni poem *Bangab-nama*. Eaton refers to "a greenish drink" made from milk and *bhang*, a concoction prepared from cannabis leaves. "The poet's advocacy of the narcotic drink seems to have been both allegorical and literal" (Eaton 1988 and online). The same commentator says that Bahri claimed to have composed his *Arus-i Irfan* while under the influence of *bhang* (Eaton 1978:258). However, "in a broader sense, the use of *bhang* symbolised the intoxicated Sufi's disaffection with the established Muslim ruling class" (ibid:260).

A possible interpretation is that the reputed "intoxication" of *majazib*, in terms of *ahwal* or spiritual states, became associated with *bhang* in the same way that wine had been symbolised for centuries by Sufi poets. The juristic *ulama* prohibited wine, which was favoured at the Bijapur court. *Bhang* was an even more evocative theme, being closely associated with Hindu *sadhus*, who were despised by the *ulama*.

It is very likely that some of the dissidents did imbibe *bhang*, and very possible that some of them were wine-drinkers. Nevertheless, the literal associations comprise a distraction from the essential situation of world-renouncing unorthodox Sufis in conflict with the wealthy orthodox Sufis, the latter being inseparable from dogmatic interests of the *ulama*. The quasi-aristocratic *pirzadas* wanted to depict the *majazib* as aberrant rivals beneath contempt, as atheists and heretics in affinity with the alien creed of Hinduism.

In relation to Sai Baba of Shirdi, the similarities are not total. Unlike Bahri, the Shirdi saint was far removed from any glorification of *bhang*, and denounced the use of alcohol. However, in other respects, there are certain parallels with the *majazib* in his case, and bearing in mind the more widespread presence of the *majzub* phenomenon in India. Like the *majazib*, Sai Baba was not rigorously orthodox in his performance of *namaz*, and his ascetic lifestyle was in strong contrast to the conveniences preferred by landowning *pirzadas*.

In the Urdu *Notebook* preserved by Abdul Baba, the Shirdi saint expresses disapproval of the *pirzada* and related categories presuming to be Sufis (Warren 1999:301). Sai Baba considered these people to be false *pirs*, and his tone of denunciation is strong. "Someone pretends to become a *pir*, showing his skills, attracting and influencing people in order to fill his coffers and amass wealth" (ibid:306).

The *pirzadas* became widespread in Western India. The *pirzada* activity in Gujarat, of more recent times, has been described in terms of the followers being "a source of revenue" rather than people to be guided (Eaton 1978:237). If we compare this trend to the *dakshina* requests of Sai Baba, an apparent similarity is a gift of cash in return for favour or blessings; the key difference was that Sai Baba did not keep any of the incoming funds for himself. Sai Baba may be interpreted in terms of echoing the older conflict with orthodox Sufis, who were so often intent upon the increase of their purse.

Dr. Marianne Warren (d.2004) entirely missed the significance of such matters in her disavowal of any resemblance between Sai Baba and the *majazib* (see Chapter 20 in this book). The Shirdi *faqir* does not fit the image of an orthodox Sufi, however flexibly this image might be presented. Sai Baba instead emerges as an independent Sufi, exercising a remarkable degree of affinity with Bhakti Hinduism.

Appendix II

Swarupananda Saraswati and Sai Baba Worship

Swami Swarupananda Saraswati is a senior and prestigious Shankaracharya of Dwaraka Math (in Gujarat). In June 2014, he commenced an ideological campaign against the worship of Shirdi Sai Baba in Hindu temples. The Swami contended that Shirdi Sai was a Muslim *faqir*, and therefore could not be worshipped in the manner of a Hindu deity.

The resulting events gained newspaper headlines and were much discussed. The Swami did have his supporters, but many Hindu observers did not agree with the attempted prohibition of Sai Baba worship. Some people in Western countries also followed these events. A general verdict was that the campaign inadvertently spotlighted an area of religious differences which should be surmounted, and not accentuated.

Devotees of Shirdi Sai were not prepared to accept the aspersions involved. In July 2014, the law court at Indore issued a summons to the Swami, requesting him to appear in court because of a complaint filed against him for making controversial statements. The Swami was able to postpone a legal confrontation. He criticised the Shirdi Sai Baba Trust (based in Shirdi) for regarding Sai Baba as superior to Hindu deities like Hanuman.

Shirdi Sai devotees countered with legal petitions, emphasising a "deliberate intent to hurt religious sentiments." As a consequence, in September 2015, Swami Swarupananda tendered an apology for the controversial statements he had made. The proceedings occurred at Madhya Pradesh High Court.

The following year, in April 2016, *The Hindu* reported reactions of Shirdi Sai devotees to the fundamentalist critique. Swami Swarupananda had interpreted the temple worship of Sai Baba in terms of creating a drought in Maharashtra. This argument was regarded as extremist by many observers. The devotees were able to negate the accusation by pointing out that drought was also prevalent in Gujarat, Madhya Pradesh, and the Punjab.

Officials of the Shirdi Sai Baba Trust defended their position. They countered the attack by saying that the Shankaracharya appeared to be suffering from a feeling of insecurity, because so many pilgrims were visiting Shirdi, instead of going for the *darshan* of Swami Swarupananda. The shrine of Shirdi Sai Baba certainly does gain a very large number of visitors, making this shrine a significant pilgrim location. No distinctions are made at that site between different religious backgrounds of visitors. Hindus, Muslims, Zoroastrians, Sikhs, Christians, and others, are all welcome as part of an expansive and pluralist policy.

The press were also able to inform readers that the Shirdi Sai Baba Trust had donated *crores* of rupees as charity aid whenever floods, earthquakes, and other calamities, had struck Maharashtra and surrounding regions.

The accusation of a Muslim identity does not cover diverse complexities of this issue. Some say that Sai Baba was born a Hindu (as many do believe, although without any proof to date for the Pathri theory supplied by V. B. Kher). Nevertheless, his identity as a Muslim *faqir* was taken for granted by many Hindus during his lifetime. That identity

Appendix II: Swarupananda Saraswati and Sai Baba Worship

requires a very flexible approach, because Sai Baba was not a typical *faqir*, and exhibited very unusual characteristics.

The liberal outlook of this independent *faqir* eliminated differences between Muslims and Hindus. He would not tolerate criticisms of Christianity even from one of his most prominent devotees (namely, Hari S. Dixit). Sai Baba welcomed Zoroastrians, and greeted the young (and then unknown) Merwan Irani (later Meher Baba) with a deferential exclamation of *"Parvardigar!"* That word had discernibly strong significations in the Urdu vocabulary of Sai Baba (see Chapter 37).

This independent *faqir* was definitely not an orthodox Muslim. Despite certain associations with Sufism, Sai Baba was not an orthodox Sufi, but instead a far more discreet type of mystic. On the basis of Abdul Baba's *Notebook*, it is certainly legitimate to describe Sai Baba as a Sufi. However, the overall details attest a substantial tangent from anything known in the Sufi Orders. Dr. Marianne Warren tended to associate Sai Baba with the Chishti Order; her theory of Chishti influence remains unconvincing (see Chapter 20). When faced with an instance of this kind, the analysis must be sufficiently thorough. Assessment should not be limited to conventional religious roles and organisations, nor to the popular stock of belief and cliché which can reduce the biographical profile.

Notes

(1) Dabholkar 1999:152. The translation reads: "his birth date can thus be roughly determined" at 1838, on the basis of a calculation that he was eighty years old at death.

(2) Govind R. Dabholkar first encountered Sai Baba in 1910. At first a magistrate in Bombay, he became a resident of Shirdi in 1916. He did not commence writing the *Shri Sai Satcharita* until 1922-3, but had been collecting information in earlier years. Dabholkar reports that his wish to write the saint's life story was communicated to Sai Baba by Shama (Madhavrao Deshpande). Sai responded with an injunction to "make a collection of all the authentic stories, experiences, conversations and talks." Sai Baba also said that Dabholkar had his full support in this endeavour. There was the accompanying proviso that Dabholkar "should subdue his ego and offer it at my feet" (Dabholkar 1999:23). Dabholkar was evidently not trying to create a biography in the manner commonly understood today. One scholar comments that it would be much easier to read the *Satcharita* if the author had written in Marathi prose. Yet Dabholkar composed in Marathi verse, attempting to make his work "acceptable within the Marathi religious milieu" (Warren 1999:5). Dabholkar here followed "the traditional Maharashtrian style of sacred literature in which precise dating is positively eschewed, modelling his work on the style of a fifteenth century revered Marathi classic text" (ibid:4). Despite the poetic casting, the *Satcharita* "contains a great deal of factual information" (ibid:5).

(3) Dabholkar 1999:xii, from the preface by Indira Kher. The lack of chronological order is obvious, but this factor does not invalidate the reporting of events in the *Satcharita*. There is a substantial amount of detail in a fair number of episodes reported by Dabholkar.

Notes

(4) Dabholkar 1999:18–19. It is not clear to what extent Dabholkar relied on these works, as he evidently had his own memories and contacts to draw upon. "The thought came to my mind, that I should write down an account of what I experienced" (ibid:21). He includes some of the *goshtis* which Sai Baba communicated. "The stories [Sai] Baba narrated were varied – some, of worldly wisdom, some of common experience and those that explained his mysterious deeds" (ibid:19). This description is not exhaustive.

(5) Das Ganu 2007. The Das Ganu version of Sai Baba's teacher, meaning Gopalrao Deshmukh, is dismissed as an error in Kher 2001:36–54. The early dating for Deshmukh, an eighteenth century figure, does not fit the lifetime of Sai Baba.

(6) Ganapat Dattatreya Sahasrabuddhe was eventually known as Das Ganu Maharaj (1868–1962). Originally a police constable, he became a *kirtankar*, singing *bhajans* and *kirtans*. Das Ganu gained repute as a devotee of Sai Baba, first meeting the saint in 1892. Yet, according to Narasimhaswami, Das Ganu was primarily a Vaishnava with commitments to the pilgrimage site of Pandharpur. He performed regularly at the Urs festival of Sai Baba from 1897, and gained widespread fame as a performer in various towns and cities. Das Ganu composed three devotional books in Marathi, including *Bhakti Lilamrit*; in these works he presented a version of numerous saints. These books included a total of seven chapters on Sai Baba, which are now known as *Sai Hari Katha*.

(7) Kamath and Kher 1991:6. The Sai Baba devotee and researcher Vishwas B. Kher was assisted by the senior journalist M. V. Kamath. Kher contradicts Dabholkar with the conclusion that Sai Baba first appeared in Shirdi between 1868 and 1872, and in the company of Chand Patel. In this version, Sai left with Patel after a few days and returned to Shirdi two months later.

(8) Narasimhaswami is associated with the theory of 1872 as the year of the second arrival in Shirdi. "According to Narasimhaswami he [Sai Baba] lived in the village [of Shirdi] for no more than forty-six years, dying at the age of sixty-six" (Rigopoulos 1993:46). In contrast, Dabholkar credits a period of sixty years residence at Shirdi. Vishwas B. Kher subsequently developed a theory which mediated between Narasimhaswami and Dabholkar. Narasimhaswami came upon the Shirdi scene during the 1930s, and gleaned much information via interviews he conducted with

devotees in 1936. His *Devotees' Experiences of Sri Sai Baba* reports the interviews. His *Charters and Sayings* is a record of statements made by, and attributed to, Sai Baba. His *Life of Sai Baba*, in four volumes, is an expanded version of the materials he collected (Shepherd 2015:328–337). From the late 1930s until the 1950s, Narasimhaswami was effectively a missionary for the Sai Baba movement, being active nationwide and establishing many regional centres.

(9) Kamath and Kher 1991:14–17; Kher 2001:6–12. In 1975, V. B. Kher visited Pathri, near Manvat, and stayed with the Chaudhari family. He interviewed all the old residents of Pathri, including the Bhusari family of *brahmans* (whose family deity was Hanuman). Kher suggests that the missing Haribhau Bhusari was Sai Baba. He urged a similarity between "the Marathi spoken by Sai Baba and the language spoken in Marathwada," but does not mention the saint's Muslim language of Deccani Urdu. Kher stated that his theory is "probable" (Kher 2001:12).

(10) Rigopoulos 1993:21; Shepherd 2005:4–5. Rating for the Jerusalem theory varies considerably. Some writers do not mention this component.

(11) Narayan 1995:16, and citing Rajarshi Bala Sanyasi (Bangalore 1949).

(12) Shepherd 2005:5, and tending to counter a suggestion of Rigopoulos that the version of Shirdi Sai by Sathya Sai Baba is more interesting than the Jerusalem legend of Narasaiyya. Sathya Sai was claiming to give details about his previous incarnation as the Shirdi saint. Cf. Rigopoulos 1993:21–25, for the account by Sathya Sai.

(13) This was Balakrishna Govind Upasani Shastri, a retired Professor of Sanskrit at Poona. He was the brother of the more famous Upasani Maharaj. The information was derived from his visit to Sai Baba, at Shirdi, in late December 1911/early January 1912.

(14) Warren 1999:344, referring to three instances, including Mule (Mulay) Shastri of Nasik and Megha Shyam the Shaiva. Megha became a devotee of Sai Baba, and died at Shirdi in 1912 (Shepherd 2015:252–254).

(15) Warren 1999:267. This commentary describes how Narasimhaswami failed to adequately convey the content of the *Notebook*. Narasimhaswami evidently saw part of the *Notebook*

Notes

during his interviews with Abdul in the 1930s, but he had no familiarity with Urdu. In his *Devotees' Experiences*, the *sannyasin* generalised about the *Notebook* by giving a disproportionate attention to the affinities with Hinduism, mentioning prayers to Maruti and references to avatars that were "dovetailing" in relation to Muhammad and numerous others (Warren 1999:265).

(16) Warren 1999:275. The author also comments that the whole manuscript "looks like a typical student's note-book, with bits of scribble and half-finished sentences interspersed with pages of serious notation" (ibid:267).

(17) Ibid:276. A few pages of the *Notebook* are in Arabic, a fact suggesting authorship by a different person. The copy of a Quranic prayer is signed by "Syed Amin Khandhar, presently a scribe in an Urdu school at Shirdi" (ibid:279). Warren does not provide any information about this obscure scribe.

(18) Rumi is well known for the lengthy poetic work *Mathnawi*. A supplement is his discourses (*Fihi Ma fihi*). See A. J. Arberry, *Discourses of Rumi* (London: John Murray, 1961). See also Schimmel 1993. Abu Yazid al-Bistami was an earlier Iranian figure of the ninth century, and credited with numerous ecstatic sayings (*shathiyat*).

(19) Warren 1999:268. The *khanwadas* mentioned in the *Notebook* include the highly visible Naqshbandi, Chishti, Qadiri, and Suhrawardi Orders. Other *khanwadas* here represented include the "Tayfuria Sufi order" named after Bistami, and the Junaydiyya. The Chishti figureheads receive more attention, but always very briefly, and merely in terms of names (Zar Zari Zar Bakhsh is one of those listed).

(20) Warren 1999:288. The same song also promotes the belief that "Sai Baba operates on two planes, in Shirdi and all over the world" (ibid). Another line states: "His speech is like that of Maulana Gausul Ajaya Dastgir" (ibid), now a rather obscure entity.

(21) Warren 1999:278.

(22) Warren 1999:279. The eclectic fusion of terms from different religious traditions is also found in the affirmation: "If you perform *upasana* according to the way prescribed, then only *Allah* will accept it" (ibid:286-287). The Sanskrit word *upasana* means worship. The same passage states that the *Vedas* and *Quran* have been transmitted "for this [purpose] alone" (ibid:287).

(23) Warren 1999:279.

(24) Ibid:280. The same passage includes a reflection that "the Islamic religious law (*sharia*) does not permit any further probe into reality" (ibid). Nevertheless, spiritual practices lead to *marifa*, translated here as "realisation of God." Yet, understanding of personal thought should come before the efforts in practise. Progress is associated with "the kingdom of the heart," a theme which is not explained in detail.

(25) Warren 1999:281.

(26) Shepherd 2015:300–303. Wordings like "Who are we?" can be read in different ways. The tendency to associate this phrase with the meditation processes of Vedanta is not necessarily accurate.

(27) Warren 1999:281-2.

(28) Warren 1999:283.

(29) Warren 1999:283. The ethical emphases of Sai Baba were pronounced, and also feature in recorded responses to Hindu devotees.

(30) Warren 1999:287. The extent to which Abdul interpolated is uncertain. The disorganised format of the *Notebook* does not readily invite any contention that the compiler was trying to systematise his jottings.

(31) Warren 1999:287. The word *avatar* appears to be employed rather loosely in the *Notebook*. The same passage states: "There are thousands of *avatars* in the Kaliyuga." There is a concession also to explicit Hindu origins of the word. "According to the conception of the Hindus from Vedic times, *avatars* rule and exercise great powers" (ibid). The two most famous *avatars* in Hinduism were Rama and Krishna, who became extensively legendised. Both of these are mentioned briefly in the *Notebook,* along with other names.

(32) Warren 1999:288. The song affirms an early belief in the abilities of Sai Baba, who "operates on two planes, in Shirdi and all over the world" (ibid). The date of composition is elusive. A belief in omnipresence can be found in the reports of some devotees.

(33) Ibid:289. Cf. the translation by V. B. Kher: "Amir, a Muslim devotee, wishes to sing the praises of Sai Baba but does he have the capacity to do so? Sai Baba's *durbar* is that of a *Kalandar* (Muslim fakir). It is not a *Math* (monastery) of a Hindu Swami. His slave Abdul regards him as his *Murshid*" (Anand 1997:19 note 2). The rather ambiguous reference to Amir apparently means Amir

Shakkar Dalal. These lines come from a *qawwali* or song by Abdul that is included in the *Notebook*.

(34) Warren interprets the reference of Abdul to mean that the Shirdi assembly of devotees was "a Court of *qalandars*, or *faqirs*, and Sai Baba was the arch-*faqir* holding court for people coming to petition him for particular blessings" (Warren 1999:331). The word *qalandar* has a more radical connotation than *faqir*, but Warren does not mention this factor. The audience of Sai Baba was largely Hindu, and many visitors did indeed petition him for benefits. The description of the Shirdi mosque assembly in terms of a *darbar* (royal court) was favoured by Hindus during the saint's last years. In general, Warren attempts to argue for the Sufi orthodoxy of Sai Baba, and to downplay radical associations such as *qalandar*. She tries to invoke the Chishti Order as a reference point, but admits that "no definite link can be made" (ibid:328). She nevertheless suggests that "Sai Baba had some connection with Chishtis as he was so fond of music" (ibid). This association is too tenuous to be convincing. She also says that "his familiarity with Rumi's poetry and song is highly suggestive of some influence" (ibid). The extent of his familiarity with Rumi is not known. Many Indian Muslims were familiar with verses of Rumi, but were not necessarily affiliates of Sufi Orders.

(35) Shepherd 2014:97ff. A distinctive *qalandar* was Shams Tabrizi, an inspirer of Rumi who was disliked by the latter's orthodox associates. "We may assume, following Golpinarli, that he [Shams] was in fact a *qalandar*, a wandering dervish without proper affiliation" (Schimmel 1993:19–20).

(36) Warren 1999:297. The earliest known account of the Sufi hierarchy is found in the *Kashf al-Mahjub* of Hujwiri, dating to the eleventh century (Nicholson 1936:213–14). This version refers to "four thousand who are concealed," three hundred *akhyar*, forty *abdal*, seven *abrar*, three *nuqaba*, and four *awtad*. Only one *qutub* is specified. In contrast, Sai Baba refers to thirteen *qutubs*, seven higher *abdal* and 357 lower *abdal*, of whom forty are *abrar*. He also mentions three hundred *nuqaba*, four *awtad*, and four thousand *mikwana*. The *Notebook* also refers to other categories of saint not found in Hujwiri.

(37) Warren 1999:300. A form of nocturnal vigil was fairly common amongst the more dedicated Sufis. Abdul was instructed by Sai Baba to keep awake at night and to read the *Quran*. He had to

meditate on what he read and also upon Sai Baba. Many years later, he disclosed such details in an interview of 1936 with Narasimhaswami. This interview was reported in the latter's book *Devotees' Experiences of Sri Sai Baba*.

(38) Warren 1999:300. The *Notebook* here refers to "the poet Shiraz" and "Maulana Shiraz." The quotation has been identified as coming from Rumi. An earlier page of the *Notebook* refers to "Maulana Rumi." The passage reads: "Maulana Rumi says that the observance of severe austerity, is a prerequisite for attaining higher levels of spirituality" (ibid). Another quotation from Rumi appears on a further page, and commences: "A man should honour and have respect for great spiritual people who should be considered to be the best of creatures" (ibid:298). The poet is again identified here as "Maulana Rumi." The same identification occurs on yet another page of the manuscript, listed as K40 (ibid:298).

(39) Warren 1999:300. There is no indication in the text as to whom Sai Baba was referring. The idiom is very disapproving. Other documentation attests that not all Sufi *pirs* in India were exemplary. Richard Burton reported the situation in Sind during the mid-nineteenth century, where many *pirs* were landowners and could have a hundred servants, and as many horses (Shepherd 2014:16). Landowner Sufis existed in other regions of India also, including Gujarat and the Deccan. They were representatives of various Sufi Orders.

(40) Warren 1999:301. The *Notebook* translation says: "These people regard the dance and song of the prostitute etc., as the best of Sufi (Chishti) mode of worship." The Chishti associations might indicate that Sai Baba was criticising the Chishti Order, in this respect, concerning a particular mode of dance and song. He was obviously complaining about some form of behaviour or habit. One should add that the tendency to song and dance was not in favour amongst all Sufi Orders. The overall criticism Sai Baba made of "false *pirs* and *faqirs*" is open-ended, in that we do not know precisely who he was referring to. It is, however, possible to conclude that the "dangerous wall of the world" (ibid:300) has implications for landowner Sufis and closely related persons. The *Notebook* warns: "Do not be a broker in this world, otherwise you will not gain the wealth of the other world" (ibid:301). See also note 39 above.

(41) Warren 1999:300. The warning from Sai Baba is strong. He evidently wanted the "dangerous wall" to be removed. On the

preceding page of the *Notebook*, the virtue of "renunciation" is approved, in a context meaning that "a man embodying these qualities is fit to be a *murshid*" (ibid). In other communications, Sai Baba is known to have referred to his own obscure teacher as a *murshid*. That Arabic word is rendered elliptically in some reports, e.g., Mowrshad.

(42) Narasimhaswami 1942:275. Narasimhaswami was largely ignorant of the *Notebook* contents, which can be viewed as supplying an alternative, and perhaps more relevant, key to the context of pulling down a wall (between the aspirant and the *murshid*). The *Notebook* languished for generations before gaining a translation. Narasimhaswami knew of that work, but he could not read Marathi or Urdu at the time he encountered Abdul in 1936. He never learned to read Urdu. The early Marathi diaries of H. S. Dixit include a reference to visitors who wanted to take a photograph of Sai Baba. They had to wait without success for two days, and then asked Shama to intercede for them. Shama advised them to greet Sai Baba when he returned from the Lendi. They complied with this cue, and Sai Baba then briefly relayed to Shama: "There is no need to take my photo. To know my Real Form, they just need to break the wall of difference between us." Sai then quickly moved away to the mosque. Dixit attributes feelings of duality (*dvaita*) to the petitioners. This episode became well known via Narasimhaswami, who favoured a Vedantic interpretation of Sai Baba's remark, which has been variously translated. Cf. Shepherd 2015:300-303.

(43) Warren 1999:306.

(44) Warren 1999:301. The reference to *pirzada* is revealing as to what the Shirdi *faqir* is complaining about. This category were landowning Sufis, whose hereditary status was closely linked to the role of Sufi shrines as mediators of *barakat* or spiritual power. See Appendix I in the present book. The *sayyad* was a descendant of the Prophet Muhammmad, with varying degrees of repute in the pedigree claimed. The *shaikh* was a teacher, frequently the representative of a Sufi Order.

(45) Warren 1999:301–302. The word *ivadat*, or *ibadat*, means "worship" (usually of God). Prayer is one form of worship; there are many others, such as singing the praises of God, serving humanity, and so forth. According to one definition, the Arabic word *ibadat* means "the canonical rites through which the relationship of the

worshipper (*'abd*) is expressed" (Trimingham 1971:304). The same scholar also interprets *ibadat*, in the Sufi context, as "devotion expressed in the traditional *zahiri* [externalist] way" (ibid).

(46) Warren 1999:308. This liberal statement reflects a tendency of some unorthodox Sufis during the generations after the Mughal monarch Akbar. It was the type of assertion appealing to *qalandars* and *majzubs* like Sarmad, an almost incredible figure executed by Islamic orthodoxy in the seventeenth century. Sarmad was an Islamised Jew who adopted the basic lifestyle of a *naga sadhu*, but with the addition of a philosophical background (derived from Iran) of a type that was comparatively rare in India. His confrontation with the prestigious adviser of Aurangzeb reportedly involved a provocative pun. That adviser (and *Qazi-ul-Quzzat*) was Itimad Khan Mulla Abdul Qawi, who loathed the *naga* practice of nudity. Sarmad would not agree to abandoning this practice, and commented "Satan is Qawi" (Shepherd 1988:133). The shock word *qawi* here meant "powerful." This idiom may be compared with Sai Baba's use of the word Satan in reference to duplicitous pseudo-Sufis, whom he called "Satans in human form" (Warren 1999:300).

(47) Shepherd 2014. There are some resemblances, and also differences, between Sai Baba and Hazrat Babajan. For instance, the matriarch of Poona was averse to the act of *darshan* homage on the part of Hindus, whereas Sai Baba eventually accommodated Hindu worship at his mosque in Shirdi. Nevertheless, Babajan gained numerous Hindu devotees.

(48) Haeri 2000:172, here distinguishing two types of *qalandar*. Hamid Qalandar wore "the saffron robe of the *qalandar*," but did not belong to "the breed of wild, itinerant *qalandars*, who roamed the land" (ibid). Hamid Qalandar was a devotee of the Chishti saint Nasiruddin Mahmud Chiragh-i-Delhi (d.1356). Hamid is described as being "in the *qalandar* tradition," remaining a celibate and owning no personal property (ibid). He was the author of *Khair al-Majalis*, recording conversations of his teacher.

(49) Shepherd 1988:118,122–35. The Italian traveller Niccolao Manucci "viewed Sarmad as an atheist who went about Delhi naked, save when in courtly company, at which times he would wear a more respectable loincloth" (ibid:124). There were many *naga sadhus* in North India, and Sarmad evidently preferred

Notes

their approach to that of eminent divines. At Delhi, Sarmad was patronised by the Mughal prince Dara Shikoh.

(50) H. K. Sherwani and P. M. Joshi, eds., *History of Medieval Deccan Vol. 1*, cited in Kher 2001:60.

(51) Shepherd 2015:22–37.

(52) Dabholkar 1999:65. Cf. the version of Sathya Sai Baba, which was reported by Swami Sai Sharan Anand at a fairly early date (Anand 1997:10). This version depicts the parents as Gangabhav and Devagiramma, who are said to have lived at Pathri. These two are described as devotees of Shiva-Parvati. "Bhagwan Shankar subjected them to a trial a number of times but they stood the test." As a consequence, Shiva took birth in their family as the third son, meaning Sai Baba. However, the parents retired into the forest for penance, "leaving the child Sai under a tree." A passing *faqir* and his wife adopted the boy, rearing him until the age of twelve. Anand observes that this story related to the declaration of Sathya Sai that he was a reincarnation of Shirdi Sai. The saint of Shirdi here became an avatar of Shiva, and a major support to the controversial avatar role of Sathya Sai Baba.

(53) Dabholkar 1999:73. Chand Patel is profiled, in the *Shri Sai Satcharita*, as an inhabitant of Dhupkhed who lost his mare during a journey to nearby Aurangabad. In the vicinity of that city, he encountered a *faqir* seated under a mango tree. The *faqir* was Sai Baba. V. B. Kher remarks that this account "seems to be based on hearsay." However, the story is to some extent supported by the testimony of Ramgiri Bua, a Shirdi villager who heard Patel describe the episode. The *faqir* had a *dhuni* fire burning, and told the wayfarer about the location of his horse, enabling the animal to be recovered. Kher emphasises that Ramgiri did not recollect any further content, meaning the miracle story, attending this incident, about lighting a pipe (Kher 2001:21–23). According to a relative of Chand Patel, Sai Baba stayed for some years in the village of Dhupkhed, before accompanying the marriage party of Chand Patel to Shirdi (ibid:25–26; cf. Kamath and Kher 1991:75–77). Kher also connects this data to the report of Swami Sai Sharan Anand that Sai Baba left home at the age of eight to travel with a *faqir*, eventually reaching Aurangabad. This detail originated with Sai Baba himself. In the Dixit memoir, Chand Patel is called "Chandbhai, the Patil," and the miracle of the pipe is included (Pradhan 1933).

(54) Dabholkar 1999:57.

(55) Dabholkar 1999:67. The disposition of Sai Baba to jokes is confirmed in the *Shirdi Diary* of Khaparde. For instance, on December 17, 1911, "he [Sai] was in a very good mood, and we enjoyed very much the jokes made by him."

(56) Dabholkar 1999:75.

(57) Das Ganu 2007:38.

(58) Kher 2001:17, relaying the report of Ramgiri Bua, found in Narasimhaswami's book *Devotees' Experiences of Sri Sai Baba*.

(59) Dabholkar 1999:75.

(60) Warren 1999:43-44, who awards some deference to the Mhalsapati "legend."

(61) Dabholkar 1999:75.

(62) The trend of "Hinduisation" was lamented by Warren, who pointed out some omissions occurring as a consequence. In this respect, a number of books have to be treated with caution on various points of exegesis. Warren made criticisms of such works as Ruhela's *What Researchers Say on Sri Shirdi Sai Baba* (Faridabad, 1994). Satya Pal Ruhela reviewed forty "researchers" on Sai Baba. This was more venturesome than numerous other works on the subject. Unfortunately, many of those "researchers" would not qualify as analytical assessors in any university sense of the word "research." Complications arise when basic factors are ignored. Warren remarks of *Researchers* that: "Although it purports to be an academic endeavour, from a scholarly point of view it is very imprecise in its research, not giving sufficient detail with regard to: original dates of publication; original language and translations; biographies of the contributors; other books written by the contributors; current availability of these books; or the details of additions and changes made to revised editions" (Warren 1999:19). Perhaps more to the point, *Researchers* "unfortunately makes no distinction between major contributions and minor works" (ibid). Also very relevant is the observation that "Ruhela quotes hagiographical stories as fact, and information given by Sathya Sai Baba about Shirdi Sai Baba without any qualification" (ibid). Indeed, any responsible researcher must treat blatantly hagiographical material with reservation (Warren herself had a difficulty in this respect). Many of the episodes and "stories" told about Shirdi Sai need careful evaluation, and Sathya Sai's version

is no exception. Sathya Sai Baba is one of the "researchers" in the presentation of Ruhela. In general, there are known instances of confusion in some reports about Sai Baba, where, for instance, one devotee is mistaken for another, and where attributions are made on the basis of mere association. The poet Das Ganu is an example of a writer who expressed some questionable attributions. Yet he also figures as one of the "researchers" in the Ruhela book. Warren critically quotes Ruhela: "Das Ganu's findings have stood the test of time; all these are today believed to be cent per cent true by all Sai devotees and researchers on Baba's divine life" (Warren 1999:19). This is a substantial error that has misled many readers. Both Bharadwaja and V. B. Kher had questioned the legend of Gopalrao Deshmukh created by Das Ganu. Kher convincingly rejected the story of Gopalrao as the guru of Sai Baba (Kher 2001:36–52). Other scholars, including Warren and Rigopoulos, have supported Kher. More popular versions continue to confuse the matter.

(63) Rizvi 1978:194.

(64) Rizvi 1978:195.

(65) Mujeeb 1967:68.

(66) Mujeeb 1967:70. The word *kuffar* is the plural for *kafir*. The same commentator observes that the *jizya* tax "was regarded as a punishment for their refusal [of the *kuffar*] to accept Islam, and was to be levied from each person in such a way as to demonstrate his abject subservience" (ibid). This tax "came to be looked upon by the Hindus as a symbol of religious intolerance and social discrimination" (ibid).

(67) Rizvi 1978:181; Haeri 2000:148–9. Zarradi is reported to have shaved his head and adopted a lifestyle of celibacy. Nizamuddin Awliya himself was a celibate *shaikh*, by no means a common event within Sufi Orders. Zarradi was engaged to be married at the time of meeting Awliya. The transition evidently involved a strong impact upon his mind.

(68) Rizvi 1978:166.

(69) Kher 2001:1–12, and urging that his theory of Haribhau Bhusari is probable. There is nothing definite in this theory. "Could it not be that Haribhau Bhusari was Sai Baba? I wonder" (ibid:12). From another angle, Swami Sai Sharan Anand was also enthusiastic about a Hindu identity for the Shirdi saint (Anand 1962; Anand 1997). According to Anand: "It is indisputable that Sai Baba regarded

himself as a Brahmin" (Anand 1997:10). However, this contention has been doubted by many others.

(70) Warren 1999:90.

(71) Flood 1996:144.

(72) Rigopoulos 2011. See also Zelliot 1988. The Mahanubhavs had become a persecuted and isolated body by the time of Eknath, who lived in the sixteenth century (Zelliot 1987:102). They were suspected of being licentious, probably because of their nuns. Orthodox biases against female renouncers, as candidates for spiritual liberation, are not attractive. This ongoing problem surfaced in the later years of Upasani Maharaj, when detractors misrepresented his creation of the Kanya Kumari Sthan at Sakori.

(73) Zelliot 1987:102.

(74) Novetzke 2008:44.

(75) Novetzke 2008:52.

(76) Novetzke 2008:41.

(77) Novetzke 2008:54–55.

(78) See further Ranade 1982.

(79) Abbott 1933:377ff.

(80) Zelliot 1987:108 note 29, and observing that the subsequent mass conversion to Buddhism in 1956, led by the untouchable leader Dr. Ambedkar, claimed most of the Mahars. Scholarly arguments about theses of Ambedkar are of some interest. Ambedkar's evocative book *The Untouchables* (Delhi 1948), has been accused of idealising the role of Buddhism in the evolution of untouchability, contradicting evidence in this regard. The *Pali Canon* and the *Jatakas* are Buddhist texts which corroborate, and supplement, the information from brahmanical sources. In the *Jatakas*, apartheid is strictly observed in relation to the *chandala*, and the taboo on accepting food from that rejected social category is inflexible. The only escape from this lifelong fate is via renunciation or joining the Buddhist monastic order. The existence of high and very low castes was becoming fully recognised towards the end of the Vedic period. There are voices of dissent, not only in the Buddhist and Jain texts, but also in the literature of Hinduism (e.g., *Brihadaranyaka Upanishad* 4.3.22; *Bhagavad Gita*, 5.18). However, the caste system was generally accepted and supported (Jha 1975:21ff). The same scholar urges that the subsequent phase of Mahayana

Notes

Buddhism developed a set of "intensely prized taboos," besides those shared with Hinduism. The *Shaddharmapundarika* explicitly prohibited contact with the *chandala*. Fear of pollution from the *matanga*, associated with the cremation ground, is strongly reflected in texts of Jainism. The untouchable castes were resented for the habit of meat-eating (ibid:31).

(81) Zelliot 1987:91.

(82) Zelliot 1987:96.

(83) Warren 1999:133, and citing Tulpule 1979. Recovering the history in these episodes is not easy. Tulpule probes the story provided by Eknath about Dattatreya appearing to him as a Sufi ascetic. Tulpule "argues that identifying Eknath's *guru* Janardhan Swami as a Hindu 'is a clever twist of the historical truth' [on the part of Eknath] in order to hide the fact that his *guru* was a Qadiri Sufi" (Warren 199:133). The implication is that Eknath traced his inspiration to Dattatreya because he intended, in this way, to avoid a conflict with orthodox *brahmans*.

(84) Zelliot 1987:94.

(85) Zelliot 1987:94.

(86) Warren 1999:136, and citing B. Nemade, *Tukaram* (New Delhi, 1980).

(87) Zelliot 1987:96. Eknath mentions some fifty *sants* in his various works (ibid:94).

(88) Zelliot 1987:107.

(89) Zelliot 1987:107.

(90) Fraser and Edwards, 1922; Chitre 1991; Ranade 1994; Eaton 2005:129ff. Different dates are given for the birth of Tukaram, including 1598 and 1608. There are strong doubts about the authenticity of many *abhangas* attributed to Tukaram. Marathi manuscripts of his poems reveal variations, and some poems are found in only one collection.

(91) The Varkari *panth* is today the biggest movement of this kind in Maharashtra, whereas "the Nath tradition survives only at a folk level of stories of nine Naths and their miracles" (Zelliot 1987:97).

(92) Flood 1996:143.

(93) Warren 1999:131, and citing K. A. Nizami, *Some Aspects of Religion and Politics in India during the Thirteenth Century* (Aligarh 1961). Another argument sometimes found is that many low caste

Hindus became Muslim converts, seeking to escape the afflictions imposed by both Islam and the brahmanical system. With regard to textual references concerning conversion, there are difficulties. For instance, British gazetteers "greatly exaggerated the role of Sufis in converting Hindus to Islam" (Ernst 1992:99). The same scholar affirms that the image of Sufis as missionaries was largely based on two late trends of interpretation, meaning "Mughul imperialism, which recast Sufis into the role of proclaimers of Mughul sovereignty, and the missionary Protestantism of British administrators" (ibid:99–100). In an earlier era, "the Khuldabad *malfuzat* texts scarcely permit one to form any picture of the relations between the Sufis and non-Muslims. The most specific reference to any non-Muslim is the occasional mention of yogis, who are regarded as alchemists (possibly fraudulent ones) with advanced knowledge of medicine and the body" (ibid:161). Professor Carl Ernst also reflects: "The first references to missionary activities among the Khuldabad Sufis come, predictably, in late biographical texts suffused with touches of imperial historiography" (ibid:164). The chronology here decodes to the seventeenth and eighteenth centuries. The use of Indian vernacular dialects by Sufis is another issue. "The immense weight of received opinion has led many to assume that the Sufis wrote in Indian languages in order to convert Indians to Islam" (ibid:166). Ernst is clearly sceptical of this assumption.

(94) Eaton 1993. In the thirteenth century, thousands of Muslim theologians and others fled to the Punjab from the Mongol invasions afflicting Central Asia and Iran. These immigrants are strongly implicated in a conversion drive. In Bengal, the outcastes proved responsive converts to Islam. Other converts were found amongst forest and pastoral peoples who were not actually Hindus, and who are now described as indigenous non-agriculturalists. Professor Richard Eaton has concluded that these non-Hindu Indians gradually became Muslim agriculturalists between the twelfth and seventeenth centuries.

(95) Warren 1999:170.

(96) Warren 1999:169. The issue of temple destruction is attended by markedly different assessments. Some claim to find evidence for the destruction of thousands of Hindu temples by Muslims. In contrast, Professor Eaton affirms that only politically relevant temples were eliminated by Islam. The total number of temples destroyed, from

the twelfth to the eighteenth centuries, here emerges as being less than a hundred (Eaton 2004).

(97) Warren 1999:170. Cf. Rigopoulos 2011:91, who describes Shah Muni as a Muslim *bhakti* poet well acquainted with Hindu theologians, and who had a partiality for Mahanubhav doctrine (because of the element of monotheism). The author further comments that some kind of mutual exchange between Mahanubhavs and Muslims undoubtedly occurred, especially with Sufis. Rigopoulos cites another commentator who is insistent that Shah Muni was a Mahanubhav. The *Siddhanta Bodha* is here viewed as containing a mixture of Mahanubhava teaching, Advaita, and Puranic stories.

(98) Warren 1999:158.

(99) Dabholkar 1999:62.

(100) Narasimhaswami 1942:36; Narasimhaswami 2006:136; Shepherd 2015:221–226. Narasimhaswami is realistic on such points. The repute of Das Ganu amongst Sai Baba devotees, in the early period, led to a substantial lack of critical assessment. Narasimhaswami avoided the glamour, despite his known appreciation of Das Ganu's poetry. In 1945, Narasimhaswami expressed a more unguarded assessment of Das Ganu, in terms of "the foremost of those who met Shri Sai Baba and still continue to broadcast his fame" (Das Ganu 2007, unpaginated Preface to First Edition, dated 1945). In *Charters and Sayings*, Narasimhaswami reported such events as: "Das Ganu gladly went to Pandharpur for Asvin, as Vittal of Pandri alone was God to him and not [Sai] Baba" (page 36). Cf. McLain 2016:54–90, for a chapter on Das Ganu entitled "Shirdi is my Pandharpur." Das Ganu extolled Shirdi and Sai Baba, but the criticism from Narasimhaswami is not thereby invalidated. Professor Karline McLain has a version of Narasimhaswami's influence on the Shirdi Sai movement (ibid:91-132).

(101) Dabholkar 1999:62. Soon afterwards, a man from another village came to Shirdi in the hope of selling pictures of "Vithoba of Pandharpur." Dixit was surprised to find the exact replica of the Vitthala he had seen in his meditation. As a consequence, he purchased one of the pictures and installed this in his *puja* room. Dabholkar emphasises "Sai's reverence towards the worship of Vitthal" (ibid:63). However, Sai Baba was also inclined to point out that devotees did not need to go to Pandharpur for communion with the deity, who could be found in Shirdi, even in a mosque.

(102) Dabholkar 1999:59.

(103) Dabholkar 1999:61.

(104) Dabholkar 1999:165.

(105) Narasimhaswami 2002:199.

(106) Dabholkar 1999:77. The passage refers to the devotee Vaman Tatya supplying Sai Baba daily with two earthen pitchers containing water, which was used for gardening. This activity appears to have been more protracted than the three years mentioned in the *Satcharita*. See further Shepherd 2015:97–98.

(107) Dabholkar 1999:67.

(108) Kher 2001:48. In contrast, many other books have repeated the beliefs about Gopalrao Deshmukh, thus contributing to widespread confusion. Kher points out that "a clear gap of thirty-six years" occurred between the death of Gopalrao and the birth of Sai Baba, even if the earlier date of birth (i.e., 1838) is favoured. "All this clearly shows that Das Ganu has no sense of time" (ibid).

(109) Kher 2001:64–5. Kher has slightly abbreviated the details of this episode. The convert's new name was Ibrahim, and the person who brought him to the mosque was the Muslim *faqir* Bade Baba (Shepherd 2015:157). We do not know if Bade Baba was directly responsible for the conversion. Bade Baba arrived at Shirdi in 1909, and the conversion episode occurred sometime after that.

(110) Ghani 1939:51.

(111) Shepherd 1986:11–12. The Khuldabad phase remains obscure and undated (Shepherd 2015:39), but is nevertheless relevant for consideration. The geography does fit other references to the Aurangabad region in connection with the early years of Sai Baba. Khuldabad was situated on the border of an extensive territory ruled by the Nizam of Hyderabad.

(112) Kher 2001:57. This contention was derived from literature of the Meher Baba movement. According to Kher, during the early years of Sai Baba, he "came to know many *faqirs*" in the Aurangabad region. Kher also urges that Bade Baba was the *faqir* "whom Sai Baba instructed for 12 years in Aurangabad" (ibid:59). A basic account here is the *Shirdi Diary* of Khaparde (ibid:55). However, Khaparde does not say that Sai gave instruction to Bade Baba. Instead, Sai begged for an old *faqir*, keeping him supplied with food for twelve years (*Shirdi Diary* entry dated December 30, 1911). Khaparde does

say that the *faqir* "came here [to Shirdi] a few years ago and lodged at the *chavadi.*" No further identity is supplied. If the Aurangabad *faqir* was old, as the source states, then it less likely that Bade Baba was the same person. Sai Baba was a young man during the period associated with Aurangabad. Bade Baba does not appear to have been much older than the saint of Shirdi, and was perhaps even a junior.

(113) Kamath and Kher 1991:291-2.

(114) Kher 2001:47.

(115) Das Ganu 2007:1-31.

(116) Cf. Rigopoulos 1993:9-14.

(117) Warren reports that the *saka* dates of 1600-1723 for Gopalrao are "clearly written on the wall of the Kesavarao Mandir in the town of Selu. . . . I witnessed this inscription myself during a field trip to Selu in 1990" (Warren 1999:39). Those dates translate to *circa* 1678-1801 in terms of the Christian era. An elaborate myth was created from "Das Ganu's weak research and then merely repeated over and over again by the majority of the secondary writers on Sai Baba" (ibid). Das Ganu pinned his theory about Gopalrao on the coincidence of a name. On one occasion, when making some allusive remarks, Sai Baba said that his guru was named Venkusha (Shepherd 2015:190). Das Ganu discovered that Gopalrao Deshmukh had the nickname of Venkusha, and assumed that Gopalrao was the same entity as Sai Baba's guru (Warren 1999:38).

(118) Shepherd 2015:106-110. The marginalised Jindewali (Jawahar Ali) requires a flexible interpretation, avoiding the rather obvious religious strictures visible in the standard version.

(119) Dabholkar 1999:727. The term *nirvikalpa samadhi* has acquired different interpretations. This phrase is a fairly common attribution, but often lacking in adequate description. According to Arthur Osborne, the term means "samadhi in a state of trance, with suspension of the human faculties" (Osborne 1954:203). The same book also employs the description: "complete absorption in the Self with resultant oblivion to the manifested world" (ibid:45). A higher state is called *sahaj samadhi*. Certain other expositors, including Meher Baba, do not refer to *nirvikalpa* in terms of trance.

(120) Dabholkar 1999:727.

(121) Dabholkar 1999:728.

(122) Kamath and Kher 1991:7. The dateline here given, for Kulkarni becoming a devotee, is "by 1878." Some episodes concerning Appa Kulkarni appear in the literature. At one time, a hostile party in Shirdi filed a complaint against him for misappropriation of funds. Kulkarni approached Sai Baba for assistance, denying the allegation. The *faqir* told him to comply with the official demands by visiting the Deputy Collector at Nevasa. However, he should first go to the "temple of Mohiniraj" at Nevasa (Nevase), "bow to the Lord and give your explanation to Him," and then visit the revenue office. The Deputy Collector decided that he was innocent. Kulkarni returned to Shirdi, and praised Sai for assisting him. The *faqir* would not take credit for this exoneration, and instead exclaimed: "What did I do? It is Narayana who gets things done. He makes impossible things possible for a devotee" (ibid:199). It is conceivable that the name of God represented here was translated from another word.

(123) Dabholkar 1999:729.

(124) Rigopoulos 1993:91–2.

(125) Warren 1999:45. According to this scholar: "After 1886, when he [Sai] apparently 'died' and came back to life after having an experience of mystical union with God, he became one of the *awliya* [saints]" (ibid:47). This version clashes with a rival theory (of Kalchuri) that high mystical achievement occurred at an earlier date, meaning the 1850s. There is currently no way of establishing such factors. See further Shepherd 2015:47,111-113, 351–2 note 58.

(126) The early Muslim commentator Dr. Abdul Ghani supplied a rather ambiguous reference. He affirms that Sai Baba early "contacted another saint near Akkalkot." No name is given. A footnote comments: "The renowned Swami of Akkalkot was Sai Baba's contemporary, and though the latter was spiritually connected with him, no other relationship as that of a Master or disciple existed between them" (Ghani 1939:51). Some readers believed that the saint contacted must have been Swami Samarth, but the clarification can be interpreted as meaning to the contrary.

(127) Bharadwaja 1994. Swami Samarth is probably one of the most interesting figures in nineteenth century Hinduism. He was photographed at an early date, apparently between 1860–1875, and a number of his images exist. Stories about him appeared in Bombay newspapers, prompting the Kodak Company to speculate that his image would be good for their business. He gained some interest

from Theosophists, as a consequence of Colonel Olcott's sojourn at Akkalkot after the saint's death. Swami Samarth was reputedly very tall, and generally wore only a loincloth (*kaupina*). Some of his habits were eccentric. He was patronised by a local aristocrat, namely Maloji Bhonsale.

(128) Narasimhaswami 1942:12.

(129) Kher 2001:112. This commentator states categorically: "Neither of them [Swami Samarth and Sai Baba] would accept disciples or give initiation" (ibid).

(130) Dabholkar 1999:158.

(131) A Western commentator construed from these details "the general impression of an assiduous practice of *hatha-yoga* on Baba's part, reproposing the [Charles White] hypothesis of a training in which Natha influences might have played a role" (Rigopoulos 1993:47). Such assumptions have led to fantastic conjectures about Yoga practices at Shirdi. Rigopoulos cites from Gunaji's 1944 adaptation of the *Satcharita*, which questionably asserts that Sai Baba "practised Yoga since his infancy." There is no proof that Sai Baba practised Hatha Yoga at any period of his life. Hatha Yoga was a speciality of the Nath Yogis. The theory of Charles White (1972) is rejected by some analysts as a simplistic version ignoring more tangible data.

(132) Shepherd 2015:241–243. See also chapter 27 in the present book.

(133) Lawrence 1978:53. Sayyid Ashraf Jahangir Simnani was originally the ruler of Simnan, in Iran. He abdicated to become a follower of Ala ad-daula as-Simnani (d.1336), who opposed the *wujudi* teaching of Ibn al-Arabi. However, Sayyid Ashraf was afterwards known as a staunch advocate of *wahdat al-wujud*. He moved to Central Asia and India, eventually settling in Bengal. Sayyid Ashraf maintained a close connection with the ruler of Jaunpur, Sultan Ibrahim Sharqi (Elias 1995:49). His *Lataif-i Ashrafi* has been described as "the most voluminous single *malfuzat* collection attributed to an Indian saint" (Lawrence 1978:53–4).

(134) Dabholkar 1999:78.

(135) Dabholkar 1999:79.

(136) Anand 1997:80; Kamath and Kher 1991:126; Shepherd 2015:128–130. The town of Sangamner was about thirty-five miles south of Shirdi.

(137) Kamath and Kher 1991:7. In the later years of Sai Baba, numerous devotees came from places like Bombay, Nasik, Poona, Kalyan, Nagpur, Amraoti, Nanded, Jamner, Thane, Sholapur, Pandharpur, and Madras. Many of the Hindu devotees apparently belonged to "Brahmin, Kayastha, and Bania communities" (Srinivas 2008:38).

(138) Narasimhaswami 2006:262ff. Chandorkar was a resident of Kalyan, and originally a *chitnis* in government service before becoming a *mamlatdar*. The Shirdi devotee Appa Kulkarni (alias Keshav Anant) told Chandorkar that Sai Baba had invited him to visit. At first Chandorkar did not believe this, but afterwards went to Shirdi for *darshan*. He soon became a devotee, and visited Shirdi frequently, sometimes being in the presence of Sai Baba for hours at a time (Pradhan 1933).

(139) Narasimhaswami 2006:216. This theory is in conflict with other materials such as the *Notebook* of Abdul Baba. Sai Baba was an Urdu-speaker. The *Satcharita* also relays that the saint constantly chanted *Allah Malik* (Dabholkar 1999:372). The devotee Raghuvir B. Purandhare testified that Sai would repeat Islamic phrases "often and at all times" (Narasimhaswami 2006:83; abridged passage in Warren 1999:168). Confirming other versions, Hari Dixit reported that Sai Baba would at times utter the phrase "*Yade Haqq*," translated by Pradhan as "I always remember God" (Pradhan 1933). Another significant detail is that the Shirdi *faqir* was in the habit of reciting *al-Fatihah*, the brief opening chapter of the *Quran* (Narasimhaswami 2006:10; Shepherd 2015:157). The Arabic, Persian, and Urdu ingredients of the saint's vocabulary do not indicate a *brahman* ancestry.

(140) Warren 1999:357.

(141) Warren 1999:357.

(142) See also Warren 1999:410–414.

(143) Dabholkar 1999:648.

(144) Warren 1999:358.

(145) Dabholkar 1999:818.

(146) Dabholkar 1999:818. The *Shri Sai Leela* magazine, in the 1920s, was originally a monthly publication, being managed by the editors Hari Dixit and Govind Dabholkar. These two made the journal an economically successful organ of the Shirdi Sansthan. When they died, the edge was lost, and the magazine became a quarterly (Pradhan 1933).

Notes

(147) Dabholkar 1999:820.

(148) Dabholkar 1999:525–526. In more general terms, the *Shri Sai Satcharita* confirms that numerous social categories existed amongst the visitors to Shirdi. This means "clerks and officials of the district, traders, businessmen, doctors, pleaders, advocates, magistrates, commission agents, priests, Muslims, Brahmins, Kayasthas, Prarthana-Samajists, Agnihotras, Hajis, Parsis, Irani gentlemen, and Indian National Congress members" (Srinivas 2008:38).

(149) Dabholkar 1999:845.

(150) Dabholkar 1999:107.

(151) Dabholkar 1999:534.

(152) Dabholkar 1999:534. The significance of *udi* was frequently emphasised by devotee commentators, including Anand 1997:265–8, who refers to cures (via *udi*) of mental disorders, the influence of drugs, lunacy, nightmare, labour pains, cholera, tuberculosis, paralysis, diabetes, typhoid, pneumonia, insomnia, snakebite, scorpion stings, and other afflictions. The list seems almost endless. As a young devotee (then Waman Patel), Anand stayed at Shirdi for nearly a year during 1913-14. Anand believed that Sai Baba was a Hindu, and more specifically, a member of the *brahman* caste. Anand became a *sannnyasin* in 1953, and died in 1982. See the biographical sketch of Anand by V. B. Kher, in Anand 1997:xi–xviii, and reporting here that Anand's main work *Shri Sai Baba* was very popular in Gujarat, achieving six editions by 1966.

(153) Dabholkar 1999:529.

(154) Dabholkar 1999:529. The same passage refers to "the skill of my Fakir, the *leela* of my Bhagavan." The original words are unknown.

(155) Dabholkar 1999:529. The translation has the words: "My Master says, 'Take, O take this away!' " The context can serve to comprise a warning against the emphasis on miracle cures favoured by some writers, including Ramalingaswami 1984, which provides a variety of stories and anecdotes. A total of 101 miracle stories are allocated here to the pre-*mahasamadhi* phase, while a further 100 are post-*mahasamadhi* stories. Each story ends with the refrain of: "Surrender [to] Shri Sai Completely! Stupendous Delectation and Deliverance be there!" The format does not appeal to all readers.

(156) Rigopoulos 1993:145. In cases where Sai Baba asked for large amounts of money, the prospective donor was wealthy. The

reminiscences of Meher Baba include a detail concerning the Sai devotee Gopalrao Buti (Buty Saheb). When this person made visits to Sai Baba, the *faqir* would ask him for a thousand rupees. That was a very substantial figure in those times, but Buti would immediately comply (Kalchuri 1998:4810). The request was not exorbitant in this instance, Buti being a millionaire, and apparently the most wealthy of the devotees.

(157) Osborne 1958:103-104. Less reliable details about *dakshina* events are found in some more recent works. For instance, the devotee Hari Vinayak Sathe was involved in activities that are misrepresented. The compilatory work of Ruhela included some purported "researcher" accounts that are factually suspect, including one from Sathya Sai Baba. We read that residents of Shirdi hated Sathe because he was collecting [*dakshina*] offerings made to Sai Baba, intending to use the monies for the erection of a temple. These people are said to have suspected Sathe of complicity in the theft of a silver chariot (Ruhela 1995:61). This reflects a confusion with the palanquin used in the *chavadi utsav*, an item which had silver-plated ornaments. On Sathe, see further Shepherd 2015:247-251.

(158) Dabholkar 1999:805. Elsewhere, the account deriving from Hari Dixit relates that, at the time of *Ramanavami*, "two huge flags" were taken in procession to the mosque by Hindu devotees. One of these flags was contributed by Nanasaheb Nimonkar, and the other by "Damushet Kasar" (Damodar Rasane) of Ahmednagar (Pradhan 1933).

(159) Dabholkar 1999:806.

(160) Dabholkar 1999:807.

(161) Dabholkar 1999:807. The wording in the translation is devotional. Dabholkar says: "Swami [Somdev] was so much engrossed at Baba's feet that by Sai's Grace he became purified and stayed at his feet, for ever" (ibid). This appears to mean that the Swami became a permanent devotee.

(162) Dabholkar 1999:435.

(163) Dabholkar 1999:436.

(164) Dabholkar 1999:437.

(165) B. V. Narasimhaswami 2002:531; Narasimhaswami 2006:6; Shepherd 2015:298-299.

(166) The *Adhyatma Ramayana* was a late text of Hinduism, dating to *circa* 1500, and presenting Rama as an avatar of Vishnu. This work is sometimes described in terms of a convergence between Rama *bhakti* and Vedanta philosophy. Not to be confused with the epic *Ramayana* of Valmiki.

(167) Dabholkar 1999:439.

(168) Dabholkar 1999:439.

(169) Dabholkar 1999:441.

(170) Dabholkar 1999:442.

(171) Klostermaier 1989:173.

(172) Dabholkar 1999:444.

(173) See Nicholson 1936. Hujwiri was a native of Ghazna, in Afghanistan, and after many travels, eventually moved to Lahore. Hujwiri complained that "there were no real Sufis left anymore, and that the few authentic figures who could still be found were 'veiled' over by a growing number of false pretenders . . . . The pretenders had multiplied to such an extent that even for genuine seekers it had become impossible to identify the real Sufis" (Karamustafa 2007:100). The issue of formalism was urgent here. Hujwiri "carefully pointed out that the master whom he considered to be his real teacher . . . did not wear the garb of the Sufis or adopt their external fashions" (ibid:101). It is not the easiest matter for anyone to establish, on the basis of popular "Sufi practices," what the essential Sufism amounted to. An earlier exponent was Abu Nasr al-Sarraj (d.988), who authored *Kitab al-Luma fi'l Tasawwuf*. Sarraj reported "a surge in the number of those who took up the subject of Sufism, and many had begun to imitate the Sufis, to refer to them often, to answer questions about them, and even to write about them. However, their written work amounted to nothing more than exercises in ostentatious display of verbal ornamentation without any real experiential basis in genuine Sufism, and those who affected knowledge of Sufis in this manner were mostly social and cultural opportunists motivated by expectations of personal gain" (Karamustafa 2007:67). Variants of such arguments appeared in later centuries, and in India sometimes featured a very pro-Islamic stance claiming Sufi credentials and casting *kafirs* (non-Muslims) in the shade.

(174) This matter of differences is covered in Shepherd 2005:47–56; idem 2015:345–346n34. In *Gurus Rediscovered* (1986), I did not

actually state that Sai Baba was a *majzub*, contrary to the implication of Warren. What I did say, in terms of identity, was: "Since Sai Baba appears never to have referred to himself as a Sufi, I propose to credit him as one, in contradistinction to many bombastic mouthpieces who use this word vainly" (Shepherd 1986:16). See also Shepherd 2015:22–37, for a description of the conflict between *majazib* and orthodox Sufis. See also Appendix I in the present book. Warren was substantially confused about the teachings of Meher Baba, mentioning (in a note) *The Wayfarers* by William Donkin, but failing to clarify in the slightest her generalising reference conflating *masts* with Bijapur *majazib*. The fact that she also attributed to me a statement not found in *Gurus Rediscovered* (which she nevertheless cited to that effect) has been a cause of wonder to some other, and more discerning, academics.

(175) Anand 1997:6. The Nath Yogi theory was promoted in a variant by Charles White, a professor of philosophy and religion who recklessly identified Shirdi Sai Baba with Sathya Sai Baba. This conflation was a rather widespread vogue during the 1970s. White formulated a "Sai Baba movement" theory which caused much confusion, a situation still continuing internationally. His well known article exhibits some unconvincing assumptions. For instance, he asserts that Sai Baba kept a fire burning "in the manner of a Nathpanthi pir." White failed to grasp that a fire was maintained by some Muslim *faqirs* also, not just Nath Yogis. He also argues: "Sai Baba was a celibate, remaining in one place, performing miracles and astonishing his disciples, and keeping a fire perpetually burning in a Dhuni. Therefore, it would not be unreasonable to assume that he was following customs already sanctified" by Nath Yogis (White 1972). This superficial argument was in line with the beliefs about miracles encouraged by Sathya Sai. White even employed, in this context, a statement that a picture of Nath Yogi founders could be purchased at the Shirdi shrine (*samadhi mandir*). The purveying of pictures is no guide to history. The shrine did not promote Nath Yoga, and nor did Sai Baba. Slightly more relevant, but still flimsy, was the argument of White about a supposed similarity between Sai Baba and Kabir. The comparison was too generalised to have any effective meaning in a scholarly argument, even the presence of dogs in Shirdi being evoked as a detail of significance. In general, the state of 1970s studies in this field was acutely deficient, being strongly influenced by popular beliefs and the reincarnation claims of Sathya Sai Baba.

The contribution of White subsequently achieved partial profile in Ruhela 1994, a presentation of diverse "researchers" that failed to remedy the extensive confusions. See also note 62 above. The neglected Urdu *Notebook* of Abdul Baba is a relevant anchorage, not becoming generally known until 1999 (and even then, assimilation of the content has been negligible on the part of many authors).

(176) A rather well known reference of Sai Baba is relevant in this eclectic context. "According to his biographers, he spoke constantly of *saburi*, a [Marathi] word derived from the Arabic *sabr*, and *nista* or its Islamic equivalent *tawakkul*" (Warren 1999:107). Warren relates *sabr* (patience) and *tawakkul* (trust) to the Sufi path (*tariqat*), which she indicates to have been an underlying feature of the saint's teaching (ibid:209ff).

(177) Warren 1999:162, and citing Narasimhaswami, *Devotees' Experiences of Sai Baba*.

(178) Dabholkar 1999:158.

(179) Dabholkar 1999:198.

(180) Warren 1999:126, and citing Narasimhaswami, *Devotees' Experiences*.

(181) Dabholkar 1999:521.

(182) Dabholkar 1999:523.

(183) Warren 1999:213–214.

(184) Shepherd 2004:149, and referring to the Chishti Sufi Abdul Quddus Gangohi (1456–1537), one of the *ulama*, and quite different from Sai Baba. See also Rizvi 1978:140, and mentioning a reluctance on the part of Khwaja Qutubuddin Bakhtiyar Kaki (d.1235) to permit *chilla-i-makus* because "such devotional exercises gave the devotee unnecessary publicity" (ibid:140 note 3). Cf. Schimmel 1975:346–7, informing that the Chishti successor of Bakhtiyar Kaki was Fariduddin Ganj-i Shakar (d.1265), who settled in the Punjab, and whose ascetic practices included *chilla-i-makus*. "His constant fasting was miraculously rewarded – even pebbles turned into sugar" (ibid:346). Facts are not always in clear evidence. See further K. A. Nizami, *The Life and Times of Shaikh Farid Ganj-i Shakar* (Aligarh 1955).

(185) Warren 1999:215–216.

(186) Warren 1999:121. The mention of two flags appears to be a cross-over reference to the *Ramanavami* festival, which accompanied the *Urs* during the last years of Sai Baba.

(187) Details of some Muslim devotees are relayed by Narasimhaswami in his *Devotees' Experiences of Sai Baba*, and also in the third volume of his *Life of Sai Baba*. See also Shepherd 2015:182–188.

(188) Dabholkar 1999:152. The idea of clear-cut divisions between Hindus and Muslims has been queried. For instance, Aurangzeb apparently incorporated more Hindus into the imperial administration than any preceding Mughal ruler. The comparatively liberal reign of Akbar saw developments in which many Sanskrit works were translated into Persian, including the Epics (Truschke 2016). The Persian-speaking Islamic elite are here viewed as conducting an exchange with traditional Sanskrit scholars, a trend enhancing the political position of Hindus and Jains.

(189) Dabholkar 1999:152.

(190) Nimbalkar 2001:133.

(191) Dabholkar 1999:106.

(192) Nimbalkar 2001:134. *Al-Fatihah* was favoured by Sai Baba in a number of situations. The relevant *surah* is very compact, consisting of only seven brief verses that are easily memorised.

(193) Dabholkar 1999:105. The number of Muslims involved in these situations is unknown. They were substantially outnumbered by Hindus during the last decade of Sai Baba's life.

(194) Dabholkar 1999:105.

(195) Dabholkar 1999:105. See also Shepherd 2015:159–161, for the *tabut* episode and some reflections on the *Muharram* celebrations in Bombay (Mumbai).

(196) Narasimhaswami 2006:140–1.

(197) Green 2009:79. On the part of Protestant Christians, "only a generation earlier it was still possible to speak of India's religious festivals with fascination rather than disdain" (ibid). The subsequent British "evangelical revival" was responsible for a mood of disapproval in relation to festivals like *Muharram* (ibid:80). Sai Baba is not known to have encountered Christian evangelists, and unlike them, was not concerned to proselytise. He was definitely in favour of liberality towards Christians, as his criticism of Hari Dixit reveals (Nimbalkar 2001:133). It could be argued that Sai Baba was primarily concerned with Indian Christians, these being the

Notes

only Christians in his direct contact. The only known encounter of Sai Baba with British colonialists occurred in the instance of Sir George Seymour Curtis and his wife (Shepherd 2015:120–122). The relevant episode of 1911 evidences the gulf existing between Indian natives and the Raj.

(198) Narasimhaswami 2002:34. According to the memoir of Hari Dixit, after the construction of Sathewada, Shirdi "began to get the appearance of a Sansthan" (Pradhan 1933). This is a reference to the increasing number of devotees residing at Shirdi, and also the communal activity via *arati* ceremonies, the *chavadi* procession, and the associated paraphernalia. The industry of Radhakrishna Ayi was considerable. The Dixit report says that this lady was responsible for the mosaic tiles featuring in refurbished floors of both the mosque and the *chavadi*.

(199) Dabholkar 1999:852. During the procession, Sai Baba would halt for about five minutes in front of the *chavadi*, looking up at the sky and making signs with his right hand (Pradhan 1933). The Dixit version contrasts with some other narrations. See further Shepherd 2015:375–376 note 449, and mentioning the Kalchuri version. The book in the name of Bhau Kalchuri, entitled *Lord Meher*, has undergone simplified representation in many reports originating from the Meher Baba movement. The translation and editing process for this multi-volume work was rather complex, and also long-term. Due explanations can be lengthy. In my 2015 book cited in this note, I conveniently followed the general belief that *Lord Meher* was solely composed by Kalchuri and translated from Hindi. This belief is deceptive. In fact, two other languages were also involved, meaning Marathi and Gujarati. The editing does not clarify such linguistic complexities, and nor other relevant matters. In contrast, I made an attempt to describe the editing process in an online article, which also rescued a notable Hindu devotee of Meher Baba (associated with New Delhi) from obscurity and misrepresentation. See further the section on *Lord Meher (Meher Prabhu)* at www.citizenthought.net/Meher_Baba_Movement.html

(200) Warren 1999:32.

(201) Dabholkar 1999:523.

(202) Narasimhaswami 2006:21. The brevity of expression is a factor tending to arouse caution at some of the longer statements in evidence. One of the more striking disclosures of Sai Baba refers

to devotees: "A slave of slaves that I am, I am indebted to you and have set out to have your *darshan*. It is indeed, by your great kindness that I have met you. I am but a worm in your faeces" (Dabholkar 1999:156). The translator mentions that the latter part of this utterance was rendered differently by Swami Sai Sharan Anand (ibid:164 note 9).

(203) Narasimhaswami 2002:571. On Narke, see also Shepherd 2015:229–235. The Narke exposition was contradicted by a misleading theory of Rigopoulos that Sai Baba taught *jnana marga*. The Western commentator relies heavily upon the Sanskritised passages adapted from Chandorkar by Narasimhaswami. Rigopoulos adds: "Unfortunately, the sources do not offer any information for an examination of Sai Baba's 'path of knowledge' in the light of Sufism" (Rigopoulos 1993:329). This was written before the publication of Abdul Baba's *Notebook*. Warren dismissed the framework adopted by Rigopoulos. "Although Rigopoulos acknowledges the saint's Muslim Sufi aspect, he does not pursue it, and never academically questions the obvious Hindu bias in his assessment and interpretation of Sai Baba. He has been content to follow the line of the previous biographers" (Warren 1999:18).

(204) Narasimhaswami 2006:27.

(205) Narasimhaswami 2006:21.

(206) Dabholkar 1999:847.

(207) Narasimhaswami 2006:21.

(208) Warren 1999:249. For a compilation, see Chitluri 2007.

(209) Dabholkar 1999:836. Apparently, one should discount from this process the numerous devotees represented in a report associated with Hari Dixit: "A very large proportion amongst the devotees of Sai Baba went to him for the fulfilment of their worldly desires" (Pradhan 1933).

(210) Dabholkar 1999:841. A less familiar source is the Marathi diary of Dixit, commenced in 1909 and continued for many years, being translated into English after his death. The title was *The Shirdi Diary of Kakasaheb Dixit*. This published document did not become well known, and the original book is very scarce. The contents describe various experiences of devotees, including cures and *dakshina* anecdotes. Dixit was evidently partial to the miraculous. One idiom reflected is: "he was saved from many diseases by intake of Udi." In some instances where Hindu devotees were slow to give

dakshina, Sai Baba allusively remarked that they were cheating a "poor brahmin."

(211) Dabholkar 1999:842. The subsequent memoir of Dixit, mediated from Marathi in an edited version, informs that he began to stay in Shirdi from about 1910 (Pradhan 1933). This memoir should not be confused with the *The Shirdi Diary of Kakasaheb Dixit,* published after his death, a book which remained relatively obscure.

(212) Dabholkar 1999:843. The memoir of Sai Baba by Hari Dixit appeared, after the saint's death, in the Marathi journal *Shri Sai Leela.* This contribution was translated into English (Pradhan 1933). These reminiscences have been compared to the *Shirdi Diary* of Khaparde. However, Dixit had not witnessed all the events he mentioned. Sai Baba was in the habit of referring to Dixit as Kakasaheb, a name common in Maharashtra, and meaning approximately "uncle." According to Warren, the memos of Dixit reflect "a view of Sai Baba at the end of his life, as encountered by a Hindu striving to understand the enigmatic saint's mystic utterances" (Warren 1999:10).

(213) Dabholkar 1999:112. The disease of Bhagoji has been reported in different versions. See Shepherd 2015:57, for an early event associated with the *hakim* ministrations of the Shirdi *faqir.* A reference in Dabholkar has been interpreted to mean that Bhagoji was losing his fingers and toes. Cf. Williams 2004:115, who briefly states that the leprosy was cured by drinking the *tirtha* water of Sai Baba, although the sufferer remained partially disfigured. The elevation of a leper as personal attendant was certainly exceptional. The inclusion of Bhagoji Shinde in the visible routine of Sai Baba appears to have caused some revulsion in orthodox Hindu ranks. The brahmanical fear of contamination was pronounced in the case of low caste lepers.

(214) Nanasaheb Chandorkar was at first a *mamlatdar,* and then a District Deputy Collector, travelling over wide areas. During his journeys, he was in the habit of performing devotional songs in honour of Sai Baba. This extension of his activity apparently had some effect of creating interest in the Shirdi saint. However, a greater response was achieved by Das Ganu, whom Chandorkar brought to Bombay. The *kirtans* of Das Ganu were well received in the metropolis, and inspired a new wave of Sai devotees. In another

direction, Das Ganu became "one of the leading Kirtankar Varkaris of Pandharpur" (Pradhan 1933, mediating the Dixit memoir).

(215) Dabholkar 1999:112. Cf. Rigopoulos 1993:156, who cites the versions of Bharadwaja and Gunaji. Sai Baba is here said to have thrust his arm into the fire. Rigopoulos describes the episode in terms of "a well known *chamatkar*" or miracle. The Western scholar adds that the sources relate how the blacksmith and his wife brought their child from the distant village "and thanked Baba for his miraculous intervention" (ibid). The saint reportedly stated, at the time he injured his hand: "Let the hand be scorched, but at least the child's life is saved" (Dabholkar 1999:111).

(216) Kher 2001:127, citing N. C. Kelkar, *Lokamanya Tilak Yanche Charitra*, Vol. 3 (1928).

(217) Tilak's *Gita Rahasya* was his major work, and parted from the Vedantic idealism often associated with the *Bhagavad Gita*. Tilak did not favour the renunciate lifestyle, but instead a course of detached action, compatible with his political activity. This has led to commentary in the vein of "karma yoga versus jnana."

(218) Rigopoulos 1993:228. Such matters have been viewed from different angles. "Tilak and many others undertook their political agitation against the British *raj* as a duty imposed on them by their religion; their aim was the restoration of Hindu India on the sociopolitical level" (Klostermaier 1989:402).

(219) Rigopoulos 1993:228. Tilak had earlier met another renunciate of unusual characteristics, namely Swami Vivekananda (d.1902). Tilak describes how, *circa* 1892, Vivekananda stayed with him at Poona for about ten days. Although Vivekananda would often talk about Advaita philosophy, "the Swami also believed like me that the Shrimad Bhagavad Gita did not preach renunciation but urged every one to work unattached and without the desire for fruits of the work" (Tilak 1961:21).

(220) The brother of R. A. Tarkhad was Sadashiv Tarkhad, who worked as manager in a textile mill at Poona. The latter became a devotee of Sai as a consequence of the example and efforts of his wife, Mrs. Tarabhai Sadashiv Tarkhad. This lady left one of the most oft-cited testimonies in Narasimhaswami's *Devotees' Experiences*, where she is called Mrs. Manager in material resulting from an interview of 1936.

(221) Dabholkar 1999:699. Thereafter, the saint would regularly eat the daily food prepared by Lakshmibai. However, he would only consume a limited quantity, and the remainder would be despatched, via Lakshmibai, to Radhakrishna Ayi, who had moved to Shirdi from Ahmednagar. Ayi was a Vaishnava who became devoted to Sai Baba; she lived at Shirdi in semi-seclusion until her death in 1916. "She was fond of eating the left-overs from [Sai] Baba's meal" (Dabholkar 1999:700). Ayi evidently regarded this food as *prasad*, a word having the general meaning of gift from a deity.

(222) Dabholkar 1999:510-11, 513. This source provides a reincarnation theory, and asks: "Is it possible that a creature will give up his physical body right in front of a saint's eyes and be liberated instantly?" (ibid:512). The *dervishes* are said to have looked sad, losing their source of revenue, but "they were happy too, that the ailing animal, on the point of death, was thus liberated" (ibid:511). Hindu beliefs are here represented. Sai Baba reputedly made remarks endorsing these beliefs.

(223) Dabholkar 1999:697.

(224) Kher 2001:134; Kamath and Kher 1991:293. Cf. Shepherd 2005:40-1, for variants of wording.

(225) Dabholkar 1999:701.

(226) Dabholkar 1999:702. Bayaji Kote is also referred to in the sources as Bayyaji Appaji Patel. His home was one of those dwellings where Sai Baba regularly appeared for alms. This devotee was one of the saint's beneficiaries in respect of a daily gift of rupees. He was known for his strength, and served as a personal attendant (*sevakari*) of Sai Baba. Cf. Shepherd 2015:196,268,280.

(227) A pro-Hindu accent is discernible in the version of Dabholkar, who evidently favoured Hindu voters led by Ramchandra Patil, "one of the village officers" (Dabholkar 1999:718). The same writer mentions that Khushalchand (Seth) and Amir Shakkar (Dalal) were on the opposing side. Khushalchand Seth was one of the earliest Hindu devotees of Sai Baba. On this figure, see Kher 2001:29-35.

(228) Kher 2001:135.

(229) Kamath and Kher 1991:296.

(230) Rigopoulos 1993:242. Bappa Baba was interviewed at Shirdi by Rigopoulos in 1985.

(231) Kamath and Kher 1991:291–292. The name of the Aurangabad *majzub* has been diversely rendered. In different accounts, one can find reference to Banne Mia, Bannemiya, Banemiyan Baba, and Bane Miyan.

(232) Ibid.

(233) Warren 1999:117.

(234) Purdom 1937:24.

(235) Warren 1999:117.

(236) Green 2009:92. It is easier to agree with Professor Nile Green that Bane Miyan has "remained a figure of more local importance" in comparison to Sai Baba (ibid).

(237) Ibid.

(238) Professor Green has suggested that Bane Miyan "was probably born during the early 1850s," which means that he was seventy years old or less when he died (Green 2009:94). This calculation is based upon an entity, reported in military records, who may not actually have been Bane Miyan, the coincidence being solely in the name Muhammad Azam (Azim) Khan. It is quite true that attributions of longevity were customarily made in the instance of both Hindu holy men and Muslim *faqirs*. However, if a need for contracted dates is felt, a lifespan of eighty or ninety years is also reasonable. Bane Miyan could easily have been born *circa* 1830. Professor Green believes that a birthdate in the early 1850s would explain why surviving accounts refer to Bane Miyan as having been introduced during childhood to his supposed mentor Afzal Shah Biyabani (d.1856). "Bane Miyan's father seems to have taken his wife and sons to receive initiation (*bayat*) at the hands of Afzal Shah" (ibid:95). Again, this detail does not prove a later date of birth. Such family initiations were "commonplace at this time" (ibid). In the *Afzal al-Karamat*, the Sufi figure Afzal Shah is said to have bestowed the nickname of "Bane Miyan." This may be an invention. Bane Miyan was certainly not regarded as a major disciple of Afzal Shah, and the linkage might be considered indirect, despite being repeated in the oral tradition maintained by the relatives of Bane Miyan.

(239) Green 2009:96–97.

(240) Green 2009:98. Bane Miyan is generally presented as the disciple of Afzal Shah Biyabani. However, only one meeting between them is recorded, which appears to fit an episode of

initiatory procedure for his family. A rather different version of affiliation is supplied by the report that Bane Miyan was a disciple of Sai Baba (Purdom 1937:24).

(241) Green 2009:101.

(242) Green 2009:102, reporting the text as saying that the private (*jawan*) was singled out for promotion by "Major-Colonel" Ross, and adding "this latter figure appears to have been the British officer Colonel Harry Ross (1869–1938)."

(243) Green 2009:100.

(244) Green 2009:117.

(245) Green 2009:102.

(246) Green 2009:103.

(247) Green 2005:627, 633.

(248) Professor Nile Green appropriately reflects that "it is difficult to judge where or how many times (and if we are truly sceptical, whether at all) Bane Miyan was incarcerated" (Green 2009:108). Certainly, the British colonialists opted to make madness a big issue, creating many native-only asylums in Indian cities. This situation led to the deplorable fact that "in colonial medical discourse the mad became quickly aligned with the bad, such that even if not expressed through illegal criminal activity, madness was symptomatic of underlying moral degeneration" (ibid:106). *Faqirs* were one target of this negative approach. A related contingency arose. "Even in cases where insanity was uncertain, the CM (cantonment magistrate) was able to detain a suspected madman for ten days for assessment of his state of mind" (ibid:110). *Ganja* and *bhang* were targeted as purported causes of insanity in asylum documentation (ibid:111). The asylum or madhouse has been viewed as a mechanism by which the British authorities controlled the presence of *faqirs*, who participated in the Sepoy Rebellion of 1857–8.

(249) There was a military cantonment at Jalna, "but no record of a public asylum" in that location (Green 2009:145). Green suggests that the British officers may have instead resorted to confining *sepoys* "in cells or infirmaries within the compounds of the barracks" (ibid). However, the anomaly involved in the hagiological claim means that the entire episode of Bane Miyan and the asylum may be an invention. A large jail existed in Hyderabad which included many "insanes" as inmates. Asylums existed at Amraoti, Nagpur,

and also Secunderabad, a cantonment zone. See also the previous note 248.

(250) Green 2009:105–106.

(251) Green 2009:107.

(252) Green 2009:98.

(253) Green 2009:111.

(254) Professor Nile Green makes the rather extreme deduction that a "frenzy" was "at times characteristic of Bane Miyan," and in a context which the commentator associates with *bhang*, a narcotic drink. Some ascetics did resort to that concoction, as was mentioned in a colonial report of 1893. The *Report on the Cultivation and Use of Ganja* stated that the frenzy induced by *bhang* was "supposed to indicate supernatural possession" (Green 2009:111). Green questionably brackets this phenomenon with the wrathful mood of *jalal* (divine majesty) credited by devotees, a disposition to which Bane Miyan was occasionally subject. Green calls this "manic fury," and further aligns the mood with a characteristic of Mughal era warrior *faqirs*. The dilation fails to mention that Bane Miyan was averse to interruption, which could disturb his otherwise placid mood. The Aurangabad *faqir* has no known connection with *bhang*, did not claim supernatural possession, and had no relation to warrior *faqirs*. Until the drug syndrome is negotiated, the outlook is less than optimistic for historical accuracy, in relation to the victims of colonial censure and contemporary misconception.

(255) Green 2009:98.

(256) Green 2009:117–120.

(257) The theme of "sepoy recreation" is favoured by Nile Green, who emphasises that the *urs* festivals would have included "feasts, a fairground and the singing of the *tawaif* (dancers, prostitutes) whose company Bane Miyan (and no doubt many other sepoys) is said in *Azam al-karamat* to have enjoyed" (Green 2009:118). This aspersion should be corrected to mean that Ismail Khan and other *sepoys* were the probable enjoyers. Ismail Khan did not stand in a difficult ascetic pose with one hand raised, but instead sought the benefits of participation in a wealthy religious class, his idea of renunciation being very minimal by comparison with that of his *faqir* uncle. The idea that Bane Miyan arranged *mahfil* (or *mehfil*), meaning a social or religious gathering with an emphasis on music, is unconvincing in view of his acutely retiring disposition. The hagiographer Ismail

Khan was the man who liked to arrange such get-togethers. Cf. Green 2009:139, who attributes "the hosting of prostitute dancers" to Bane Miyan, a figure more realistically discernible as an ascetic intent upon retreating into a simple cell (*hujra*) made of clay (Green 2005:630). The Sufi shrines were, to some extent perhaps, venues of *mahfil*, but no proof exists that these were frequented by Bane Miyan.

(258) A hagiological invention of contemporary scholarship is afforded by the phrase: "*Faqirs* like Baba Jan and Bane Miyan continued to work miracles for their sepoy followers as late as the 1920s" (Green 2009:148). Babajan did not work miracles, and *sepoys* were a bare minority amongst her followers during the 1920s. She did not cater for their preferences, even if they did actually want miracles (which is not known). Bane Miyan died in 1921, and there is no convincing report of his having worked miracles to satisfy *sepoys*. In 1918, the ex-soldier Imambai Chota Khan had to wait for some time before he could even approach Bane Miyan with a brief message. There was no possibility of miracles in such a reclusive setting.

(259) Green 2009:119.

(260) Narasimhaswami 1942:261; Narasimhaswami 2006:220.

(261) A reminiscence from Meher Baba is worded as: "Gustadji was with him [Sai Baba] at the time, since he was residing in Sai's ashram at Shirdi" (Kalchuri 1998:4810). The source is a translation from an unspecified Indian language. Sai Baba did not actually have an *ashram*. A handful of Hindu devotees are named in other well known reports describing the death of Sai Baba at the mosque, e.g., Kamath and Kher 1991:293. It is known that other persons were also present, but they escaped record. Gustad Hansotia was very likely one of these.

(262) One report concerning Gustad is Brabazon 1978:40ff. The content was gleaned, after Gustad's death, by Australian poet Francis Brabazon from a prominent Parsi adherent of Meher Baba named Eruch Jessawala, who was relaying information given by Gustad many years earlier, the details being known to the *mandali* of Meher Baba. The Brabazon version is not complete, and some details are missing. Oral reports of the 1960s stressed the complexity of Gustad's relationship with Sai Baba. Those reports were not found amongst devotees of Sai Baba, but amongst devotees of

Meher Baba, to whom Gustad transferred allegiance after the death of Sai. Gustad was forgotten at Shirdi, and does not appear in the coverages of Dabholkar and Narasimhaswami. This omission was not intentional on the part of those writers, but does illustrate how some events can pass into oblivion. A reminder of the missing Parsi entity was afforded in my *Gurus Rediscovered* (1986), utilising the Meher Baba literature and oral reports, and drawing upon my unpublished manuscript *Life of Meher Baba*. Cf. Kalchuri 1986:260.

(263) Kalchuri 1986:217–221; Shepherd 2015:269–271. Kalchuri was a Hindu and part author of *Lord Meher*. His original text was in Hindi, later translated into English with amplifications. His account of the meeting between Sai Baba and Merwan Irani has poetic touches. The translation refers to *Parvardigar* in terms of "the Mohammedan name for Lord Vishnu" (Kalchuri 1986:218). *Parvardigar* was evidently a component of Sai Baba's Urdu vocabulary as an independent Sufi mystic.

(264) Shepherd 1986:78–79 note 55, informing that Meher Baba awarded Sai Baba the status of *qutub-e-irshad*, an assertion appearing in print in 1961. This role means the leader of the "spiritual hierarchy" emphasised in Sufism. The reference "has to date largely escaped attention" (ibid:79).

(265) For instance, according to Meher Baba, there were three places where Sai Baba slept during his last years, and in succession every three days. The first day in the mosque, the second day at the *chavadi*, and the third day in a small hut (Kalchuri 1998:4810). The Kalchuri version erroneously refers to the tomb instead of *chavadi*. Diverse linguistic sources have been blamed for some errors in *Lord Meher* (translations from Hindi, Marathi, and Gujarati were made into English). The first two of the Shirdi sites mentioned are well known in the Sai Baba literature, but the third is very obscure. The same report also mentions that "no talk ever took place about spirituality" (ibid). This refers to the situation at Shirdi concerning Sai Baba, who did not discourse or teach in the manner that visitors often expected. The reference of Meher Baba may be taken as confirming various accounts which relay that Sai Baba did not preach Vedanta, Yoga, or other subjects. The Shirdi *faqir* preferred allusive speech and brief ethical reflections.

(266) The details in this chapter come from Shepherd, *Upasani Maharaj of Sakori: A Biography* (unpublished).

Bibliography

Abbott, Justin E., *Stories of Indian Saints: An English Translation of Mahipati's BhaktiVijaya* (2 vols, fourth edn Pune 1933; repr. Delhi: Motilal Banarsidass, 1982).

Anand, Swami Sai Sharan, *Shri Sai the Superman* (Shirdi: Shri Sai Baba Sansthan, 1962).

---------*Shri Sai Baba*, trans. V. B. Kher (New Delhi: Sterling Publishers Pvt. Ltd., 1997).

Babuji, Sainathuni Sarath, *Arati Sai Baba: The Psalm Book of Sri Sai Samadhi Mandir at Shirdi* (Hyderabad: Saipatham, 1996).

Bharadwaja, Acharya Ekkirala, trans., *Sree Guru Charitra* by Gangadhar Saraswati (Ongole: Sai Baba Mission, 1987).

---------*The Supreme Master: Shri Akkalkot Maharaj* (Ongole, Andhra: Guru Paduka Publications, 1994).

---------*Sai Baba the Master* (1978; new edn, Ongole, Andhra: Guru Paduka Publications, 1996).

Brabazon, Francis, *The Silent Word: Being Some Chapters of the Life and Time of Avatar Meher Baba* (Bombay: Meher House, 1978).

Chitluri, Vinny, *Baba's Rinanubandh – Leelas during his Sojourn in Shirdi* (New Delhi: Sterling Publishers Pvt. Ltd., 2007).

Chitre, Dilip, trans., *Says Tuka: Selected Poetry of Tukaram* (London: Penguin 1991).

Dabholkar, Govind R., *Shri Sai Satcharita: The Life and Teachings of Shirdi Sai Baba*, trans. Indira Kher (New Delhi: Sterling Publishers Pvt. Ltd., 1999).

Das Ganu Maharaj, *Sai Hari Katha*, trans. Rabinder Nath Kakarya (New Delhi: Sterling Publishers Pvt. Ltd., 2007).

Dhere, Ramchandra C., *Muslim Marathi Sant Kavi* (Pune: Padmagandha Prakashan, 2008).

---------*The Rise of a Folk God: Vitthal of Pandharpur* (New York: Oxford University Press, 2011).

Donkin, William, *The Wayfarers: An Account of the Work of Meher Baba with the God-intoxicated, and also with Advanced Souls, Sadhus, and the Poor* (Ahmednagar: Adi K. Irani, 1948).

Eaton, Richard M., *The Sufis of Bijapur 1300-1700: Social Roles of Sufis in Medieval India* (Princeton, NJ: Princeton University Press, 1978).

---------"Bahri, Mahmud," in *Encyclopaedia Iranica* Vol. 3 (1988), and at www.iranicaonline.org/articles/bahri-mahmud-b (Accessed April 15, 2016).

---------*The Rise of Islam and the Bengal Frontier 1204–1760* (Berkeley and Los Angeles: University of California Press, 1993).

---------*Temple Desecration and Muslim States in Medieval India* (Gurgaon: Hope India Publications, 2004).

---------*A Social History of the Deccan 1300-1761: Eight Indian Lives* (New York: Cambridge University Press, 2005).

Elias, Jamal J., *The Throne Carrier of God: The Life and Thought of Ala ad-daula as-Simnani* (Albany: State University of New York Press, 1995).

Ernst, Carl W., *Eternal Garden: Mysticism, History, and Politics at a South Asian Sufi Center* (Albany: State University of New York Press, 1992).

---------"Situating Sufism and Yoga," *Journal of the Royal Asiatic Society* (2005) 15 (1):15–43.

Ernst, Carl W., and Lawrence, Bruce B., *Sufi Martyrs of Love: The Chishti Order in South Asia and Beyond* (New York: Palgrave Macmillan, 2002).

Flood, Gavin, *An Introduction to Hinduism* (Cambridge: Cambridge University Press, 1996).

Fraser, James Nelson, and J. F. Edwards, *The Life and Teaching of Tukaram* (London: Probsthain, 1922).

Ghani (Munsiff), Abdul, "Hazrat Sai Baba of Shirdi," *Meher Baba Journal* (March 1939) 1(5):46–56.

Green, Nile, "Making a 'Muslim' Saint: Writing Customary Religion in an Indian Princely State," *Comparative Studies of South Asia, Africa and the Middle East* (2005) 25(3):617–33.

---------*Indian Sufism Since the Seventeenth Century: Saints, Books and Empires in the Muslim Deccan* (New York and London: Routledge, 2006).

---------*Islam and the Army in Colonial India: Sepoy Religion in the Service of Empire* (New York: Cambridge University Press, 2009).

---------*Sufism: A Global History* (Chichester: Wiley-Blackwell, 2012).

Gunaji, Nagesh Vasudev, *Shri Sai Satcharita or the Wonderful Life and Teachings of Shri Sai Baba: Adapted from the Original Marathi Book by Hemadpant* (1944; Shirdi: Shri Sai Baba Sansthan, 1999). [N.B., this very influential work, frequently reprinted, has been criticised for abridgment and some misleading adaptation of the original]

Haeri, Muneera, *The Chishtis: A Living Light* (Karachi: Oxford University Press, 2000).

Hartsuiker, Dolf, *Sadhus: Holy Men of India* (London: Thames and Hudson, 1993).

Jha, V., "Stages in the History of Untouchables," *Indian Historical Review* (1975) 2:14-31.

Kalchuri, Bhau, F. Workingboxwala, D. Fenster *et al*, *Lord Meher Vol. One* (North Myrtle Beach, SC: Manifestation, 1986).

---------*Lord Meher Vol. Thirteen* (Asheville, NC: Manifestation, 1998).

Kamath, M. V., and Kher, V. B., *Sai Baba of Shirdi: A Unique Saint* (Bombay: Jaico Publishing House, 1991).

Karamustafa, Ahmet T., *Sufism: The Formative Period* (Edinburgh: Edinburgh University Press, 2007).

Khaparde, Ganesh S., *Shirdi Diary of the Hon'ble Mr. G. S. Khaparde* (Shirdi: Sri Sai Baba Sansthan, n.d.).

Kher, V. B., *Sai Baba: His Divine Glimpses* (New Delhi: Sterling Publishers Pvt. Ltd., 2001).

Klostermaier, Klaus K., *A Survey of Hinduism* (Albany: State University of New York Press, 1989).

Lal, Kishori Saran, *Muslim Slave System in Medieval India* (New Delhi: Aditya Prakashan, 1994).

Lawrence, Bruce B., *Notes from a Distant Flute: Sufi Literature in Pre-Mughal India* (Tehran: Imperial Iranian Academy of Philosophy, 1978).

Lehmann, Fritz, review of R. M. Eaton, *Sufis of Bijapur 1300-1700*, in *Journal of Asian Studies* (1980) 39(2):387–8.

Major, Andrea, *Slavery, Abolitionism and Empire in India, 1772–1843* (Liverpool University Press, 2012).

McLain, Karline, *The Afterlife of Sai Baba: Competing Visions of a Global Saint* (Seattle: University of Washington Press, 2016).

Mujeeb, M., *The Indian Muslims* (London: George Allen and Unwin, 1967).

Narasimhaswami, B. V., *Sri Sai Baba's Charters and Sayings* (Madras: All India Sai Samaj, first edn 1939; fifth edn, 1944).

--------*Devotees' Experiences of Sri Sai Baba* (3 vols, Madras: All India Sai Samaj, 1940; first edn composite volume, Mylapore, Chennai: All India Sai Samaj, 2006).

--------*Life of Sai Baba* (4 vols, Mylapore, Chennai: All India Sai Samaj, 1955-6; first edn composite volume, 2002).

Narayan, B. K. *Saint Shah Waris Ali and Sai Baba* (New Delhi: Vikas, 1995).

Nicholson, Reynold A., trans., *Kashf al-Mahjub of Al Hujwiri*:

The Oldest Persian Treatise on Sufism (1911; new edn London: Luzac 1936).

Nimbalkar, M. B., *Shri Sai Baba: Teachings and Philosophy* (New Delhi: Sterling Publishers Pvt. Ltd., 2001).

Novetzke, Christian Lee, *Religion and Public Memory: A Cultural History of Saint Namdev in India* (New York: Columbia University Press, 2008).

Osborne, Arthur, *Ramana Maharshi and the Path of Self-Knowledge* (London: Rider, 1954).

---------*The Incredible Sai Baba* (Calcutta, 1957; London: Rider, 1958).

Parthasarathy, Rangaswami, *God Who Walked on Earth: The Life and Times of Shirdi Sai Baba* (New Delhi: Sterling Publishers Pvt. Ltd., 1996).

Pradhan, Moreshwar W., *Shri Sai Baba of Shirdi: A Glimpse of Indian Spirituality* (Shirdi: Shri Sai Baba Sansthan, 1933).

Purdom, Charles B., *The Perfect Master: The Life of Shri Meher Baba* (London: Williams and Norgate, 1937).

Ramalingaswami, *Ambrosia in Shirdi: A Book Never Before* (Shirdi: Ramalingaswami, 1984).

Ranade, R. D., *Mysticism in Maharashtra* (Poona 1933; repr. Delhi: Motilal Banarsidass, 1982).

---------*Tukaram* (Albany: State University of New York Press, 1994).

Rigopoulos, Antonio, *The Life and Teachings of Sai Baba of Shirdi* (Albany: State University of New York Press, 1993).

---------*The Mahanubhavs* (London and New York: Anthem Press, 2011).

Rizvi, Saiyid Athar Abbas, *A History of Sufism in India* (2 vols, New Delhi: Manoharlal, 1978–1983).

Ruhela, Satya Pal, *What Researchers Say on Sri Shirdi Sai Baba* (1994; second edn, New Delhi: M D Publications Pvt. Ltd., 1995).

Schimmel, Annemarie, *Mystical Dimensions of Islam* (Chapel Hill: University of North Carolina Press, 1975).

---------*The Triumphal Sun: A Study of the Works of Jalaloddin Rumi* (1980; Albany: State University of New York Press, 1993).

Shepherd, Kevin R. D., *Gurus Rediscovered: Biographies of Sai Baba of Shirdi and Upasni Maharaj of Sakori* (Cambridge: Anthropographia, 1986).

---------*From Oppression to Freedom: A Study of the Kaivani Gnostics* (Cambridge: Anthropographia, 1988).

---------*Some Philosophical Critiques and Appraisals* (Dorchester: Citizen Initiative, 2004).

----------*Investigating the Sai Baba Movement: A Clarification of Misrepresented Saints and Opportunism* (Dorchester: Citizen Initiative, 2005).

----------*Hazrat Babajan: A Pathan Sufi of Poona* (New Delhi: Sterling Publishers Pvt. Ltd., 2014).

----------*Sai Baba of Shirdi: A Biographical Investigation* (New Delhi: Sterling Publishers Pvt. Ltd., 2015).

----------"Shirdi Sai Baba and the Sai Baba Movement." www.kevinrdshepherd.info/shirdi_sai_baba_and_sai_baba_movement.html (Accessed April 15, 2016).

---------"Meher Baba and Yazd" www.kevinrdshepherd.info/Meher_Baba_and_Yazd.html (Accessed December 20, 2016).

Sontheimer, Gunther-Dietz, *Pastoral Deities in Western India*, trans. Anne Feldhaus (Oxford: Oxford University Press, 1989).

Srinivas, Smriti, *In the Presence of Sai Baba: Body, City and Memory in a Global Religious Movement* (Leiden: Brill, 2008).

Swahananda, Swami, ed. and trans., *Panchadashi* (Madras: Ramakrishna Math, 1967).

Tilak, Bal Gangadhar, Chapter 2 (21-2), in *Reminiscences of Swami Vivekananda* by his Eastern and Western Admirers (Calcutta: Advaita Ashrama, 1961).

Trimingham, J. Spencer, *The Sufi Orders in Islam* (Oxford: Oxford University Press, 1971).

Truschke, Audrey, *Culture of Encounters: Sanskrit at the Mughal Court* (New York: Columbia University Press, 2016).

Tulpule, Shankar G., *Classical Marathi Literature: From the Beginning to A.D. 1818* (Wiesbaden: Otto Harrassowitz, 1979).

Warren, Marianne, *Unravelling the Enigma: Shirdi Sai Baba in the Light of Sufism* (New Delhi: Sterling Publishers Pvt. Ltd., 1999).

Weissmann, Itzchak, *The Naqshbandiyya: Orthodoxy and Activism in a Worldwide Sufi Tradition* (New York: Routledge, 2007).

White, Charles S. J., "The Sai Baba Movement: Approaches to the Study of Indian Saints," *Journal of Asian Studies* (1972) 31:863–878.

Williams, Alison, *Experiencing Sai Baba's Shirdi: A Guide* (Shirdi: Saipatham, 2002; revised edn 2004).

Zelliot, Eleanor, "Eknath's *Bharuds*: The Sant as Link Between Cultures" (91–109) in K. Schomer and W. H. McLeod, eds., *The Sants: Studies in a Devotional Tradition of India* (Delhi: Motilal Banarsidass, 1987).

---------"The Orthodoxy of the Mahanubhavs" in E. Zelliot and M. Berntsen, eds., *The Experience of Hinduism: Essays on Religion in Maharashtra* (Albany: State University of New York Press, 1988).

INDEX

'abd, 198n.45
abdal, 195n.36
Abdul Baba, 7, 144, 189, 193n.15, 194n.30, 195n.34, 210n.139, 218n.203; Sai Baba spoke to him in Urdu, ix; served Sai Baba for thirty years, 5; lived at Shirdi under personal instructions, 6, 10, 195n.37; his *qawwali* or song, 9; referred to Sai Baba in a *qalandar* context, 13,194n.33; his Urdu *Notebook* is an important source, 5-6, 87; one of the Muslim minority of devotees, 102; received stern treatment from Sai, 150; the only follower allowed into the Lendi garden, 152; his *Notebook* not generally known until 1999, 215n.175. See also *Notebook*
Abdul Qadir Jilani, 166
abhangas (Tukaram), 32, 203n.90
abrar, 195n.36
Adhyatma Ramayana, 81, 213n.166
Adil Shahi dynasty, 184
Advaita Bhashya (Shankara), 58
Advaita Vedanta, 30, 35, 176, 205n.97
advaita-bhakti, 30
Advaitendra Saraswati (Gholap Shastri), 85
Afghanistan, 213n.173
Afzal al-Karamat (Muhyiuddin Qadiri), 222n.238
Afzal Khan, 34

Agnihotra, 73, 84
Agnihotra Brahmin, 84, 85
Ahmad Gujarati Shattari, 157
Ahmednagar, 45, 118, 128, 155, 156, 162, 173, 221n.221
ahwal, 185
ajnana, 58, 59, 111
Akbar (Mughal emperor), 33, 198n.46, 216n.188
Akkalkot, 48, 85, 209n.127
Akkalkot Swami Maharaj (Swami Samarth), 48. See also Swami Swamarth
Alakh, viii
alchemists, 204n.93
Ali (Caliph), 12, 97
alim, 11, 22, 94
Allah, 6, 9, 10, 11, 12, 35, 36, 38, 47, 74, 97, 98, 112, 113, 122, 134, 142, 158, 163, 173, 185, 193n.22
Allah Bhala Karega, 145
Allah Malik, vii, 48, 74, 142, 210n.139
Allah Vali Hai, vii
Ambedkar, Bhimrao R., 168, 202n.80
Aminbhai of Shirdi, 19
Amir Shakkar Dalal: a Muslim devotee who inaugurated a "sandal procession" at Shirdi, in accompaniment to the *Urs* festival, 102; mentioned in the *qawwali* composed by Abdul Baba, 194n.33; represented the Muslim contingent during

the friction concerning the burial of Sai Baba, 221n.227
Amraoti (Amravati), 123, 125, 144, 145, 168, 210n.137, 223n.249
Amuli, Haji-yi, 180
Anand, Swami Sai Sharan (Waman Patel), 218n.202; a *sannyasin* who furthered the "Hinduising" interpretation of Sai Baba, 96; reported beliefs about Sai relating to Nath legends, 96; relayed the explanation from high caste devotees as to why Sai Baba wore Muslim garb and adopted some Muslim observances, 96; believed that Sai Baba was a *brahman*, 201n.69, 211n.152; stayed at Shirdi for nearly a year during 1913-14, 211n.152; emphasised cures relating to *udi*, 211n.152
Anandgiri, 59
ancient Greeks, 117
Andhra, 51
Appa Kulkarni, 47, 208n.122
Arabia, 158, 182
Arabian Nights, 14
Arabic language, 3, 5, 6, 13, 14, 97, 98, 193n.17, 197n.41, 197n.45, 210n.139, 215n.176
Arabs, 158, 161
arati (*arti*), 83, 85, 86, 109, 110, 132, 134, 138, 139, 141, 143, 152, 217n.198; *kakad arati*, 134, 137, 139, 142, 144; *shej arati*, 135, 137, 142
Arus-i Irfan (Bahri), 185

asana, xii, 85
astrologers, 72
astrology, 71, 84, 181
asylums, 223n.248, 223n.249
atman, 10
Attar, Fariduddin, 180
Aurangabad, xii, 2, 19, 26, 43, 44, 45, 64, 94, 103, 157-167, 199n.53, 206n.112, 222n.231
Aurangabad cantonment, 160
Aurangabadi, Nizamuddin, 94, 95, 157, 165
Aurangzeb (Mughal emperor), 15, 90, 167, 184, 198n.46, 216n.188
avatars, 9, 48, 81, 193n.15, 194n.31
awliya, 208n.125
awtad, 195n.36
Ayi, Radhakrishna, 125, 129-130, 131, 136, 139, 142; a *brahman* widow and *bhakta* who lived at Shirdi until her death, 68; desired a Shirdi version of Vaishnava festivities at Pandharpur, 108; uncertainty about the precise degree of contact between Ayi and Sai Baba, 134, 140; her considerable industry at Shirdi, 217n.198
Azam al-Karamat (Muhammad Ismail Khan), 160, 161, 162, 163, 164, 166, 224n.257

Baba Gholap Shastri (Gholap Swami), 85, 86. See also Advaitendra Saraswati
Baba Palekar, 144, 145
Babas, viii
Baba Tahir, 14

Index

Babuji, Sainathuni Sarath, 109
Bade Baba (Fakir Baba), 206-207n.112; a Muslim *faqir* who, in 1909, arrived at Shirdi, 206n.109; brought the convert Ibrahim to the Shirdi mosque, 206n.109; and Trimbak Rao, 143-144; credited by Khaparde with spiritual advancement, 146
Baghdad, 21, 133
Bahadur Shah II, 15
Bahira Jatadeva, 33
Bahri, Mahmud, 184, 185, 186
bai'at, 178
Bakhtiyar Kaki, Khwaja Qutubuddin, 215n.184
Balakrishna Govind Upasani Shastri, 192n.13
Balkrishna Khaparde, 124
Bane Miyan (Muhammad Azam Khan), xii, xiii, 157-167, 222n.236; his name, 222n.231; his date of birth, 222n.238; as disciple of Sai Baba, 44, 223n.240; his retiring existence, 158, 159; his receipt of Sai Baba's message, 158; lived like a Hindu *sadhu*, 159; affinities with Hindu holy men, 167; his Hindu followers, 167; granted an income by the Nizam, 161; the Urdu hagiography, 159, 160, 161-162, 163, 166; reputedly consigned to an asylum by the British, 163; the Jalna legend, 163-164; his alleged incarceration, 223n.248; repute as a *majzub*, 164; and *jalal*, 224n.254; no relation to warrior *faqirs*, 224n.254; and miracles, 225n.258; and his cell (*hujra*), 225n.257; the *sanad-e-khilafat*, 165-166; his nephew Muhammad Ismail Khan becomes *sajjada nashin*, 165; in contrast to Ismail Khan, 224n.257; his funeral, 167
Bangab-nama (Bahri), 185
Bania, 210n.137
Bappa Baba, 221n.230, 156
barakat, 17, 180, 181, 197n.44
Barani, Ziyauddin, 21
Bayajibai Kote, 61
Bayaji Kote (Bayyaji Appa Kote Patil): a devotee in Shirdi who became a personal attendant of Sai Baba, 61; present at the death of Sai, 154-155; one of the saint's beneficiaries, 221n.226
Bedar, 64
Bengal, 50, 204n.94, 209n.133
Bengali *bhakti*, 30
Bhagavad Gita, xi, 30, 57, 58, 82, 128, 202n.80, 220n.217, 220n.219
Bhagavata Purana, 29
Bhagoji Shinde, xii; a leper who became a personal attendant of Sai Baba, 69; would prepare the tobacco pipe for Sai Baba, 70; as *sevakari*, 121-122; present at the death of Sai Baba, 154; the brahmanical fear of contamination, 219n.213

bhajan, 135
bhakri, 60, 153, 169
bhaktas, 70
bhakti, 26ff, 98, 110, 111, 112
Bhakti Lilamrit (Das Ganu), 68, 191n.6
Bhakti sants, xi, 26ff
Bhakti Saramrit (Das Ganu), 44
Bhakti-Sufi traditions of Maharashtra, 96
bhang, 91, 106, 185, 186, 223n.248, 224n.254
bhangis, 177
Bharadwaja, Acharya E., 52, 100, 114, 169, 201n.62, 220n.215
bharudas (Eknath), 31
Bhate, Balasaheb, 126, 130, 145
Bhavartha Ramayana, 119, 135
Bhishma, Krishnashastri, 135, 139
Bhorgad mountain, 175
Bhusari, Haribhau, 192n.9, 201n.69
bidi, 103
Bijapur, 15, 16, 17, 32, 89, 91, 182-185
Bijapur majazib, 214n.174
Bismillah ar-Rahim, 12
al-Bistami, Abu Yazid, 6, 9, 99, 193n.18
Biyabani, Afzal Shah, 101, 161, 166, 222n.238, 222n.240
black magic, 114
Bombay (Mumbai), 63, 68, 77, 106, 107, 118, 122, 125, 148, 150, 171, 177, 110n.2, 208n.127, 210n.137, 216n.195
Bombay High Court, 63
Book of Shirdi Aratis, 149
Brabazon, Francis, 225n.262

Brahma, 12, 97
brahman, xi, xii, xiii, 2, 23, 29, 30, 33, 57, 68, 117, 147, 175, 210n.139, 211n.152
Brahman, 176
brahman devotees, 176
brahmans (Brahmins), 27, 29, 31, 55, 94, 104, 148, 181, 192n.9, 203n.83, 211n.148
Brahmin, 202n.69, 210n.137
Brihadaranyaka Upanishad, 202n.80
British administrators, 204n.93
British army, 3
British cantonment magistrate, 163, 223n.248
British colonialists, 223n.248
British educational system, 57
British gazetteers, 204n.93
British government, 57, 125
British government of Bombay, 65
British military officers, 10, 163, 223n.242, 223n.249
British Raj, 128, 138, 161, 163, 164, 167, 217n.197, 220n.218
British rule, 128
bua, 67
buddhi, 7
Buddhism, 117, 202n.80
Buddhism in Iran, 181
Buddhist monastic order, 202n.80
Buddhists, 181
Burton, Richard, 196n.39
Buti, Bapusaheb (Shrimant Gopalrao Mukund): a rich landowner from Nagpur who resided at Shirdi from 1910 as a devotee of Sai

Index

Baba, 67; would comply with substantial requests for *dakshina*, 212n.156; and the astrologer, 71; the intermediary between Mulay Shastri and Sai Baba, 84; remained silent when in the presence of Sai Baba, 123; present on the occasion in 1917 when Tilak visited Shirdi, 126; constructed a stone house at Shirdi which became known as Butiwada, 146; accompanied Sai Baba on his evening begging round, 153; the Butiwada became the tomb of Sai Baba, also known as *samadhi mandir*, 154, 156. See also Butiwada
Butiwada, 67, 146, 154, 155, 156, 172. See also *samadhi mandir*
Butya, 145

cannabis, viii, 91, 160, 164, 165, 185
caste discrimination, 38
caste system, 202n.80
celibacy, 93
Chakradhar Swami, 27
chakras, 96
chamatkar, 220n.215
chandala, 203n.80
Chand Bodhale, 29, 35
Chandorkar, Narayan Govind (Nanasaheb), xi, 142, 218n.203; this *brahman* devotee in government service was told by Sai Baba that he did not perform miracles, 56; first encountered Sai in 1891, and initially resisted because of the saint's Muslim identity, 57; his conversation with Sai Baba circa 1900-1902, concerning *Gita* 4:34, became famous, 57-59; brought the *kirtankar* Das Ganu to Bombay, 68, 219n.214; instrumental in creating the contact between Hari Dixit and Sai Baba, 118-119; brought the medic Paramanand from Bombay to tend the saint's hand, but without success, 122; and Ganesh Khaparde, 132; noted for Sanskrit learning, 145; and Appa Kulkarni, 210n.138
Chand Patel (Patil), 18, 19, 191n.7, 199n.53
charas, viii
Charters and Sayings (Narasimhaswami), 7, 57, 58, 99, 139, 173, 192n.8
chattra, 121
Chatushloki Bhagavata (Eknath), 30
chavadi, 78, 107-109, 123, 126, 129, 134, 136, 142, 144, 156, 207n.112, 217n.198, 217n.199, 226n.265
chavadi procession, 68, 78
chavadi utsav, 108, 109, 110, 129, 143, 212n.157, 217n.198, 217n.199
chilla, 100
chilla-i-makus, 101, 215n.184

chilum, viii, xii, 65, 70, 137, 164
chilum mantras, viii
Chishti hagiographies, 95
Chishti Order, 15, 22, 23, 41, 43, 92, 93, 94, 95, 101, 179, 184, 189, 193n.19, 195n.34, 196n.40
Chishti Sufis, 34, 49, 198n.48, 215n.184
Chishti Sufism, 93
chitnis, 210n.138
Chokhamela, 28
Christian army chaplains, 10
Christian evangelists, 163, 216n.197
Christianity, 189
Christians, 4, 104, 106, 188, 216n.197
CID (Criminal Investigation Department), 128, 143
Constantinople, 133
conversion to Islam, 15, 32, 33, 204n.93, 204n.94
Curtis, Sir George Seymour, 217n.197

Dabholkar, Govind Raghunath (Hemadpant), 3, 63, 70, 72, 78, 80, 81, 191n.7, 191n.8, 205n.101, 226n.262; a magistrate of Bombay who met Sai Baba in 1910, and later became a resident of Shirdi, 190n.2; a devotee poet who composed the *Shri Sai Satcharita*, ix, 1-2, 190n.2, 190n.3; his book included *goshtis* or parables communicated by Sai Baba, 191n.4; supported Sai Baba's

ajnana argument, xi, 59, 111; sceptical of lore concerning the obscure tomb at Shirdi, 18; his theme of "neither Hindu nor Muslim," 19; acknowledged the Muslim identity of Sai Baba, 24, 25; on the early years of Sai Baba, 39, 40; and Jawahar Ali, 44, 45; and *nirvikalpa samadhi*, 46; on Sai Baba as a wrestler, 52, 53; in 1923 launched *Shri Sai Leela* with Hari Dixit, 71, 210n.146; viewed Sai Baba's *dhuni* in the light of Vedic associations, 73; his unfamiliarity with Islam and Sufism, 95; commenced the "Hinduising" interpretation, 96; rarely used the word *faqir*, 98; attributed a lengthy recital to Sai Baba, 100; reported that Sai Baba tried to bridge the gap between Hindus and Muslims, 104; informs that Sai Baba ate meat and fish in the company of *faqirs*, 105; indicates that the major affinity of Sai Baba, in relation to Hinduism, was the *bhakti* tradition, 110; referred to telepathic communication of the saints, 113; and *rinanubandha*, 117; and the *vimana* of Dixit, 120; on Swami Somdev, 212n.161; on the death of Sai Baba, 155, 221n.227. See also *Shri Sai Satcharita*

Index

dacoits, 65
Dada Kelkar, 145
Dakhni, 185
dakshina, x, 76-77, 85, 86, 127, 152, 171, 212n.157
damaru, vii
Dara Shikoh, 15, 199n.49
dargah, 17, 102, 159, 182
darshan, 72, 137, 138, 78, 79, 198n.47, 218n.202
darwish-i qalandar, 14
Das Ganu (Ganapat Dattatreya Sahasrabuddhe), 19, 68; a Marathi poet who contributed a legendary version of Sai Baba's guru, x; a *kirtankar* who eulogised saints, 1, 191n.6; a Vitthala *bhakta* who importuned Sai Baba for a vision of Vitthala, 37-38; one of the leading *kirtankar* Varkaris of Pandharpur, 220n.214; criticised by Narasimhaswami, 38, 57, 68, 191n.6, 205n.100; associated the name Venkusha with Gopalrao Deshmukh, 40; was influential in creating the misleading story of Gopalrao Deshmukh, 44, 191n.5, 201n.62; identified Sai Baba as a reincarnation of Kabir, 44; his *kirtankar* performances at urban venues aroused interest in Sai Baba, 57; devotees influenced by his narration of miracle stories, 68; reported that Sai Baba occasionally sang Muslim songs, 93; averse to *tirtha* water, 148; his *kirtans* well received in Bombay, 219n.214. See also *Bhakti Lilamrit* and *Bhakti Saramrit*
Datta Maharaj, 114
Dattatreya, 27, 29, 37, 48, 96, 99, 115, 203n.83
Deccan, 15, 17, 43, 45, 179, 196n.39
Deccani Sufi poets, 35-37
Deccani Urdu, 4, 5, 192n.9
Dehu, 31
Delhi, 21, 90, 94, 179, 198n.49
Dengle, Nanasaheb, 55
Deo, Balkrishna V., 152
dervish, 153,
dervishes, 221n.222
Devagiri (Daulatabad), 29
Devidas, 45
Devotees' Experiences of Sri Sai Baba (Narasimhaswami), 56, 192n.8, 193n.15, 196n.37, 216n.187, 220n.220
dharma, 30
Dharmasastras, 37
dhauti, 50
Dhere, Ramchandra, 36
dhobi caste, 168
dhuni, vii, 41, 61, 121
dhuni wala, vii
Dhupkhed, 18, 43, 199n.53
Diary of Kakasaheb Dixit, 119, 197n.42, 218n.210, 219n.211
Dixit, Hari Sitaram (Kakasaheb), 86, 135, 136, 140, 145, 152, 154, 212n.158, 217n.198, 217n.199, 218n.209; a *brahman* of Khandwa who became a

prominent devotee, 117; a lawyer who met Sai Baba in 1909, 119; his informative early memoranda, x; his report known as *A Sketch of the Life and Teaching of Shri Sai Baba*, 63-71, 219n.211, 219n.212; and *rinanubandha*, 117; a Vitthala *bhakta*, 37; his "*darshan* of Vitthal," 38, 205n.101; admonished by Sai Baba for criticising Christians, 104, 189, 216n.197; constructed at Shirdi the large house called Dixitwada, 170; enjoined by Sai to read *bhakti* texts of Eknath, 119; influential in the conflict over Sai Baba's burial, 155; his early Marathi diaries, or *The Shirdi Diary of Kakasaheb Dixit*, 63, 197n.42, 218n.210, 219n.211; became editor of *Shri Sai Leela*, 210n.146; his death, 120; Sai Baba's reference to *vimana*, 119, 120
Dixitwada, 67, 119, 126, 132, 134, 135, 142, 170
drishtipath, 136
dvaita, 197n.42
Dwaraka, 38
Dwaraka Math, 187

East India Company, 34
East Pakistan, 33
Eaton, Richard M., 178, 179, 184, 185, 204n.94, 204n.96
eclectic Sufis of Maharashtra, 35-37, 97

Eknath, xi, 28-31, 33, 36, 96, 119, 202n.72, 203n.83, 203n.87
Eknathi Bhagavata, 29, 83
Ernst, Carl, 204n.93
exorcism, 49, 50

Fakir, 211n.154
faqir (fakir), xii, 3, 6, 7, 10, 11, 13, 14, 47, 101, 152, 158, 161, 162
Faqir as *Allah*, 74
faqiri, 11, 62, 77, 91, 98, 107
faqirs, viii, xiii, 10, 87, 103, 165, 166, 206n.112, 223n.248
Fariduddin Ganj-i Shakar, 215n.184
Fasle, Madhav, 121
al-Fatihah, 210n.139, 216n.192

Gabaji, 67
Gadge Maharaj: a saint of Maharashtra, born a *shudra*, xii, xiii; championed the cause of untouchables (*harijans*), xiii; a social reformer in the villages and cities of Maharashtra, 168; his encounters with Sai Baba and Meher Baba, 169
Ganesha, 36, 128
Gangapur, 56
Gangohi, Abdul Quddus, 215n.184
ganja, viii, 223n.248
Gaudiya Vaishnavism, 30
Ghani (Munsiff), Abdul: author of an early and independent article on Sai Baba; influenced by Das Ganu on the subject of Gopalrao Deshmukh, 40;

Index

his ambiguous reference concerning Swami Samarth of Akkalkot, 208n.126
Ghai, S. K., v
ghats, 132
Ghazan Khan Mahmud, 181
Ghazna, 34, 213n.173
Ghaznawi, Sayed Nuruddin Mubarak, 21
ghee, 122
Gisudaras, Sayed Muhammad Husaini, 94, 179-180
Gita Rahasya (Tilak), 82, 220n.217
Godavari Mataji, 177
Godavari river, 115
God-realisation, 30, 97
Gogi, 184
Golpinarli, 195n.35
Gopalrao Deshmukh, 40, 44, 191n.5, 201n.62, 206n.108, 207n.117
Gopalrao Gund, 66
gopi, 140
goshtis, 4, 100, 137
Green, Nile, 162, 222n.236, 222n.238, 223n.248, 223n.249, 224n.254, 224n.257
Gujarat, 2, 186, 187, 188, 196n.39, 211n.152
Gujarati language, 217n.199, 226n.265
Gulbarga, 94, 179
Gunaji, Nagesh Vasudev, 47, 49, 209n.131, 220n.215
Gurus Rediscovered (Shepherd), 214n.174, 226n.262

Habib Allah, 182
habs-i nafs, 48
hadith, 5
Haji Siddiq Falke (Haji Saheb), 133
Hallaj, 6, 99
hajj, 3
hakim, 219n.213
Hamid Qalandar, 198n.48
Hanafi-Maturidi scholarship, 88
Hansotia, Gustad N., a Parsi devotee who visited Sai Baba from 1910 onwards, and whose stay at Shirdi in 1918 was distinctive, 170-172; apparently present at the death of Sai Baba, 225n.261; complexities of reporting, 225-226n.262
Hanuman, 187
Hari, 108
harijans (untouchables), 168
Hari Ram, 185
Hatha Yoga, 50, 96, 209n.131
havildar, 35, 160
Hazrat Babajan: like Sai Baba, the *faqir* of Poona claimed no *silsila*, 13; likewise independent in relation to medical treatment, 122; in 1915, urged Merwan Irani (Meher Baba) to visit Sai Baba at Shirdi, 172-173; her resemblances to, and differences from, Sai Baba, 198n.47; did not work miracles, 225n.258; and Abdul Khader, 103
hereditary leadership (in Sufi Orders), 181
Hidaya, 22

high caste Hindus, 3, 4, 20, 21, 55, 67, 69, 70, 76, 86, 148, 170, 219n.213
Hindi language, 28, 217n.199, 226n.263, 226n.265
Hindu *arati* ceremonies, 16, 26
Hindu ascetics, 4, 56, 64, 101, 164
Hindu *avatars*, 9
Hindu *bhakti* movements, 26
Hindu *bhakti* poets, 97
Hindu *chelas*, 36
Hindu deities and avatars, 97
Hindu devotees, 16, 20, 23, 24, 26, 37, 60, 98, 102, 103, 105, 107, 133, 172, 198n.47, 212n.158, 218n.210, 221n.227, 225n.261
Hindu Epics, 180
Hindu fundamentalism, 20
Hindu holy men, 14, 15, 40, 92, 158, 163, 167, 222n.238
Hindu India, 220n.218
Hindu orthodoxy, 37
Hindu religion, 6
Hindu *sadhus*, 16, 167, 185
Hindu slaves, 34
Hindu temples, 37, 204n.96
Hindu theologians, 205n.97
Hindu-Turk Samvad (Eknath), 33
Hinduism, 12, 20, 26, 36, 57, 76, 110, 117, 180, 185, 186, 193n.15, 203n.80, 208n.127, 213n.166
Hinduisation tendency, 20, 200n.62
Hinduisation theme (Warren), 87, 96
Hindus, 4, 5, 12, 15, 20, 21, 32, 33, 36, 66, 88, 91, 155, 163, 167, 178, 183, 184, 188, 195n.34, 201n.66, 204n.93, 204n.94, 216n.188, 216n.193, 226n.263
hujra, 225n.257
al-Hujwiri, 88, 92, 195n.36, 213n.173
Hulmaniyya, 88
huqqa, 132
Hyderabad, 2, 160, 166, 184, 223n.249
Hyderabad Contingent, 160
Hyderabad State, 103, 159

ibadat (*ivadat*), 11, 197-198n.45
Ibn al-Arabi, 180, 209n.133
Ibrahim, 206n.109
Iltutmish (Sultan), 21
Imambai Chota Khan: a Muslim devotee from Aurangabad, originally a soldier; at first found difficulty in being accepted by Sai Baba, 8, 103; informed that Sai Baba knew Arabic, 97; in 1918, acted as an emissary from Sai Baba to the Sufi saints Shamsuddin Miyan and Bane Miyan of Aurangabad, 157-158, 225n.258
inam, 182
in'amdar, 182
in'amdar-pirzada, 182
independent Sufis, 179
Indian Christians, 296n.197
Indian Independence, 128
Indian Muslims, 195n.34
Indian National Congress, 211n.148
Indian natives, 217n.197
Indian Slavery Act of 1843, 34

Index

Indian Sufism, 48, 178, 179
Indore law court, 187
initiation, 48, 49, 81; multiple initiations, 48, 49, 94, 95
Iran, 174
Irani Buddhism, 181
Irani Zoroastrians, xii, 170, 172, 174
Islam, 20, 21, 26, 27, 35, 109, 163, 181, 184, 201n.66, 203-204n.93
Islamic legalism, 88
Islamic philosophers, 21

Jagale (Jagle), Appa, 64
Jahanabadi, Shah Kalimullah, 94, 95
Jainism, 27, 117, 203n.80
Jains, 33, 216n.188
Jain texts, 202-203n.80
jalal, 150
Jalna, 163, 164, 223n.249
Jamner, 210n.137
Janardhan Swami, 29, 36, 203n.83
janmas, 117
Jatakas, 202n.80
Jaunpur, 50, 209n.133
Jawahar Ali (Bapu Shah Jindewali), 45, 207n.118
jawan, 223n.242
jazb, 163, 164
Jerusalem, 2, 3
Jerusalem theory, 2, 3, 192n.10, 192n.12
Jessawala, Eruch, 225n.262
Jewish Kabbalah, 117
jihad, 22, 181
jihadi, 15
jizya, 33, 34, 201n.66

jnana, 57, 58, 59, 111
jnana marga, 218n.203
Jnana Yoga, 112
Jnaneshvar (Jnaneswar), 59, 96
Jnaneshwari, 30, 83
jnani, 59, 110, 111
Jog, Bapusaheb (Sakharam Hari), 129, 145; a learned *brahman* devotee from Poona who became the *arati* officiant at Shirdi, 82-83; told by Sai Baba to read Tilak's commentary on the *Gita*, 82-83; present in May 1917 when Tilak visited Shirdi, 126; and his wife, 131; in 1912, replaced Megha Shyam as the *arati* officiant and attended the Vedanta study group of Khaparde, 139; like Abdul Baba, received correction from the disciplinary *satka*, 150; the *satka* thrown at Jog and his wife, 143; eventually became an ascetic 152; established an enduring connection with Upasani Maharaj, 152
Junayd of Baghdad, 9
Junaydiyya, 193n.19

Kabir, 27, 32, 36, 44, 66, 131
kafirs, 21, 23, 32, 34, 35, 91, 201n.66, 213n.173, 183
kafni, 4, 10, 53, 169
kalam, 88
Kalchuri, Bhau, 208n.125, 217n.199, 226n.263. See also *Lord Meher*

Kaliyuga, 194n.31
Kaliyuga *avatar*, 9
Kalyan, 210n.137, 210n.138
Kamath, M. V., 191n.7
Kannada-speaking Hindus, 184
Kanphata (Nath) Yogis, 73, 96
Kanya Kumari Sthan, 202n.72
karmamarga, 82
Karma Yoga, 112, 169, 172, 220n.217
Kashan, 90
Kashf al-Mahjub (Hujwiri), 195n.36
Kasim (son of Bade Baba), 157, 158
Kaula Tantrism, 96
Kaulgi, Lakshmibai, 139-140, 145
kaupina, 209n.127
Kayastha(s), 210n.137, 211n.148
Kelkar, Narasimha Chintaman (Tatyasaheb), 126, 127
Khader, Abdul, 103
Khair al-Majalis, 198n.48
khalifa, 165
khanaqah, 17, 32, 62, 180, 183
khanda yoga, 49
Khandesh, 24
Khandoba, 36
Khandoba temple (Shirdi), 19, 39, 53, 119, 176
Khandwa, 117
khanwadas, 9, 92, 193n.19
Khaparde, Balvant, 134, 138
Khaparde, Ganesh S., a lawyer and politician who visited Shirdi several times from 1911 onwards, 125; in early 1912, conducted a Vedanta study group at Shirdi, 123; a close colleague of Bal Gangadhar Tilak, 124; in 1917, he accompanied Tilak on a visit to Sai Baba, 126-127; his Shirdi Diary, 129-146; and Krishnashastri Bhishma, 147; smoking the *chilum* of Sai Baba, 149; and Upasani Maharaj, 176; on the old *faqir* of Aurangabad, 206n.112
Kharagpur, 176
Kher, Indira, 190n.3
Kher, Vishwas B., 126, 145, 191n.7, 191n.8, 206n.109, 206n.112; his influential Pathri theory, 2, 188, 192n.9; dismissed the legend of Gopalrao Deshmukh created by Das Ganu, 40, 44, 201n.62, 206n.108; his version of the begging rounds, 61; his critical assessment of the *Shri Sai Satcharita*, 72; on Chand Patel, 199n.53
Khuda, 173
Khuldabad, 43, 206n.111
Khuldabad *malfuzat* texts, 204n.93
Khuldabad Sufis, 204n.93
Khurasan, 180
Khushalchand Seth, 221n.227
Kichhauchha, 50
kirtankar, 1, 5, 7, 147, 191n.6
Kirtankar Varkaris, 220n.214
kirtans, 168
Kitab al-Luma (Sarraj), 88, 213n.173
Kodak Company, 208n.127

Index

Kondaji, 65
Kopargaon, 78, 119, 135
Kote, Appa, 142
Krishna, 27, 30, 37, 140, 194n.31
Krishna worship, 57
kshatriya, 28, 31
Kubravi Order, 180
kuffar, 22, 201n.66
Kulkarni, Appa (Keshav Anant), 47, 208n.122, 210n.138
kundalini, 96, 112
Kusha Bhav: a Tantric Yogi who became a follower of Sai Baba; apparently a Nath Yogi, dabbled in Tantric magic, x; Sai Baba was severe in this instance of sorcery, 50; the Bharadwaja version, 114-115; Kusha Bhav encouraged belief in his purported miracles, 115; interviewed in 1936 by Narasimhaswami, 116; reversion to "miracle" exhibitionism, 50
Kutba, 11

Lakshmibai Shinde: a resident devotee at Shirdi, and the only woman allowed into the mosque at night, 153; Sai Baba would eat simple food that she daily prepared, 221n.221; she was present at the death of Sai Baba, 154
landed Sufis, 182-183
landowner Sufis, 196n.39, 196n.40, 197n.44
langar, 22, 157
langot, 53
langoti, 156
Lataif-i Ashrafi (Simnani), 209n.133
leela, 211n.154
Lendi, 85, 121, 129, 135, 140, 152, 173, 197n.42
lepers, 121, 168
leprosy, 121-122, 219n.213
Life of Sai Baba (Narasimhaswami), 2, 47, 56, 192n.8, 216n.187
linga, 184
Lingayat community, 36
Lingayats, 184
Lodi dynasty, 15
Lonavla, 118
London, 118, 124
Lord Meher (Kalchuri *at al*): a multi-volume biography of Meher Baba generally attributed to Bhau Kalchuri, but actually the product of various contributors, and involving translations from different languages; a complex editing process was involved, 217n.199; Kalchuri the part author of *Lord Meher*, his original text (*Meher Prabhu*) being in Hindi, 226n.263; some errors known in this work, 226n.265. See also Kalchuri, Bhau
lota, 127
low caste Hindus, 203n.93

Madani Saheb, 161
Madhava Bhat, 98-99
Madhusudan, 59
Madhya Pradesh, 188

Madhya Pradesh High Court, 188
madness, 223n.248
Madras, 210n.137
madrasah, 100
magic, 181
Mahanubhava *panth*, 27
Mahanubhavs, 202n.72, 205n.97
Maharashtra, xi, xiii, 12, 15, 26ff, 39, 99, 128, 168, 169, 177, 188, 203n.91, 219n.212
Maharashtrian *bhakti*, 30
Mahars, 28, 31, 72
Mahayana Buddhism, 202n.80
Mahbub Ali Khan (Nizam), 161
mahfil, 10, 224n.257, 225n.257
Mahipati, 28, 32, 33, 36
majazib, 16, 89, 90, 166, 182-186, 214n.174
majzub, 11, 14, 15, 16, 32, 44, 55, 89, 90, 158, 159, 162, 164, 166, 182-186, 198n.46, 214n.174, 222n.231
Makanji Khatau Mills, 150
Malik al-maut, 12
Maloji Bhonsale, 209n.127
mamlatdar, 23, 130, 155, 210n.138, 219n.214
Manmad, 151
mantra, 48, 49, 52, 81, 96
mantras, 50, 114, 115
mantrika, 52
Manucci, Niccolao, 198n.49
Manwat (Manvat), 44, 64, 192n.9
Maratha army, 34
Marathi language, 1, 5, 19, 28, 29, 31, 35, 36, 63, 72, 74, 90, 97, 115, 124, 127, 190n.2, 191n.6, 192n.9, 197n.42, 203n.90, 215n.176, 217n.199, 219n.211, 226n.265
marifa, 6, 194n.24
Martand (son of Mhalsapati), 138
Maruti, 192n.15
Maruti (Hanuman) temple (Shirdi), 39, 66
mast (God-intoxicated), 89, 214n.174
matanga, 203n.80
Maulana Gausul Ajaya Dastgir, 193n.20
maulavi, 46, 47
mauna, 55
McLain, Karline, 205n.100
Mecca, 2, 3, 22, 133
Medina, 161
Megha Shyam, 136, 139, 143, 192n.14
Meherabad ashram, 173
Meher Baba (Merwan S. Irani), xii, 172-174, 189, 207n.119, 217n.199; his ancestral location on Yazd plain, 174; and Gustad Hansotia, 225n.261, 225-226n.262; and Hazrat Babajan, 172-173; and Upasani Maharaj, 173, 174; visit to Shirdi in 1915, 172; the *Parvardigar* greeting, 173, 189; his remarks about Sai Baba, 173; reminiscences of Sai Baba, 226n.265; on the Sufi status of Sai Baba, 226n.264; and Khuldabad, 43; his version of *majzub*, 89; his liberal teaching, 174; and Gadge Maharaj, 169;

Index

and Marianne Warren, 89, 90, 214n.174
Meher Baba literature, 44
Meher Baba movement, 206n.112, 217n.199
Mhalsapati, one of the earliest devotees at Shirdi, 55; and the name Sai, 3, 19, 200n.60; and the Khandoba temple, 19, 39, 55; introduced Sai Baba to Kashiram Shimpi and Appa Jagale (Jagle), 64; kept guard over Sai Baba when he seemed to be dead, 46-47; innovated *puja* at the Shirdi mosque, 53, 54; local Muslims objected to the worship, 53, 104; a *sevakari*, 55
mikwana, 195n.36
miracles, 56, 115, 225n.258
miracles as sleight of hand, 51
Mirikar, Kakasaheb, 118
Modi script, 5
Moglai, 64
moulu, 157
Muazzam, Muhammad, 183
Mudha Pangula, 36
mufti, 11
Mughal emperor, 22
Muhammad Ismail Khan, 160, 165, 166, 224n.257
Muhammad, Prophet, 5, 12, 93, 178, 193n.15, 197n.44
Muharram festival, 106, 216n.195, 216n.197
Muinuddin Khan, 160
Mulay Shastri, xii, 84-86, 192n.14
mulla, 46
Mulla Qawi, 90

mullas, 11, 16
Munindra Swami, 37
Muntoji Bahamani (Brahmini), 36, 96
murshid, 87, 98, 194n.33
mushriks, 21
Muslim, ix, xi, xii, 3, 6, 52, 69, 208n.126
Muslim agriculturalists, 204n.94
Muslim *bhakti* poet, 205n.97
Muslim converts, 204n.93
Muslim devotees, 97, 102-103, 108, 172, 216n.187
Muslim *faqir*, 20, 147
Muslim *faqirs*, 16, 41, 73, 77, 92, 222n.238
Muslim reformists, 10
Muslims, 4, 6, 11, 15, 33, 37, 52, 117, 149, 154, 155, 167, 188, 204n.93, 204n.96, 205n.97, 211n.148, 216n.188, 216n.193
Muslims of Aurangabad, 163

naam-saptah, 37
Nabhadas, 28
nafs, 88
naga sadhu, 90
naga sadhus, vii, 198n.46, 198n.49
Nagpur, 67, 71, 78, 147, 148, 177, 210n.137, 223n.249
namaz, 11, 92, 182, 186
namaz-i-makus, 101
Namdev, 27-28
Nanak (Sikh Guru), 27, 73
Nandaram Marwari, 61
Nanded, 210n.137
Naqshbandi order, 34, 43, 94, 95, 193n.19
Narasaiyya, Shri Mittha Lakshmi, 2

Narasimhaswami, B. V., the *sannyasin* who created a "Shirdi revival," and who authored a number of books on Sai Baba, 2, 58, 98, 99, 112, 114, 139, 191-192n.8, 195-196n.37, 218n.203, 220n.220, 226n.262; interviewed many informants in 1936 at Shirdi, 56; his acceptance of the Sepoy Rebellion episode, 3, 53; and Abdul Baba's *Notebook*, 5, 7, 192-193n.15, 197n.42; criticism of Das Ganu, 38, 57, 68, 191n.6, 205n.100; credited the story of Gopalrao Deshmukh which has since been rejected by scholars, 40; on Jawahar Ali, 45; his theory of Sai Baba's "mission," 47; an enthusiast of miracles, 56; his nationwide missionary campaign, 56; his interview with Kusha Bhav, 116; regarded Ganesh Khaparde as an outsider, 140; his Vedantic interpretation of "Who are we?" 151-152; provided details of Muslim devotees, 216n.187
Narayan (deity), 97
Narayana, 208n.122
Narayanpur, 36
Narayan Teli, 61
Narke, Ganpatrao G., an academic devotee of Poona; testified that Sai Baba did not teach *kundalini* or *siddhis*, 96; his description of Sai Baba, 112-113; on reincarnation, 117; and Ganesh Khaparde, 145; the Narke exposition contradicted by a misleading theory that Sai Baba taught *jnana marga*, 218n.203
Nasik, 168, 169, 175, 210n.137
Nasiruddin Mahmud Chiragh-i-Delhi, 93, 198n.48
Natekar (Swami, Hamsa), 124, 125, 143
Nath tradition, 203n.91
Nath Yoga, 27
Nath (Gorakhnathi) Yogis, vii, viii, 41, 50, 73, 96, 209n.131
Navanaths, 96
Neemgaon, 55, 67, 134
Nevasa, 69, 208n.122
Nevaskar, Balaji Patel, 68-69
Nilanga, 184
Nimonkar, Nanasaheb, 153, 154, 212n.158
nine Naths, 203n.91
nirguna, 35
Nirguni Nirakar, 35
nirvikalpa samadhi, 46, 47, 207n.119
nista, 215n.176
Nizam of Hyderabad, 2, 37, 43, 64, 103, 157, 161, 206n.111
Nizamuddin Awliya, 22, 93, 201n.67
Noolkar, Tatyasaheb, 123
Notebook (Abdul Baba): a record of communications in Urdu from Sai Baba, 193n.16, 193n.19, 194n.30, 210n.139; did not become

Index

generally known until 1999, 215n.175; confirms a strong Muslim Sufi dimension in the outlook of Sai Baba, ix; composed in Urdu and Modi script, 5; survey of content, 5-12; reveals an "unorthodox Sufi" context, 13; the contents to some extent supported the exegesis of Marianne Warren, who argued against "Hinduisation," 87; Warren believed that the *Notebook* showed more familiarity with the Chishti Order, 92; the contents do not indicate that Sai Baba was illiterate, 94; the eclectic components reminiscent of Shah Muni, 97; the *Notebook* expresses disapproval of the *pirzada*, 11, 186, 197n.44; supports description of Sai Baba as a Sufi, 189; analysis of behaviour, 7-8; ethical teaching, 8-9; lists of Sufi figures, 9; a few pages are in Arabic, 193n.17; the word *avatar* is employed, 194n.31; the *qawwali* or song by Abdul Baba, 9, 194n.32, 194n.33; the Sufi hierarchy of saints, 9, 195n.36; quotations from Jalaluddin Rumi, 196n.38; reference to false *pirs*, 10, 11, 196n.39; criticism of dance and song, 10, 196n.40; Narasimhaswami generalised about the content, which he could not read, 192-193n.15, 197n.42. See also Abdul Baba

nuqaba, 195n.36
Nuruddin Ishaq Qadiri, 184

oil vendors, 141
Olcott, Colonel Henry, 209n.127
onions, 61
opium, 14
opium shops, 164
orthodox Sufis, 12, 16, 17, 21, 32, 34, 91, 159, 166, 180, 181, 182, 186, 214n.174
orthodox Sufism, 15, 17
Osborne, Arthur, 207n.119
ovala, 85

pagal, 164
pagalkhana, 163
Paithan, 28, 29
Pali Canon, 202n.81
palmistry, 84
Panchadashi (Vidyaranya), 123, 176
Panchikarana (Shah Muntoji), 36
Pandharpur, 26, 27, 28, 35, 38, 56, 57, 64, 68, 108, 147, 168, 169, 191n.6, 205n.100, 210n.137
Paramanand (medic), 122
Parsi Zoroastrians, 170-172, 211n.148
Parvardigar, 99, 173, 189, 226n.263
Patanjali Yoga, 49, 96
Pathri, 2, 44, 63-64, 192n.9, 199n.52
Persian language, 13, 14, 33, 36, 97, 165, 173, 185, 210n.139, 216n.188
pesh-imam, 11

Peston Jamas, Cursetji Shapurji, 170
pir, 11, 66, 182, 186
pirs, 10, 186, 196n.39
pirzada, 182, 185, 186
pirzadas, 11, 17, 165, 182
pirzada Sufis, 183, 184, 185
Poona (Pune), 31, 112, 148, 168, 210n.137, 220n.219, 220n.220
pothi, 81, 95, 100
Pradhan, Moreshwar, 63, 98
prana, 7
pranayama, 49, 96, 112, 175
Prarthana Samaj, 150, 211n.148
prasad, viii, 71, 74, 80, 114, 127, 140, 221n.221
Protestant Christians, 216n.197
puja, 83, 104, 147
Punjab, 163, 188, 204n.94
Puranas, 30, 37, 100
Purandhare, Raghuvir B., 108, 210n.139
Puttaparthi, 51, 90

Qadiri Order, 36, 97, 101, 182, 193n.19
Qadiri Sufi, 203n.83
qadis, 12
qalandar, 9. 13, 14, 15, 195n.35, 198n.48
qalandari, 14
qalandars, 64, 164, 198n.46, 198n.48
qawi, 198n.46
Qawi, Itimad Khan Mulla Abdul, 198n.46
qawwali, 6, 9, 41, 157
Qazi of Sangamner, 53, 54
Qazipeth, 101
Qazi-ul-Quzzat, 198n.46

Qila Arak (Aurangabad), 167
Quran, 6, 11, 22, 94, 97, 98, 102, 105, 193n.22, 195n.37, 210n.139
Qushayri, 88
qutub, 195n.36
qutub al-aqtab, 9
qutubs, 9, 195n.36

Radhakrishna Ayi; see Ayi
Rahata, 40, 45
Rahuri, 175
Raja Yoga, 112, 169
Rajarshi Bala Sannyasi, 192n.11
Rama, 81, 96, 98, 105, 119, 148, 194n.31, 213n.166
Rama *bhakti*, 213n.166
Ramalingaswami, 211n.155
Ramananda, 44
Ramanavami festival (Shirdi), 102, 105, 212n.158, 215n.186
Ramayana (Valmiki), 30, 119, 213n.166
Ramchandra Patil, 221n.227
Ramdas Swami, 104
Ramdasi Bua, 81
Ramgiri Bua, 199n.53, 200n.58
Rameshwar, 64
Rani of Jhansi, 3
Rasane, Damodar, 169, 212n.158
Rasane, Nanasaheb, 169
Rege, M. B., 80-81
reincarnation, 221n.222
Report on the Cultivation and Use of Ganja (1893), 224n.254
Rifai Order, 101
Rigopoulos, Antonio: author of a well known scholarly book on the life and teachings of Shirdi Sai; on the version

Index

of Shirdi Sai by Sathya Sai, 192n.12; supported V. B. Kher in the critical reception of Gopalrao Deshmukh lore, 201n.62; on Shah Muni as a Muslim *bhakti* poet, 205n.97; deferred to the Charles White hypothesis of Nath Yogi influence on Shirdi Sai, 209n.131; his misleading theory that Shirdi Sai taught *jnana marga*, and also his curtailment of the Sufi factor prior to the revealing publication of Abdul Baba's Urdu *Notebook*, 218n.203; on the popular *chamatkar* concerning a blacksmith family, coinciding with the burned hand of Shirdi Sai, 220n.215; in 1985 interviewed Bappa Baba at Shirdi, 221n.230

riyaz, 6
Rizvi, Saiyid Athar Abbas, 14
Rohilla, 145
Ross, Colonel Harry, 162, 223n.242
royal land grants, 17
Ruhela, Satya Pal, 200-201n.62
Rumi, Jalaluddin, 6, 92, 93, 94, 180, 193n.18, 195n.34, 196n.38

sabr, 215n.176
saburi, 215n.176
sadhana, 175
sadhu, 78, 185
sadhu dhuni, 41
sadhus, viii

safi, 10
sahaj samadhi, 207n.119
Sai Baba Sansthan (Shirdi), 59, 71, 146, 187, 188, 210n.146
Sai Hari Katha (Das Ganu), 191n.6
sajjada nashin, 165, 183
Sakori (Sakuri), 175, 177
Sakori ashram, xiii, 202n.72
sama, 92
samadhi (tomb), 66
samadhi mandir, 156; see also Butiwada
Samana, 22
sanad-e-khilafat, 165
Sangamner, 85, 126, 209n.136
sannyasin, 40, 77, 78, 79, 177, 211n.152
Sanskrit language, 3, 7, 29, 33, 46, 57, 58, 81, 83, 84, 94, 97, 152, 177, 180, 193n.22, 216n.188
sant, 26ff, 203n.87
Sarmad, 15, 90, 198n.46, 198n.49
al-Sarraj, Abu Nasr, 88, 92, 213n.173
Satan, 10
Satana, 175
Satara, 37, 148
Sat-Chit-Ananda, 147
Sathe, Hari Vinayak, 146, 212n.157
Sathewada, 83, 129, 134, 146, 217n.198
Sathya Sai Baba of Puttaparthi, 200n.62, 201n.62, 212n.157; encouraged belief in his performance of miracles, 51; repudiated by Marianne Warren, formerly his

devotee, 90; claimed to be a reincarnation of Shirdi Sai, 192n.12; his version of the birth of Shirdi Sai, 199n.52
satpurush, 151
Sayed Sadr ad-din (Chiragh-i Hind), 50
sayyad, 197n.44
Sayyads, 11
Secunderabad, 224n.249
Selu (Shelu), 44, 64, 207n.117
Sepoy Rebellion (1857-58), 3, 15, 52, 223n.248
sepoys, 10, 161, 166, 223n.249, 224n.257, 225n.258
sevakari, 55, 69, 121, 172, 221n.226
Shaddharmapundarika, 203n.80
Shafii-Ashari scholarship, 88
shahada, 92
Shah Aminuddin Ala, 32, 90, 183
Shah Muni, 36, 96, 97, 205n.97
Shah Muntoji Bahamani, 36
Shah Sibghat Allah, 182
Shah Sokhta Miyan, 165
Shahpur Hillock, 183, 184
shaikh, 163, 178, 197n.44, 201n.67
Shaikh al-Islam, 21
Shaikh Muhammad (Shekh Mahammad), 35-36, 96, 97
Shaiva, vii
Shaiva *sadhus*, viii, 41
Shama (Madhavrao Deshpande): school teacher, an early devotee, and resident of Shirdi, who was frequently the intermediary between Sai Baba and visitors, 65, 126, 132, 140, 143, 145, 197n.42; interviewed by Narasimhaswami, 56; one of the first devotees, he would prepare the tobacco pipe for Sai Baba, 66; a direct witness of Sai Baba's attitude to proffered sacred books, 80; and Ramdasi Bua, 81-82; and Hari S. Dixit, 118-119; pulled Sai Baba away from the *dhuni* in an emergency, 121-122; interceded with Sai on behalf of Ganesh Khaparde, 125; intermediary with Ramachandra Tarkhad, 151; intermediary with Govind Dabholkar, 190n.2
Shams Tabrizi, 195n.35
Shamsuddin Miyan, 157, 159
Shankara(charya), 58, 59
Shankara (Dashanami) Order, xi
sharia, 34, 194n.24
shariat, 180
shastri, xiii
shathiyat, 99, 193n.18
Shattari Order, 182
Shaykhs, 11
Shedgaon, 168
Shia Islam, 106
Shia Muslims, 21
shimpi, 28
Shimpi, Kashiram, 64-65
Shimpi, Lakshman Bala, 143, 154
Shinde, 176
Shirdi Diary (Dixit), 63, 197n.42, 218-219n.210, 219n.211
Shirdi Diary (Khaparde), x, 123, 124, 129-146, 147, 149, 199n.55, 200n.55, 206n.112, 219n.212
Shirdi Sai Baba, as independent mystic, ix; as independent

faqir, 13, 17, 23, 41, 90, 93; as independent Sufi, 186, 189, 226n.263; attributed dates of birth, 1, 190n.1; theory of Hindu birth at Pathri, 26; disputed *brahman* ancestry, 210n.139; left home at age of eight, 199n.53; following a Muslim *faqir*, 2; first and second arrivals at Shirdi, 2, 18, 39, 43, 191n.7, 191n.8; accompanies the marriage party to Shirdi, 18, 43; and Chand Patel, 199n.53; the Khuldabad phase, 43, 206n.111; turned away from Khandoba temple, 19; the obscure tomb or cell at Shirdi, 18, 39; and the *turbat*, 66; and gardening, 206n.106; renunciation and celibacy, 10; as Urdu-speaker, ix, 210n.139; his Urdu vocabulary, 189, 226n.263; his white *kafni*, 16, 86, 98; green *kafni*, white *kafni*, 64; orange *kafni*, 64; as a "mad *faqir*," 55-56, 77, 89; as wrestler, 52, 53, 138; and Tambuli, 52-54; retreat to Lendi wilderness, 53; his Sufi aspect, ix, xi; his Sufi identity, 4; not a Tantric Yogi, x; did not act like a Yogi, 110; not a preacher of Islam, 98; did not preach Vedanta or Yoga, 226n.265; and *dakshina*, x, 76-77, 85, 86, 127, 139, 186, 218-219n.210; and the Shirdi *taqiya*, 41; and the Shirdi mosque, xii, 4; *brahmans* fear contamination at Shirdi mosque, 34, 86; the priestly issue of contamination, 69; high caste reaction, 57; high caste aversion to a Muslim, 98-99; recipient of orthodox Hindu stigma, 37; and the *dhuni*, vii, 41, 73; offering to the *dhuni*, 61; burns his hand in the *dhuni*, 121-122, 220n.215; and *udi*, vii, 41, 74, 126, 131, 135, 138, 145; as *hakim*, 41; his reputed cures, 211n.152; his *chilum*, 137, 147, 148, 149; the Muslim and Hindu dimensions of Sai, ix; his religious liberalism, ix, 6, 12, 20, 21, 170, 189; his temperament, xi; did not preach religious doctrines, v, 4, 20; and the eclectic trend, xi; and Hindu worship, xi, 198n.47; and sacred books, xi; wanted unity between Hindus and Muslims, xii, 20, 41-42, 104, 105, 145, 146; as *faqir*, v, vii, xi, xii, 13, 19, 20, 23, 37, 42, 46, 53, 55, 57, 60, 62, 65, 70, 76, 78, 79, 82, 98, 104, 107, 114, 115, 123, 126, 127, 128, 129, 130, 132, 138, 144, 147, 171, 172, 186, 187, 188, 189, 195n.34, 199n.53, 208n.122; his *faqir* garb, 53; as a Muslim, 24, 55; as a Hindu, 2, 3, 201n.69, 211n.152; his Muslim characteristics, 4;

discourses to Abdul Baba, 6; no claim of *silsila*, 13, 23; his disapproval of the *pirzada*, 186, 197n.44; his allusive speech, 4, 20, 42, 113, 141; associated with *majzub* category, 16; and Jawahar Ali (Jindewali), 40, 45; and Swami Samarth, 48, 208n.125, 209n.129; and Abdul Baba, 5, 13, 195n.37; and Bade Baba, 146, 206n.112; and Govind Dabholkar, 1, 2, 190n.2; and Shama, 56, 66, 80, 81-82; and Bhagoji Shinde, xii, 69-70, 121-122, 219n.213; and Hari S. Dixit, 117-120; and Bapusaheb Jog, 82-83, 143; and Mulay Shastri, xii, 84-86; and Krishnashastri Bhishma, xii, 147-149; and Gadge Maharaj xiii, 169; and Bane Miyan, xii, 44, 157-159; and Meher Baba, xii, 172-173, 189, 226n.263; and Upasani Maharaj, xiii, 175-176, 177; and Imambai Chota Khan, 103; and Abdul Khader, 103; and Hazrat Shamsuddin Miyan, 157; and *Parvardigar*, 173; comparison with Hazrat Babajan, 198n.47; his analysis of behaviour, 7, 8; self-analysis, 8; and brain faculties, 7; his ethical teaching, 8, 9, 13, 70-71, 75, 194n.29; "Who are we?" 7, 8, 194n.26; "dangerous wall of the world," 196n.40, 196n.41, 197n.42; "break the wall of difference," 197n.42; his daily begging rounds, x, 60-62, 153; his ablutions, 70, 130, 132; his disposition to jokes, 18, 133, 142, 200n.55; his religious tolerance, 4; his Sufi affinities, 5; credited as a Sufi, 214n.174; his teacher as *murshid*, 197n.41; his criticism of dance and song, 196n.40; his unorthodox Sufi role, 9; and independent Sufis, 87, 91; Warren's theory of Sufi orthodoxy, 195n.34; his *darbar* (*durbar*), 9, 13, 70, 194n.33, 195n.34; as *qalandar*, 9, 194n.33, 195n.34; "neither Hindu nor Muslim," 19, 20; cooked free meals at Shirdi, 23; and *nirvikalpa samadhi*, 46-47; theory of his mystical union with God, 208n.125; and the Rama devotee, 23-25; affinity with *bhakti* temperament, 26; affinity with *bhakti* tradition, 110; affinity with Bhakti Hinduism, 186; convergence with *sant* attitude, 30; prescribes *Eknathi Bhagavata* for Hari Dixit, 30; and Hindu beliefs about liberation, 221n.222; and Hatha Yoga, 209n.131; was constantly repeating *Allah Malik*, 38, 74, 112; chanted *al-Fatihah*, 94, 216n.192; and *namaz*, 186; and Hindu holy men, 40;

Index

and Venkusha, 40, 207n.117; frowned upon conversion to another religion, 42, 104; he permitted *chavadi* procession, 37; honoured as *maharaja*, 37; and *Vitthaldarshan*, 38; and Vitthal worship, 205n.101; and British colonialists, 217n.197; had no ashram, 225n.261; anecdote of vomiting intestines, 49; and Kusha Bhav, 50, 114-115; and Sathya Sai Baba, 51; did not dispense *mantra* or initiation, x, 48, 209n.129; and Muslim devotees, 102, 103; and Hindu devotees, 55-59, 218n.209; and *brahman* devotees, 148; disclosure to devotees as "a slave of slaves," 217-218n.202; and Mhalsapati, 53, 54, 55; and Radhakrishna Ayi, 68, 134, 140, 221n.221; and Nanasaheb Chandorkar, 56, 210n.138; conversation with Chandorkar (about *Gita* 4:34), 57-58, 111; and Sanskrit, 58; his *ajnana* argument, xi, 111; "miracle" of lighting mosque lamps with water, 68; and miracles, 56; and Das Ganu, x, 1, 38, 205n.100; and the disputed Gopalrao Deshmukh, 201n.62, 206n.108, 207n.117; not a vegetarian, 105; the *darshan* situation, 71, 75; and *darshan* petitioners, 103; his theme of "oil-monger's wall," 61; his *goshtis*, 98, 191n.4; spoke many languages, 98; his claim of foreknowledge, 56; his claim of omnipresence, 56; the devotee belief in omnipresence, 194n.32; encouraged the practice of repentance *(taubat)*, 101; discouraged addiction to alcohol, 101, 186; the *Urs* festival at Shirdi, 102, 215n.186; the Muslim "sandal procession," 102, 105; disposed of a *tabut*, 106; and *Ramanavami*, 102, 105; the mosque in need of repair, 107; and the *chavadi*, 107, 108, 109; and *chavadi utsav*, 108, 109; and the palanquin, 108, 110; and jewellery, 108, 110; despised pomp, 108; danced when leaving the *chavadi*, 144; places where he slept, 226n.265; independence from ritual, 106; his impatience with routine *arati*, 141; assessment by Professor Narke, 112-113; he would not advocate renunciation, 112; his role as a devotee of *Allah*, 112; constantly uttering Islamic phrases, 112; and *Allah Bhale Karega*, 113; and the *Faqir (Allah)*, 74, 75, 139; as *qutub-e-irshad*, 226n.264; his use of the word Satan, 198n.46;

paranormal abilities, 113; telepathic communication, 113; operating on two planes, 193n.20, 194n.32; and reincarnation, 88, 117, 137; and *rinanubandha*, 117-118; and Swami Somdev, 78-79, 212n.161; and Gopalrao (Bapusaheb) Buti, 67, 212n.156; and Ramdasi Bua, 81-82; and Lakshmibai Kaulgi, 139-140, 145; and Lakshmibai Shinde, 153, 154, 221n.221; and Appa Kulkarni, 208n.122, 210n.138; and Ram Maruti Bua, 138; and the intrusive *faqir*, 137, 141; his *satka*, 74, 134, 143, 150, 152; doing manual work, 71; denied expectations about sacred books, 80; his own views about sacred books, 80-81; and the astrologer, 71; as Sainath Maharaj, 96; as the tenth Nath, 96; and Charles White, 214n.175; not a Nath Yogi or Tantric Yogi, 96; his teachings similar to those of Shah Muni, 97; *saburi* and *nista*, 215n.176; as *pir* to the itinerant Sufis, 97; comparison with Bistami and Hallaj, 99; and *chilla-i-makus*, 100-101; his asthma, 145, 153; independence from medical treatment, 122; his tendency to counter social degradation, 122; and Ganesh Khaparde, 123-128, 129-146; and Bal Gangadhar Tilak, 126-128; his "yogic glances," 124, 136; and *tirtha* water, 127, 148; his daily routine, 129; his varying moods, 130; abusive language, 150; contrasting reports of his disposition, 133; and Ramachandra Tarkhad, 150-152; his reference to Kabir, 131; his allusions to Teli and Marwadi, 131; resisting the *teli* or *vani*, 140; and the feigning holy man, 142; hard words against internal enemies, 142; and five *laddus*, 148; and Zoroastrian visitors, 170-174, 189; the *dervishes* and tiger, 154; his death and burial, 154-156; his worship in Hindu temples, 187; Sai worship was criticised by Swami Swarupananda Saraswati, 23

Shirdi Sai Baba Trust; see Sai Baba Sansthan
Shirdi Sai devotees, 187, 188
Shirdi Sai movement, 205n.100
Shiva, viii, 12, 35, 36, 96
Shiva-Parvati, 199n.52
Shivaji, 34, 104
Shivanand Shastri, 142
Shree Guru Charitra, 115
Shridhar, 59
Shrigonde, 35
Shri Sai Baba (Anand), 211n.152
Shri Sai Leela magazine, 59, 71, 124, 210n.146, 219n.212

Shri Sai Satcharita (Dabholkar): the major work on Sai Baba, with hagiographical elements; the author, 190n.2; assessment by V. B. Kher, 72; a Marathi religious text (*pothi*), 1; a lack of chronological order, 190n.3; an erroneous Western belief, ix; on the early phase at Shirdi, 18; version of the name Sai, 19; "neither Hindu nor Muslim," 19; description of Sai Baba as a Muslim, 24; on Das Ganu, 37-38; the name of *Allah*, 38; 1886 episode of *nirvikalpa samadhi*, 46-47; Sai Baba did not prescribe *yogasanas* or *pranayama*, 49; the bizarre practice of *khanda yoga*, 49; Sai and Tambuli as wrestlers, 52; on Balaji Nevaskar, 69; supplies a list of *darshan* contingents who visited Sai Baba, 72-73; on the *dhuni*, 73; on *Allah Malik*, 74, 210n.139; on the *Faqir* (*Allah*), 74, 75; on Swami Somdev, 78-79; on Sai Baba and sacred books, 80-83; on Mulay Shastri, 84-86; losses with regard to Sufism, 95; on the patched *kafni* of Sai Baba, 98; a lengthy recital attributed to Sai Baba, 100; bridging the divide between Hindus and Muslims, 104; the *Muharram* festival, 106; on Bhagoji Shinde, 121-122; and Haji Siddiq Falke, 133; on Vaman Tatya, 206n.106; visitors to Shirdi included numerous social and religious categories, 211n.148. See also Dabholkar, Govind Raghunath

Shri Sainath Sagunopasana, 149
shudra, xiii, 28, 31, 37, 168
siddhis, 96, 112, 114, 115
Siddhanta Bodha (Shah Muni), 37, 205n.97
Sikh Guru Arjun, 34
Sikhism, 27
Sikhs, 4, 73, 188
silsila, 13, 16, 23, 43, 93
Simnan, 209n.133
Simnani, Ala ad-Daula, 180, 181
Simnani, Sayyid Ashraf Jahangir, 49, 50, 209n.133
Sirhindi, Ahmad, 34
Sketch of the Life and Teaching of Shri Sai Baba (Dixit), 63
slave trade, 34
Smith, Henry, 163
sonar, 55
sovala, 84
Sufi, 10, 11, 45, 97, 98, 106
Sufi-bhakti concepts, 37
Sufi discipline, 6
Sufi folk tradition, 109
Sufi hierarchy of saints, 6. 9, 195n.36, 226n.264
Sufi ideas, 6
Sufi Order, viii
Sufi Orders, ix, 5, 11, 13, 16, 17, 22, 23, 32, 48, 49, 89, 92, 94, 95, 179, 181, 189, 195n.34, 196n.39, 196n.40, 201n.67
Sufi path, 101

Sufi *pirs*, 196n.38
Sufi shrines, 197n.44, 225n.257
Sufi *tariqat*, 97
Sufi themes, 174
Sufis, xi, 32, 50, 88, 156, 195n.37, 213n.173
Sufis and Yogis, 51
Sufis as missionaries, 204n.93
Sufis of Bijapur, 88
The Sufis of Bijapur (Eaton), 178
Sufism, 12, 14, 15, 21, 22, 26, 27, 35, 36, 43, 50, 93, 95, 157, 178-186, 189, 213n.173, 218n.203, 226n.264
Sufi tombs, 17, 33
Suhrawardi Order, 21, 50, 193n.19
Suhrawardi, Shihabuddin Abu Hafs, 21
Sultan Ahmad Bahmani, 179
Sultan Firuz Shah Bahmani, 179
Sultan Ibrahim Sharqi, 209n.133
Sultan Sikandar Adil Shahi, 184
Sunni Islam, 106
Swami Sai Sharan Anand, 63, 199n.52, 199n.53
Swami Samarth (Akkalkot Swami), 48, 85, 95, 208n.126, 208-209n.127
Swami Somdev (Somadeva), xi, 212n.161
Swarupananda Saraswati, Swami, xi, 23, 187-189
Swatmasukha (Janardhan Swami), 36
Syed Amin Khandhar, 192n.17

tabut, 106, 216n.195
talismans, 52, 182
Tambuli, Mohiuddin: a Muslim inhabitant of Shirdi, xii; a recurring friction with Sai Baba, xii; the wrestling match, 52-53; objected to the Hindu worship occurring at the Shirdi mosque, 53-54, 104
tanasukh, 88, 117
tantra, 49
Tantric attitudes and customs, vii
Tantric magic, 50
Tantric trick, x
Tantric Yoga, 49, 112, 114, 169
Tantric Yogi (Kusha Bhav), 50
tapas, 6
Tarabhai Sadashiv Tarkhad (Mrs. Manager), 220n.220
tariqat, 215n.176
Tarkhad, Ramachandra Atmaram (Babasaheb), xi, 150-152, 220n.220
Tarkhad, Sadashiv, 220n.220
taubat, 101
tawaif, 224n.257
tawakkul, 215n.176
Tayfuria Sufi Order, 193n.19
temple destruction, 204n.96
Thane, 210n.137
Theosophists, 209n.127
Thosar (Tozer, Swami Narayan), 132
Tilak, Bal Gangadhar (alias Lokamanya): the nationalist politician and colleague of Ganesh Khaparde, xi, 82, 125, 134, 220n.218; in 1908, imprisoned by the British

Index

on charges of sedition, 124; in May 1917, visited Sai Baba at Shirdi, 126-128; his reason for visiting Shirdi is unknown, 128; his major work *Gita Rahasya*, 220n.217; and Swami Vivekananda, 220n.219
tirtha water, 69, 127, 148, 219n.213
tobacco, viii, 52, 65
toda, 105
transmigration, 117
trikalajnani, 149
Trimbak Rao (Maruti), 135, 143, 144
tripundra, 147
trishul, vii
Tukaram (carpenter), 67
Tukaram (poet), xi, 28, 31-32, 96, 203n.90
Tulpule, Shankar G., 203n.83
turbat, 66
Turkish Sultans of Delhi, 22

udi, 41, 50, 51, 122, 126, 127, 218n.210
ulama, 11, 15, 16, 23, 33, 90, 94, 166, 178, 179, 183, 185, 215n.184
unorthodox Sufis, 106, 198n.46
unorthodox Sufism, 16,
untouchable castes, 203n.80
The Untouchables (Ambedkar), 202n.80
untouchables (*harijans*), xiii, 27, 28, 31, 168
upadesha, 48
upasana, 193n.22

Upasani Maharaj, xii, xiii, 83, 173, 174, 175-177, 192n.13; early renunciate life, 175; householder phase, 175; breathing ailment, 49, 175-176; at the Khandoba temple, 119, 176; and the Vedanta study group of Khaparde, 139, 145, 176; sojourn at Kharagpur, 176-177; settles at Sakori, 177; and Bapusaheb Jog, 152; and Meher Baba, 173; and the Kanya Kumari Sthan, 177, 202n.72
Upasani Kanya Kumari Sthan, 177
Urdu language, 5, 99, 101, 159, 173, 193n.15, 197n.42, 210n.139
Urdu mystical songs, 93
Urs, 159, 166
Urs festival (Shirdi), 102, 105, 191n.6, 215n.186
Uttar Kashi, 78

vaidh, 175
Vaidya, 122
Vaishnava, vii, viii, 147, 191n.6, 221n.221
Vaishnava *bhakta*, 68
Vaishnava *brahmans*, 2
Vaishnava devotionalism, 26
Vaishnava *gosavis*, 72
Vaishnava *sadhus*, 41
Vaishnava *sant*, 26
Vaishnava worship, 148
Vaishnavas, 64
Vallabhacharya, 30

Vaman Tatya, 206n.106
Varkari *bhaktas*, 30
Varkari *panth*, 27, 32, 203n.91
Varkaris, 28
Veda, 96
Vedanta, 26, 30, 57, 71, 110, 111, 112, 139, 194n.26, 213n.166
Vedanta *sannyasins*, 72
Vedantic teachings, 11, 174
Vedas, 9, 37, 97, 193n.22
Vedic fire rituals, 73
Vidyaranya, 123
vimana, 119, 120
Virashaivas, 184
Vishishtadvaita Vedanta, 176
Vishnu, 12, 35, 97, 108, 213n.166, 226n.263
Vishnusahasranaam, 81
Vithoba, 205n.101
Vittal of Pandri, 205n.100
Vitthala (Vithoba), 27, 28, 31, 35, 38, 108, 147, 205n.100
Vitthala *bhaktas*, 29, 37
Vivekananda, Swami, 220n.219

wada (Butiwada), 154, 155
wahdat al-wujud, 180, 181, 209n.133
Waman Gondkar Patil, 61
Waman Sakharam Shelke, 61
Waman Tatya, 142
Warren, Marianne: the author of *Unravelling the Enigma*, which profiled the Sufi background of Shirdi Sai, xi; had the Urdu *Notebook* of Abdul Baba translated into English, 5; suggested a Chishti influence on Shirdi Sai, 41, 92-95, 189, 195n34; suggested his direct experience of union with God, 47, 208n.125; emphasised a Sufi context for the *ajnana* theme of Shirdi Sai, 58; her counter to "Hinduisation" via explicating Shirdi Sai as a Sufi, 87-99, 200n.62; her misunderstanding of the *majzub* issue, 89-90, 186, 214n.174; and Sathya Sai Baba, 90; on *chilla-i-makus*, 100; on *taubat*, 101; rejected Das Ganu's theory of Gopalrao Deshmukh as the teacher of Shirdi Sai, 207n.117; on *saburi* and *nista*, 215n.176; criticism of Rigopoulos, 218n.203; on Hari Dixit, 219n.212
The Wayfarers (Donkin), 214n.174
wazir, 7
West Bengal, 176
West Pakistan, 33
White, Charles, theory of Nath Yogi influence on Shirdi Sai, 209n.131, 214n.175; identified Shirdi Sai with Sathya Sai, 214n.175; formulated a "Sai Baba movement" supposition, 214n.175; compared Shirdi Sai with Kabir, 214n.175; and Ruhela, 215n.175
wine, 14, 91, 184, 185

Index

wrestling, 105
wujudi ideas, 181
wujudi teaching, 209n.133

Yade Haqq, vii, 210n.139
yantra pooja, 49
Yazd plain, 174
Yeola, 126
Yoga, 26, 71, 112, 136
Yogasamgrama (Shaikh Muhammad), 35, 36, 97
Yogasanas, 49
Yogi, 175
Yogis, vii, viii, 204n.93. See also Nath Yogis

yoginis, 96

zahiri, 198n.45
zamindar, 67
Zarradi, Maulana Fakhruddin, 22, 201n.67
Zar Zari Zar Bakhsh, 193n.19
zikr, 48, 95, 142, 181
Zoroastrian fire rituals, 73
Zoroastrians, 4, 73, 163, 170-174, 188, 189
Zubairi, Maulana Muhammad, 90, 182

Our Books on SHIRDI SAI BABA

Shirdi Sai Baba is a household name in India as well as in many parts of the World today. Sterling are well known for publishing the largest number of books on Shirdi Sai, indeed far more than any other publisher. We endeavour to be comprehensive in the range of author and content. We also publish books on other saints and masters.

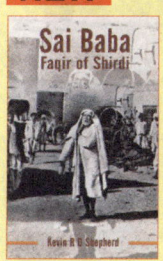

NEW
Sai Baba: Faqir of Shirdi
Kevin R.D. Shepherd
ISBN 978 93 86245 06 9
₹ 350

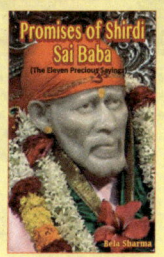

NEW
Promises of Shirdi Sai Baba
(The Eleven Precious Sayings)
Bela Sharma
ISBN 978 93 85913 98 3
₹ 200

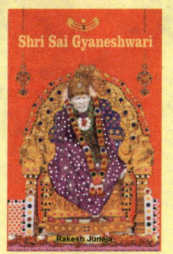

NEW
Shri Sai Gyaneshwari
Rakesh Juneja
ISBN 978 93 86245 05 2
₹ 300

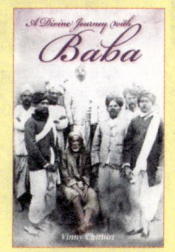

NEW
A Divine Journey with Baba
Vinny Chitluri
ISBN 978 81 207 9859 5
₹ 200

SHIRDI within & beyond
A collection of unseen & rare photographs
Dr. Rabinder Nath Kakarya
ISBN 978 81 207 7806 1
₹ 750

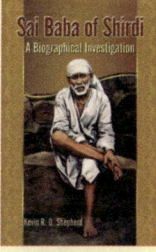

Sai Baba of Shirdi:
A Biographical Investigation
Kevin R. D. Shepherd
978 81 207 9901 1
₹ 450

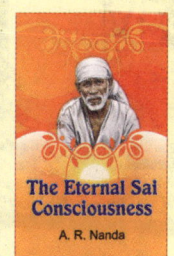

The Eternal Sai Consciousness
A. R. Nanda
ISBN 978 81 207 9043 8
₹ 200

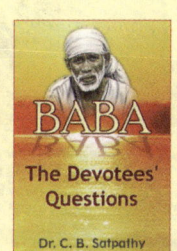

BABA:
The Devotees' Questions
Dr. C. B. Satpathy
ISBN 978 81 207 8966 1
₹ 150

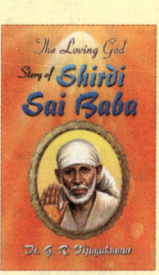

The Loving God:
Story of Shirdi Sai Baba
Dr. G. R. Vijayakumar
ISBN 978 81 207 8079 8
₹ 200

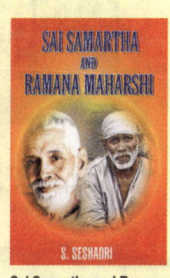

Sai Samartha and Ramana Maharshi
S. Seshadri
ISBN 978 81 207 8986 9
₹ 150

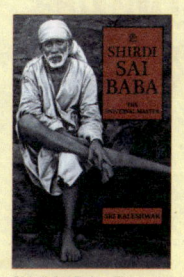

Shirdi Sai Baba: The Universal Master
Sri Kaleshwar
978 81 207 9664 5
₹ 150

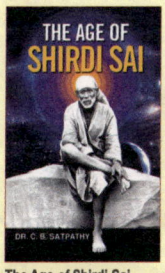

The Age of Shirdi Sai
Dr. C. B. Satpathy
ISBN 978 81 207 8700 1
₹ 225

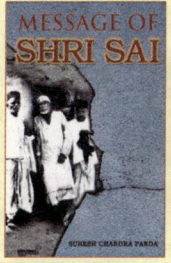

Message of Shri Sai
Suresh Chandra Panda
ISBN 978 81 207 9512 9
₹ 150

Sree Sai Charitra Darshan
Mohan Jagannath Yadav
ISBN 978 81 207 8346 1
₹ 200

Shri Sai Baba Teachings & Philosophy
Lt Col M B Nimbalkar
ISBN 978 81 207 2364 1
₹ 100

STERLING

SHIRDI SAI BABA

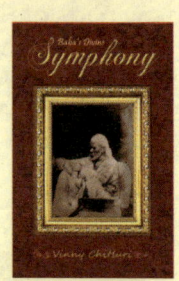

Baba's Divine Symphony
Vinny Chitluri
ISBN 978 81 207 8485 7
₹ 250

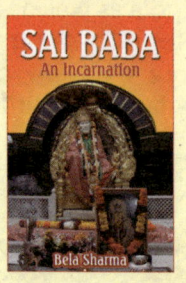

Sai Baba an Incarnation
Bela Sharma
ISBN 978 81 207 8833 6
₹ 200

Shirdi Sai Baba: The Perfect Master
Suresh Chandra Panda & Smita Panda
ISBN 978 81 207 8113 9
₹ 200

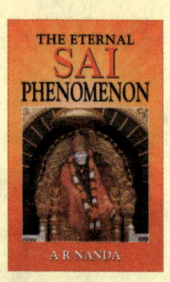

The Eternal Sai Phenomenon
A R Nanda
ISBN 978 81 207 6086 8
₹ 200

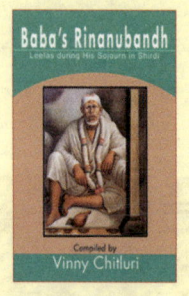

Baba's Rinanubandh Leelas during His Sojourn in Shirdi
Compiled by Vinny Chitluri
ISBN 978 81 207 3403 6
₹ 200

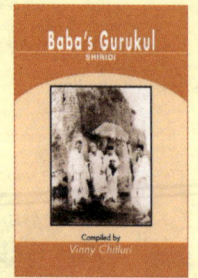

Baba's Gurukul SHIRDI
Vinny Chitluri
ISBN 978 81 207 4770 8
₹ 200

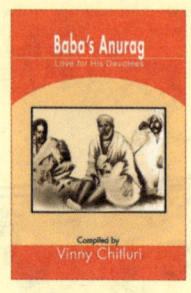

Baba's Anurag Love for His Devotees
Compiled by Vinny Chitluri
ISBN 978 81 207 5447 8
₹ 125

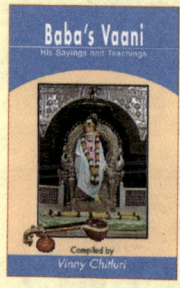

Baba's Vaani: His Sayings and Teachings
Compiled by Vinny Chitluri
ISBN 978 81 207 3859 1
₹ 200

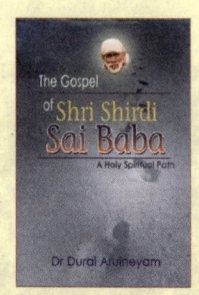

The Gospel of Shri Shirdi Sai Baba: A Holy Spiritual Path
Dr Durai Arulneyam
ISBN 978 81 207 3997 0
₹ 150

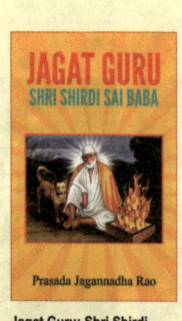

Jagat Guru: Shri Shirdi Sai Baba
Prasada Jagannadha Rao
ISBN 978 81 207 8175 7
₹ 100

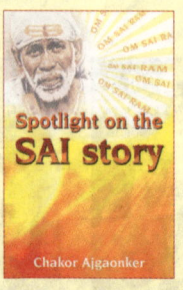

Spotlight on the Sai Story
Chakor Ajgaonker
ISBN 978 81 207 4399 1
₹ 125

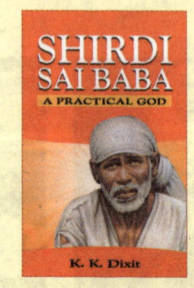

Shirdi Sai Baba A Practical God
K. K. Dixit
ISBN 978 81 207 5918 3
₹ 75

STERLING

Sab Ka Malik Ek

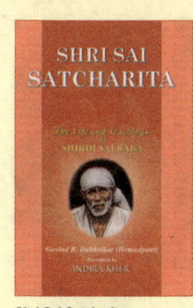

Shri Sai Satcharita
The Life and Teachings of Shirdi Sai Baba
Translated by Indira Kher
ISBN 978 81 207 2211 8 ₹ 550(HB)
ISBN 978 81 207 2153 1 ₹ 450(PB)

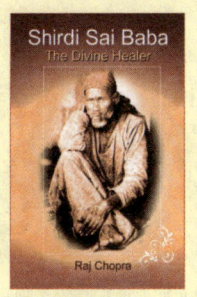

Shirdi Sai Baba
The Divine Healer
Raj Chopra
ISBN 978 81 207 4766 1
₹ 100

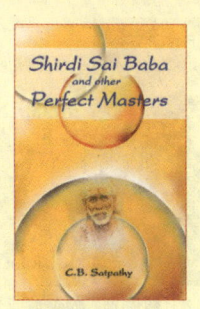

Shirdi Sai Baba and other Perfect Masters
C B Satpathy
ISBN 978 81 207 2384 9
₹ 150

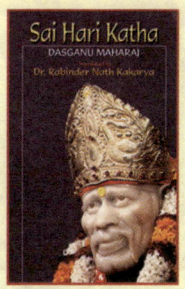

Sai Hari Katha
Dasganu Maharaj Translated by
Dr. Rabinder Nath Kakarya
ISBN 978 81 207 3324 4
₹ 100

Unravelling the Enigma:
Shirdi Sai Baba in the light of Sufism
Marianne Warren
ISBN 978 81 207 2147 0
₹ 400

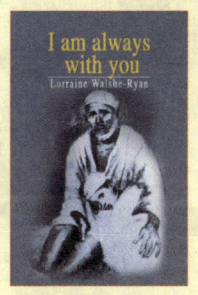

I am always with you
Lorraine Walshe-Ryan
ISBN 978 81 207 3192 9
₹ 150

BABA- May I Answer
C.B. Satpathy
ISBN 978 81 207 4594 0
₹ 150

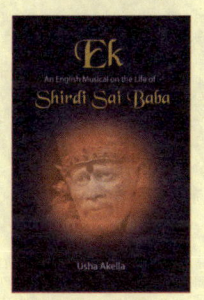

Ek An English Musical on the Life of Shirdi Sai Baba
Usha Akella
ISBN 978 81 207 6842 0
₹ 75

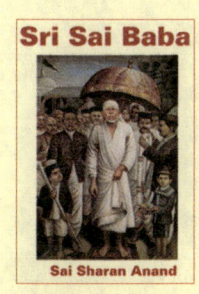

Sri Sai Baba
Sai Sharan Anand
Translated by V.B Kher
ISBN 978 81 207 1950 7
₹ 200

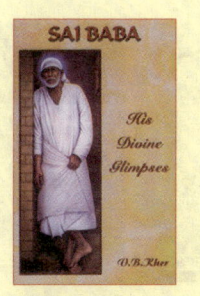

Sai Baba: His Divine Glimpses
V B Kher
ISBN 978 81 207 2291 0
₹ 95

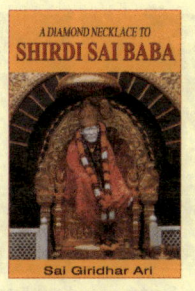

A Diamond Necklace To: Shirdi Sai Baba
Giridhar Ari
ISBN 978 81 207 5868 1
₹ 200

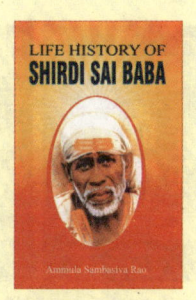

Life History of Shirdi Sai Baba
Ammula Sambasiva Rao
ISBN 978 81 207 7722 4
₹ 200

STERLING

SHIRDI SAI BABA

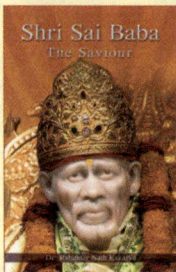

Shri Sai Baba- The Saviour
Dr. Rabinder Nath Kakarya
ISBN 978 81 207 4701 2
₹ 100

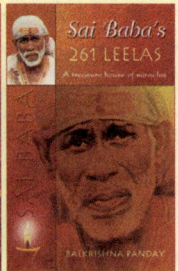

Sai Baba's 261 Leelas
Balkrishna Panday
ISBN 978 81 207 2727 4
₹ 125

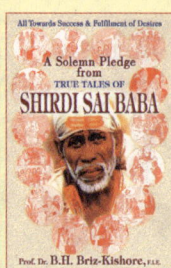

A Solemn Pledge from True Tales of Shirdi Sai Baba
Dr B H Briz-Kishore
ISBN 978 81 207 2240 8
₹ 95

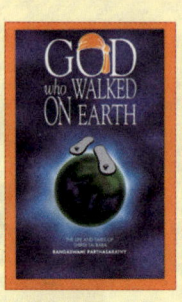

God Who Walked on Earth: The Life & Times of Shirdi Sai Baba
Rangaswami Parthasarathy
ISBN 978 81 207 1809 8
₹ 150

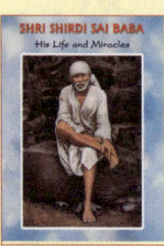

Shri Shirdi Sai Baba: His Life and Miracles
ISBN 978 81 207 2877 6
₹ 30

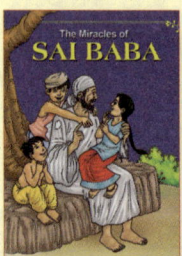

The Miracles of Sai Baba
ISBN 978 81 207 5433 1 (HB)
₹ 250

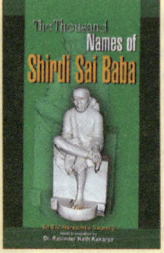

The Thousand Names of Shirdi Sai Baba
Sri B.V. Narasimha Swami Ji
Hindi translation by
Dr. Rabinder Nath Kakarya
ISBN 978 81 207 3738 9
₹ 75

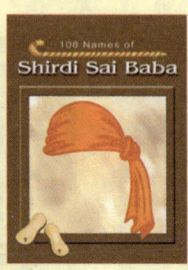

108 Names of Shirdi Sai Baba
ISBN 978 81 207 3074 8
₹ 50

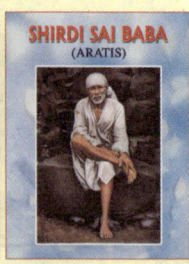

Shirdi Sai Baba Aratis
ISBN 978 81 207 8456 7
(English)   ₹ 10

Shirdi Sai Speaks... Sab Ka Malik Ek
Quotes for the Day
ISBN 978 81 207 3101 1
₹ 200

Divine Gurus

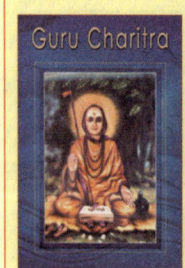

Guru Charitra
Shree Swami Samarth
ISBN 978 81 207 3348 0
₹ 200

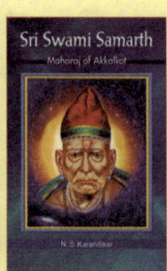

Sri Swami Samarth Maharaj of Akkalkot
N.S. Karandikar
ISBN 978 81 207 3445 6
₹ 200

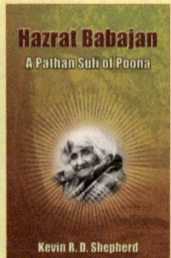

Hazrat Babajan: A Pathan Sufi of Poona
Kevin R. D. Shepherd
ISBN 978 81 207 8698 1
₹ 200

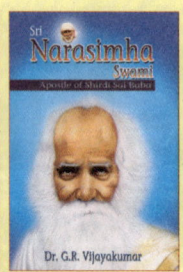

Sri Narasimha Swami Apostle of Shirdi Sai Baba
Dr. G.R. Vijayakumar
ISBN 978 81 207 4432 5
₹ 90

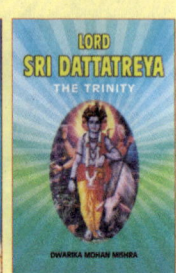

Lord Sri Dattatreya The Trinity
Dwarika Mohan Mishra
ISBN 978 81 207 5417 1
₹ 200

STERLING

श्री शिरडी साई बाबा

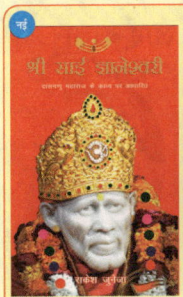

श्री साई ज्ञानेश्वरी
राकेश जुनेजा
978 81 207 9491 7
₹ 250

साई ही क्यों?
राकेश जुनेजा
978 81 207 9610 2
₹ 200

जेल में साई साक्षात्कार
राकेश जुनेजा
978 81 207 9507 5
₹ 150

शिरडी साई बाबा के ग्यारह अनमोल वचन
बेला शर्मा
978 93 85913 97 6
₹ 75

श्री साई सच्चरित्र
श्री शिरडी साई बाबा की अद्भुत जीवनी तथा उनके अमूल्य उपदेश
गोविंद रघुनाथ दाभोलकर (हेमाडपंत)
978 81 207 2500 3
₹ 300 (HB)

श्री साई चरित्र दर्शन
मोहन जगन्नाथ यादव
978 81 207 8350 8
₹ 200

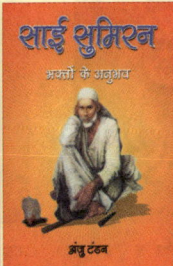

साई सुमिरन
अंजु टंडन
978 81 207 8706 3
₹ 90

बाबा की वाणी-उनके वचन तथा आदेश
बेला शर्मा
978 81 207 4745 6
₹ 100

बाबा का अनुराग
विनी चितलुरी
978 81 207 6699 0
₹ 100

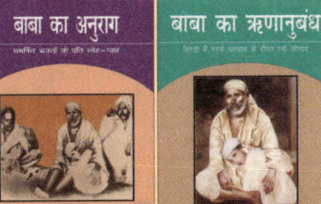

बाबा का ऋणानुबंध
विनी चितलुरी
978 81 207 5998 5
₹ 150

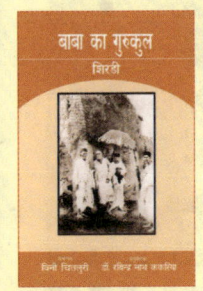

बाबा का गुरूकुल-शिरडी
विनी चितलुरी
978 81 207 6698 3
₹ 125

बाबा-आध्यात्मिक विचार
चन्द्रभानु सतपथी
978 81 207 4627 5
₹ 150

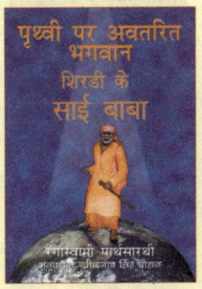

पृथ्वी पर अवतरित भगवान शिरडी के साई बाबा
रंगास्वामी पार्थसारथी
978 81 207 2101 2
₹ 150

शिरडी अंतः से अनंत
डॉ. रबिनाथ ककरिया
978 81 207 8191 7
₹ 750

STERLING

श्री शिरडी साईं बाबा

श्री शिरडी साईं बाबा एवं अन्य सद्गुरु
चन्द्रभानु सतपथी
978 81 207 4401 1
₹ 90

साईं शरण में
चन्द्रभानु सतपथी
978 81 207 2802 8
₹ 150

साईं - सबका मालिक
कल्पना भाकुनी
978 81 207 9886 1
₹ 200

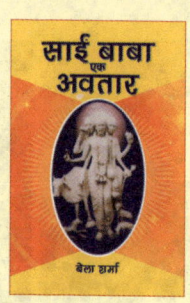

साईं बाबा एक अवतार
बेला शर्मा
978 81 207 6706 5
₹ 100

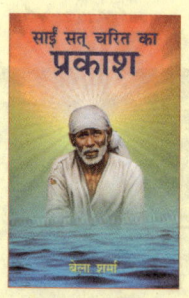

साईं सत् चरित का प्रकाश
बेला शर्मा
978 81 207 7804 7
₹ 200

श्री साईं बाबा के परम भक्त
डॉ. रबिन्द्रनाथ ककरिया
978 81 207 2779 3
₹ 75

श्री साईं बाबा के उपदेश व तत्त्वज्ञान
लेफ्टिनेंट कर्नल
एम. बी. निंबालकर
978 81 207 5971 8   ₹ 100

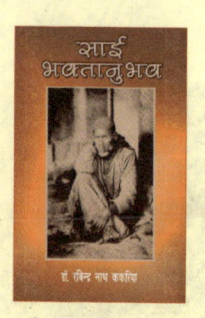

साईं भक्तानुभव
डॉ. रबिन्द्रनाथ ककरिया
978 81 207 3052 6
₹ 125

श्री साईं बाबा के अनन्य भक्त
डॉ. रबिन्द्र नाथ ककरिया
978 81 207 2705 2
₹ 100

साईं का संदेश
डॉ. रबिन्द्र नाथ ककरिया
978 81 207 2879 0
₹ 125

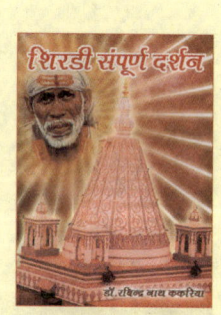

शिरडी संपूर्ण दर्शन
डॉ. रबिन्द्रनाथ ककरिया
978 81 207 2312 2
₹ 50

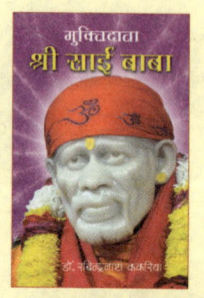

मुक्तिदाता - श्री साईं बाबा
डॉ. रबिन्द्रनाथ ककरिया
978 81 207 2778 6
₹ 65

STERLING

सबका मालिक एक

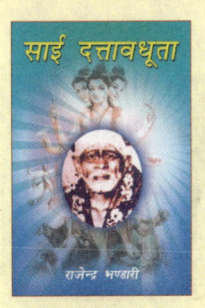

साई दत्तावधूता
राजेन्द्र भण्डारी
978 81 207 4400 4
₹ 75

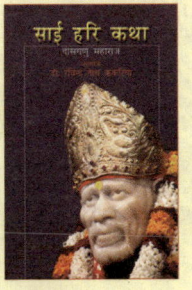

साई हरि कथा
दासगणु महाराज
978 81 207 3323 7
₹ 65

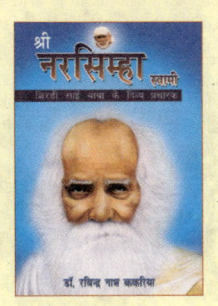

श्री नरसिम्हा स्वामी
शिरडी साई बाबा के
दिव्य प्रचारक
डॉ. रबिन्द्र नाथ ककरिया
978 81 207 4437 0   ₹ 75

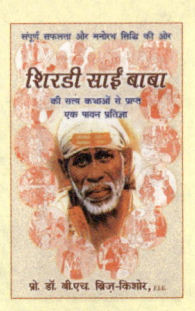

शिरडी साई बाबा - की सत्य
कथाओं से प्राप्त - एक पावन
प्रतिज्ञा
प्रो. डॉ. बी.एच. ब्रिज-किशोर
978 81 207 2346 7   ₹ 80

**शिरडी साई बाबा की दिव्य
लीलाएँ**
डॉ. रबिन्द्र नाथ ककरिया
978 81 207 6376 0   ₹ 150

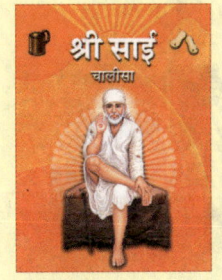

श्री साई चालीसा
978 81 207 4773 9
₹ 50

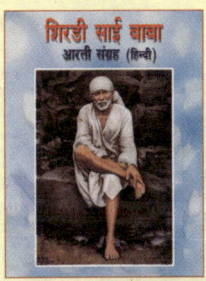

शिरडी साई बाबा आरती
978 81 207 8195 5
₹ 10

आरती संग्रह (Boardbook)
ISBN 978 81 207 9057 5
Size: 10.70 cm x 15.45 cm
₹ 100

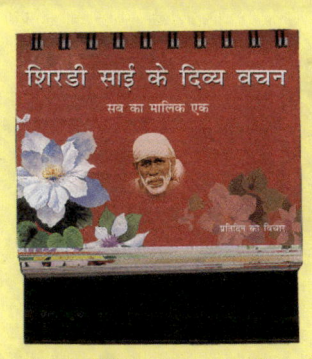

शिरडी साई के दिव्य वचन-सब का मालिक एक
प्रतिदिन का विचार
978 81 207 3533 0
₹ 180

STERLING

Other Indian Languages

Oriya Language

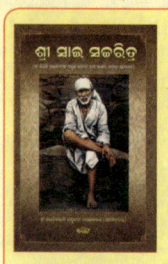

ଶ୍ରୀ ସାଇ ସଚରିତ୍ର
ଶ୍ରୀ ଗୋବିନ୍ଦରାଓ ରଘୁନାଥ ଦାଭୋଳକର
(ହେମାଡ଼ପନ୍ତ)
978 81 207 8332 4 ₹ 300

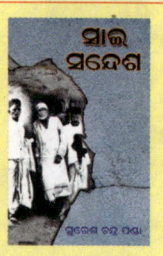

ସାଇ ସନ୍ଦେଶ
ସୁରେଶ ଚନ୍ଦ୍ର ପଣ୍ଡା
978 81 207 9534 1 ₹ 100

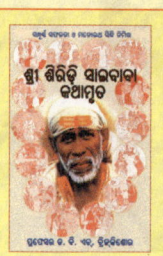

ଶ୍ରୀ ଶିରିଡ଼ି ସାଇବାବା କଥାମୃତ
ପ୍ରଫେସର ଜ. ବି. ଏଚ୍. ବ୍ରିଜକିଶୋର
978 81 207 7774 3 ₹ 80

ଶ୍ରୀ ସାଇବାବାଙ୍କ ଉପଦେଶ ଓ ତତ୍ତ୍ୱଜ୍ଞାନ
978 81 207 9982 0 ₹ 125

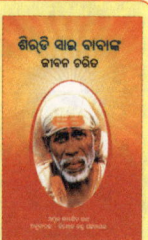

ଶିରଡ଼ି ସାଇ ବାବାଙ୍କ ଜୀବନ ଚରିତ (Oriya)
ଅନୁବାଦକ - ବିଶ୍ୱନାଥ ଚନ୍ଦ୍ର ପଟ୍ଟନାୟକ
978 81 207 7417 9 ₹ 125

Kannad Language

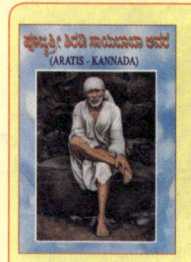

Shirdi Sai Baba Aratis (Kannada) ₹ 10

ಬಾಬಾರವರ ಉಪದೇಶಗಳು
ಎನ್. ಚಿಟ್ನೂರ್
978 81 207 9500 6 ₹ 200

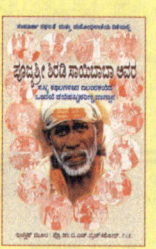

ಶ್ರೀ ಶಿರಡಿ ಸಾಯಿಬಾಬಾ ಅವರ (Kannada)
ಪ್ರೋ. ಡಾ. ಬಿ.ಎಚ್. ಬ್ರಿಜ್-ಕಿಶೋರ್
978 81 207 2873 8 ₹ 80

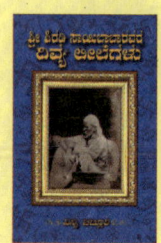

ಶ್ರೀ ಶಿರಡಿ ಸಾಯಿಬಾಬಾ ಚರಿತ್ರೆ ಅಮೃತಧಾರಾ
ಎನ್. ಚಿಟ್ನೂರ್
978 81 207 8930 2 ₹ 225

Marathi Language

शिर्डी साईबाबांची दिव्य वचने (Marathi)
सबका मालिक एक
दैनंदिन विचार
978 81 207 7518 3 ₹ 180

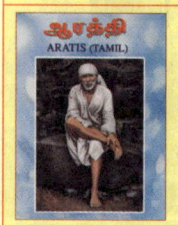

Shirdi Sai Baba Aratis (Tamil) ₹ 10

ஷீரடி சாயிபாபாவின் (Tamil)
உபதேசங்களும்தத்துவஞானமும்
பெருமைகளும் ஆசீர்வாதம்
ப்ரோ. டா. பி.எச். ப்ரிஜ்-கிஷோர்
978 81 207 2876 9 ₹ 80

Shirdi Sai Baba Aratis (Telugu) ₹ 10

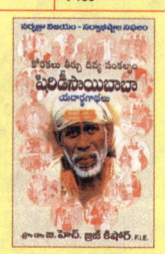

షిరిడి సాయిబాబా (Telugu)
ప్రో. డా. బి.హెచ్. బ్రిజ్-కిషోర్
978 81 207 2294 1 ₹ 80

Sterling Publishers Pvt. Ltd. Regd. Office: A1/256 Safdarjung Enclave, New Delhi-110029.
For Online order & detailed Catalogue visit our website:
www.sterlingpublishers.com, E-mail : mail@sterlingpublishers.com, Tel. 91-11-26386165, 26387070
Office and Works: Plot No. 13, Ecotech-III, Greater Noida - 201306, Uttar Pradesh, India